Education Contested

Education Contested

Changing Relations between
State, Market and Civil Society
in Modern European Education

Edited by: Jules L. Peschar & Marieke van der Wal

Taylor & Francis
Taylor & Francis Group
LONDON AND NEW YORK

Library of Congress Cataloging-in-Publication Data

Applied for

Published by Taylor & Francis
2 Park Square, Milton Park, Abingdon, Oxon, OX14 4RN
270 Madison Ave, New York NY 10016

Transferred to Digital Printing 2010

Typeset by: digiTAAL ontwerpen groningen bv

ISBN 90 265 1630 4 (hardback)

Contents

Part 3: Civil Society

Preface

Recently, there has been an increasing interest in comparative education. However, since it seems to be contradicted by daily experience, this statement should be further explained. Apart from the politicians and policy makers' assertions of high societal relevance, little interest is apparent in everyday life. Students go to school, teachers teach, directors direct, parents are usually satisfied and life goes on.

Nevertheless, the publication of the yearly *Education at a Glance* of OECD yields great interest from newspapers, policy maker, politicians and the public. Suddenly all that is known about education becomes visible. How much do we spend, how good are we, do we pay teachers enough or what do students achieve? And, most relevant: all this is presented in a comparative perspective, both in time and between countries. This however, is all relatively new: most of the data have become available after 1992 and the interest and investment in these data are increasing.

Here we can certainly speak of a real paradoxical situation. Hasn't there been a steady decrease in the interest to the long academic tradition of comparative education that begun at the end of the 19th century? And is it not the case that only a few of these insights were adopted by policy makers and practitioners? Were there no discussions about the practical relevance of academic comparative education? So how can we explain this paradox?

This book is one result of the 18th Conference of the Comparative Education Society of Europe (CESE), held at the University of Groningen, the Netherlands in July 1998. The conference aimed to bring together two parties: academic comparative educational scientists and policy makers and practitioners. The theme: 'State-Market-Civil Society' allowed the participants to address the above-mentioned paradox from various angles and merge views from *academia* and *politica*.

The following organisations contributed to making the conference and the publication of this book possible: The Dutch Royal Academy of Sciences (KNAW), The Dutch Ministry of Education, Culture and Science (OC&W), The European Union (DGXII), the Province and the City of Groningen, The University of Groningen and Swets & Zeitlinger Publishers. We also thank the Board of the CESE for their great confidence in the organisation of what is considered to be a highlight in the CESE activities: the bi-annual European conference.

But, no conference organisation is without its hard working and loyal staff. In particular we want to thank Hilde Steenbergen, Liesbeth Bargerbos and Cathrynke Dijkstra for their skilful work.

This book is dedicated to our collegue and friend Gijs Rupert of the Department of Education at the University of Groningen. Gijs was a long time participant in CESE activities and he took the initiative for housing the 18th Conference in Groningen. His serious illness prevented him from participating in the preparations and in taking part in what had to become 'his' conference. Just a few days later he sadly passed away.

We, organisers and CESE members, will commemorate him.

Jules L. Peschar
Marieke van der Wal

Department of Sociology
University of Groningen

1

Central Issues and Changing Perspectives in European Comparative Education

Jules L. Peschar & Marieke van der Wal

1. Transparency in Education

It is often said that there is a great resemblance between education and water: both are commodities. Usually, at least in the western world, people do not care very much about water as long as it is clear, does not taste and flows regularly. Only when a disruption of the water flow occurs, when the colour is different or when it tastes like mud, do the public and responsible policy makers show any concern.

Similar attitudes can be noted about education and the quality of teaching. In general the public, and thus policy makers, seem to be satisfied with education. Only at certain moments do emotions erupt: for example with the student movement in the sixties, with the introduction of educational reforms or with changing patterns of financing the system. Suddenly public and policy are highly aware of a delicate balance in the education system.

This balance, however, seems to have become an even more delicate balance then in the past. One only needs to scan the newspapers of the more recent months to see an increasing attention in schools, the learning process, in moral values regarding education or the workloads of students and teachers. Dutch students strike and demonstrate against the increased workload in upper secondary schools (the 'studiehuis'). In France 7000 special police personnel will be assigned to schools to maintain order and thus to reduce violence. In Germany, students protest against crowded classes at the Universities. In The United Kingdom the large amount of testing time in schools ('preparing for the test') is almost permanently under dispute.

Coming back to the resemblance between water and education, the availability and the constant quality of water was mentioned as being the most prominent problem of the 21st century (*Atlas of the Future 2000* as quoted in Trouw). Does that also hold for education? Can we feature education more prominently on the agenda? At least an increased interest in the following issues during the last decade can be noticed.

- *League tables and hit lists of schools*

In several countries, data on school achievement are available in the public domain. Educational authorities in the United Kingdom yearly publish the outcomes of secondary schools: the ratio of students that achieve the general certificate of secondary schooling and the score of students on these tests. Newspapers transform this information into League Tables that yield a high interest from parents and educational policy makers. Recently similar information for primary education has become available.

Also other European countries make such information available, for instance France and the Netherlands. However, this is not always an easy process. In the Netherlands for instance, the nation-wide newspaper *Trouw* had to resort to the courts in order to get access to the information on participation, grade repetition and the awarded diplomas of schools. This resulted in a –now yearly— publication of the ranking of schools as well as heavy debates occurring about the reliability and validity of such practices (Veenstra et al 1998 and Dronkers 1998). Much of these practices however, depend of the structure of the state and the educational system. In Federal States relatively high thresholds to making such information available appear to exist apparently due to the risk of internal comparisons (for instance in Germany or Austria)

- *Comparative studies on achievement*

Since 1966 the International Association for Educational Achievement (IEA) began their comparative studies and these have received much public attention. Within IEA great expertise in the international comparison of mathematics, science and reading has been developed, allowing large-scale studies in more then 50 countries to be conducted. In this area the so-called SIMSS and TIMSS-studies on mathematics and science have set a standard for comparative research on achievement.

It was during this same period, that an interest in educational indicators arose. The Organisation for Economic Co-operation and Development (OECD) launched their Indicators of Educational Systems (INES) programme in 1988. Massive effort was required to standardise the available data so as to allow the comparative evaluations of countries. Since 1992, indicators on participation, financing and achievement have been published in *'Education at a Glance'*. From 2000, the OECD will gather data on a regular three-yearly basis, about students in their Programme for International Student Assessment (PISA). There has been much investment in the development of equivalent instruments, not only with regard to subject matter, but also for cross-curricular competencies: so-called CCC's (see OECD 1997).

In most countries national education indicator activities have been launched to monitor educational developments in detail (For instance France, Belgium, Denmark and Austria). Clearly, this all indicates the importance of comparative education reflected in policy.

- *Accountability of education*

In many countries the accountability of the educational system is a central issue. How much is being invested and spent in education and what 'does one get back'? Is the investment worthwhile and if so for whom? Especially since *Education at a Glance* can provide countries, and teacher unions, with reliable data on expenditures for education, attention to financial aspects has been growing. The quality control within countries may have had a positive incentive effect with the availability of such educational indicators and it is highly plausible that inspectors have redefined their functions.

- *Evaluations of innovations and reform*

Educational researchers, by nature, long for the evaluation of educational innovations and reforms. But educational policy makers do not automatically share this interest: evaluations may show unreachable goals, ineffective organisation or a lack of positive results. During the last decades both the quality and scope of evaluation research has clearly improved. To a certain extent this may be related to the interest in indicators, however it may also be linked to the accountability issue: why spend large amounts of money on reforms if the expected outcomes fail to be realised. Evaluation –in some countries—is a parallel activity to the introduction of a reform. The focus on and search for effective schools can be seen as one aspect of this development (see for instance Bosker, Creemers & Stringfield 1999) and certainly has resulted in an increased attention in education and (comparative) education research.

Summarising: there is a growing interest in the information, indicators and studies that render the educational system and the learning process transparent. This increasing transparency serves policy makers, teachers and those who have a choice: students and parents.

2. Central Issues in Education

According to Cummins (1999, 414) the important questions facing contemporary education are:
- Who controls education?
- What is the purpose of education?
- How do children learn?
- How much is spent on education?
- Why are schools so resistant to change?
- Taking the structure into consideration, what is the likely future of education?

There is no reason to disagree over these issues: these are undoubtedly relevant questions, but these questions cover only a part of the spectrum. Some important elements are still to be uncovered.

For the purpose of our argument we represent the education process by a rather simple causal chain:

Goals - Means - Effects.

This chain generates most of the relevant education issues to date.
1. The selection of educational goals is the first stage in the education process:
    *   Which goals are selected?
    *   What is the underlying philosophy?
    *   Who selects these goals?
2. The selection of means specifies under which conditions the goals must be met:
    *   How many resources will be allocated?
    *   How will this process be organised?
    *   Who will be involved?
    *   How will the quality be controlled?
3. The third stage is the issue of whether the anticipated effects will indeed occur:
    *   Which dimensions, matched to the goals, should be evaluated?
    *   How should these dimensions be measured? (certificates, achievement, competencies, citizenship etc)
    *   What is the distribution of these dimensions? (equality, basic competencies)
    *   How are the effects evaluated? (methods, average level,)
    *   When are goals reached? (norms, minimum thresholds)

The above sketched process can be refined further in great detail and so has been done before. Our main argument here is that this representation of the education process shows where the main effort in research has been focused on and suggests where new approaches might be needed in the future.

In this respect, three observations are relevant.

Firstly, few studies cover the complete chain from goals to effects. That may be due to the fact that such studies require a heavy investment of time and resources. But this is regrettable since we are left only with information about partial processes. Nevertheless one study should be mentioned as an example of what is feasible. Blom (1995) studied the impact of educational philosophies on equity in France and the Netherlands in the post-war period. She found large differences with regard to participation and achievement within and between the two countries. These outcomes were clearly related to the educational paradigms and policies.

Secondly, it appears not many studies are available on alternative means structures. Given one selected goal of education, in practice various ways of realisation can be chosen or are already at work. Especially within countries the examples are obvious: differences in effects between public and private education, differences in financing arrangements, differences in organisational arrangements of control.

Thirdly, the nature of this above presented research paradigm implies that a comparative approach will be the most profitable. Given the goals, which alternative means produce the anticipated effects? Given the goals and means, which alternative measures of effect can be designed and which will show the anticipated results? And finally, do different goal settings indeed produce different results? Comparative studies, being either quantitative or qualitative, will produce the relevant knowledge.

In this abstract form such questions may not look very attractive. But in fact these are the underlying questions in most of the international comparative studies on educational achievement. The research process however, is reversed in time. On the basis of differences in achievement scores (effect) between countries, the search for factors that may explain these differences (means or goals) is conducted. But this assumes that a wide knowledge of these two elements in the causal chain is to hand, and this may not always be the case.

The foregoing argument must not be seen as a negative evaluation of existing studies or insights. The purpose is to underline the comparative aspects of the study of educational processes, to emphasise studies that focus on the complete 'causal' chain and to focus upon the relevance of studies of alternate means of educational 'production'.

This last issue is the central subject of this book and again we wish to make a simple yet important point. In the realisation of goals one may choose either for a strict regulation of the process or for leaving the organisation to societal forces i.e.: in fact this incorporates the issue of state regulation versus the market. Presently much of the debate on this issue is concentrated at the theoretical level and is less focused on the realisation of effects. This, of course, has much to do with empirical reality: do we find the same educational practices under conditions of state regulation as we do in a competitive market? New Zealand is such a rare case and fortunately some empirical work has been codepiled (see Waslander & Thrupp 1997). The study points to a decreasing equality in achievement after the transition from state regulation to a market situation.

In addition another issue, namely the dimensions of the educational effects becomes relevant. In practice all too easy the effects are described in terms of achievement in school subjects and in particular those that can be assessed relatively 'easily' . In practice this means that the educational goals are being evaluated only in terms of a subset of the intended effects, usually mathematics, science or reading.

Again, this must not be understood as a negative evaluation of ongoing or developing comparative enterprises. On the contrary, it should be seen as a strong plea for the development of a broad set of socially relevant criteria.

Let us be more concrete: In most countries educational goals explicitly refer to characteristics of the civil society and point to the development of individual competencies in three main dimensions (OECD 1997, Granheim 1998):

- preparation for the labour market
- preparation for active citizenship
- personality development

If one wishes to evaluate whether these goals are being realised through different means structures (public versus private, state versus market, effective schools and so on), then the effect measures must be congruent to the goals. So, a large developmental task lies ahead for the coming years. When the goals are described in civil society terms, then we also need the matching criteria.

On the basis of this conceptual exercise we can now focus on the three elements that constitute the core of this book: state, market and civil society.

3. Education between State-Market-Civil Society: European Perspectives

It may be relevant to mention here some relevant issues in the area of organisation of education and in particular the relation between market and state intervention. This will act as a kind of heuristic framework to generate the issues throughout the rest of this book. For this purpose we refer to Figure 1 in which Core relations (relations A, B and C) within a Context (conditions X, Y and Z) are distinguished.

Figure 1   *Relations around the Education System.*

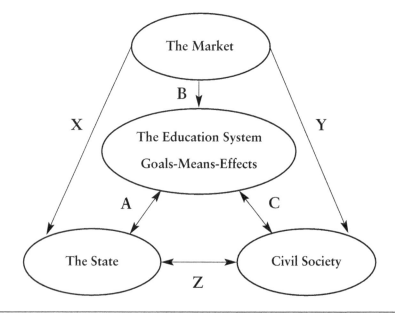

The Core
A State Intervention and Education
In most countries while educational goals are defined at the state level, the extent of state regulation can differ widely between countries. In some countries all

details of the curriculum, of schedules and of examinations are regulated by official state agencies. In other countries the state only defines the general framework whilst leaving the specifics to other actors in the process. The organisation of quality control is likely to differ greatly between these two extremes but that does not automatically mean that either student outcomes or equality (the effects) will differ. An even more interesting issue is what happens when much of the organisational details are left to the market. This may have substantial effects on organisation and the execution of processes. But to what degree do these effects vary? It is this domain that most of the discussion on goals and means should be placed.

B Market and Education: two sides of the same coin.
In economy education is a scarce good, not in an absolute but in a relative sense. Such positional goods can be traded on the market, which is the basis for the human capital theories. Investing in education can be done at the individual level, but is also evident at the government level. At both levels the market pays a price for education: individuals earn an income in a competitive market; countries earn national incomes in international competition. This is one side of the market in education coin, but this will not be discussed here.

The other side of the coin is that actors in the education process (schools and school boards) can act as if they are entrepreneurs on an educational market and have to compete with each other. It is especially this kind of issues that have recently become relevant and result in many questions emerging. This refers to the strategic behaviour of schools. Is organisation by the market as effective as it is by the state? Can educational goals be met with similar investment as is made by the state? Which educational goals can be more easily reached in a market-organised education system and which goals are neglected? How is quality control organised in a market when the state withdraws? And finally, how can we guarantee a minimum level of results for students?

C Education and Civil Society
This relation is clearly a two-sided one. Firstly the relevant actors in civil society determine the educational goals as well as the available and relevant means. In this process the role of actors is precisely described, as are the (implicit or explicit) expectations of the anticipated effects. Evaluation must show whether these effects really match with expectations. The core issue here is the definition of relevant educational goals for civil society.

On the other hand, irrespective of the way the education process is organised, the quality and effects of education also have their impact on society. Apart from explicit educational goals, more implicit expectations are also formed. Democratic values, an emphasis on justice and equality or the cooperative attitudes that are relevant for civil society. Most citizens expect that education will enhance these attitudes. But how much do we really know about this? To what degree has the education system contributed in this respect, to mention just two emerging questions.

The Context
The above three mentioned relations explicitly refer to the effects of state, market and civil society on education. But we have to remember that such effects are not autonomous: they depend on the societal arrangements and a wider context. Thus three other relations X, Y and Z also have to be taken into account. These act as *contingencies* for the educational system.

X Shift from State to Market
In many countries the state privatises not only education but many of its public services. Railways, toll roads and tunnels, telecom services, social security services and health care are just a few examples of this massive shift from 'collective responsibility' to 'market efficiency'. Usually the assumption is that the market can organise and provide such services, with equal justice, much more efficiently than the state can.

Y Effects of Marketisation on Civil Society
In the wider societal context of marketisation, both individuals and institutions will behave differently. Privatised public services will focus less on the realisation of societal goals (such as equality) than on efficiency and profit. Individuals may shift their focus from cooperation and solidarity with others to competition (the post-materialistic society). It is not necessary here to evaluate this development but we wish to emphasise that such changing societal arrangements affect the thinking on educational issues and thus are relevant to the framework of this book.

Z Civil Society and the State: a matter of trust
In various different societies discussions take place about the quality of the performance of the state. Some of the questions that arise are whether the goals of society are successfully realised by the institution of the State? How well organised is it and how effectively can it be evaluated? More and more the character of such evaluations shows elements of distrust. Often this relates to the private or corporate conduct of state officials. Here, the intention is not to take a moral position, but to emphasise that conditions of decreasing trust in the state and its institutions are not conducive to the realisation of the goals of a civil society. An important contingency for educational policy is the credibility of the state in educational intervention and innovation.

Comparative context
From a methodological point the above mentioned questions can best be studied in a comparative context. Transitions from state regulation to a competitive education market will allow studying the relative advantages of both organisational forms. Refinement of educational goals and curricula may show, over time, the impact on achievement and the extent of the realisation of educational goals. Furthermore, in the same way, the non-realisation of educational goals, such as personality formation or citizenship, which have important consequences for society, can be examined.

4. About this Book

The contributions to this book fit quite neatly into the model outlined in figure 1. It shows that almost all contributions do not solely relate to the relation between state and educational system but instead involve an interaction between state and civil society in relation to the educational system. The same applies to the other components of our model: Market - Civil Society and Market - State in relation to the educational system. Nevertheless, we can order the chapters on the basis of the emphasis led on state, respectively market and civil society. In the first part entitled 'State' we combined several chapters focussing on the role of the State in the educational system.

Part One: State

In the second chapter of this book the relation between state and education system effects is explored. Reynolds, Creemers, Teddlie and Stringfield describe an extensive study on school effectiveness in Asian countries. The authors show that a clear education policy by the state and a stable educational climate is beneficial for students' achievement. Although not explicitly mentioned in the text, it can be argued that the explored relation between state and effect can be expanded by civil society in the sense that effective schools should create equal opportunities for all students, given their personal abilities, socio-economic status and other background characteristics. Some authors even go a step further claiming that an effective school prevents a growing cleavage between low and high achieving students. If doing so the effective school contributes to equality both in school and later in civil society.

Kotthoff (chapter 3) provides an insight into the operation of the reformed British Inspection of Education (OFSTED). He also compares the British Inspection with the Inspection of Education of other European countries. The chapter focuses on the core relations between state and goals, means, effects, with a particular emphasis on effects. The author makes clear that the British Inspection of Education concentrates on the outcomes of education by taking efficiency and effectiveness, principles of the market, as leading principles. The British Inspection shows the relevance of the context relation X, where a state institution is ruled and organised by the market principles to a great extent.

Moutsios studies the fundamental differences between the British and Greek Inspections of education. This fourth chapter concentrates on the core relation between state and the educational system (goals, means and effect). The author argues that the difference between England and Greece relates to a difference in philosophy on inspection. Whereas in England the inspection concentrates on the effects of education, in Greece the inspection concentrates on the pedagogy i.e. the means structure. This chapter demonstrates how much countries may vary in how far the state permits the market to feature in education policy (context relation X).

The last chapter (5) in this section on the state deals with decentralisation policies in education in Russia and France. Although Russia and France are very different in their political and social history, they are comparable in their pursuit to change what is a very centralistic education policy into one that is a more decentralised. Folliet and Leclercq explore the core relation A between state and education. They give their thoughts on how decentralisation can be implemented without losing the guarantee that children, adolescents and young adults in every part of the country receive adequate and sufficient education.

Part Two: Market

In the first chapter in this section on market perspectives, Weiler describes how universities in many countries are forced by the state to act and behave increasingly according to market principles (chapter 6). The author focuses on how incentives are build into the financing of the universities. Again we see the relevance of the context relation X. Due to the opinion of the state that the market can organise the education system better than the state itself, universities are stimulated to act as a commercial organisation; universities have to compete with other universities both at home and abroad to attract enough students; students are becoming clients or consumers whilst their diploma become products with a certain price. Weiler elaborates on the consequences that these developments might have for universities.

Cowen argues in chapter 7 that the university-of-today is the result of an interplay between state, market and civil society. This explains a great deal of the differences between countries such as the USA, Germany, France and the UK. His analysis focuses on the nationally formulated goals in the different countries. In doing so, Cowen does not concentrate on the market in particular. This changes when he focuses on the university-of-the-future. Here he argues that a global university is emerging through new ICT-technology and further globalisation and internationalisation. Old patterns of state, market and civil society cannot easily be traced in this new context. The relevance of state and civil society seems to diminish or at least still has to develop in the global society, and therefore market seems to be the dominant mechanism of influence in the development of the global university.

The third issue in the section on market focuses on a rather 'old' phenomenon of markets in the education system, namely private schools (chapter 8). Dijkstra and Dronkers describe the situation of private schools in the Netherlands. They discuss how these schools came into existence and how they can be maintained in a primarily secularised society. Dutch private schools are equally financed by the state as public schools are. The organisation of education is shaped in such a way that state and civil society meet on a sort of marketplace. The state is the provider of money, the civil society, in the form of interest groups such as parents and churches, is the manager of the private schools. This chapter is a good example of civil society as an actor in the education system, driven by ideological and market principles (core relation C and context relation Z and Y).

In the last chapter of this part Renkema en De Hoop describe two case studies on the development of higher education in developmental countries. Chapter 9 shows that universities in third world countries function in a market environment; their main goal is to provide employees for the (local) market. In their description, the authors concentrate on the capacity building programme. Universities in developmental countries receive funds and are advised by a Dutch foreign aid organisation on development of education programmes. This chapter shows that the functioning of the university is highly related to developments in the market and civil society (political and ethnic), whereas the market is of decisive interest to the end result.

Part Three: Civil society

The section on civil society opens with a contribution by Thélot (chapter 10). He discusses the relation between the state and goals of the educational system on the one hand and the effects of it on civil society on the other. By taking four main goals, knowledge, qualification for profession, preparation for citizenship and equality, he shows us how well the French education system has succeeded in realising its goals. These results are confronted with the finances invested in the system. Although the increase of the costs is higher than the increase of the results, Thélot argues that a cleavage between the level of education in general and the needs of the French society and economy is more worrying than the money spent in education.

In a next chapter (11) Guyot investigates in how far the civil society has influenced the increasing demands for adult education at the university. He approaches this question from a contingency and a culturalist framework. Both frameworks contribute to the understanding of the increase of adult education. Moreover, Guyot provides a possible explanation for why certain studies such as psychology or education are moving into this area more than other studies.

Hansen focuses in chapter 12 on the situation of Pakistani students in secondary education in Oslo, Norway. First she describes the policy of the Norwegian government towards Pakistani and other foreign students in secondary education. This policy emphasises integration, in a sense that students are offered education in their own language. However, Norwegian values and norms on education and personal development are maintained and taught also to Pakistani students. Furthermore the author discusses the perceptions of Pakistani pupils on education in relation to their cultural and family background. So here the issue is whether a certain policy indeed generates the intended effects on civil society.

In chapter 13 another market perspective on education is presented. The contribution of Murdoch, Paul and Zanzala focuses on the relation between market (selectivity), effects and civil society (employment / status): context relation Y. The authors approach the education system from an economical point of view. In their opinion the individual's returns of education is whether (s)he will find employment and earn a salary. The analyses investigate whether selectivity of universities in England and France influences the chances of employment after students leave the university with a diploma. Secondly differences between the two countries are analysed. Murdoch and his colleagues contrast human capital theory and filtering theory to get more insight into the relation between selectivity and returns of education. The analyses show that students from selective schools find more easily a job and earn more money than students from less selective schools. They find that selectivity increases the efficiency of education (less dropouts) but also endangers equity.

Conclusion

The chapters of this book focus on important perspectives in modern European education: the mutual relationships between state, market and civil society. It has not been attempted to cover all potential aspects in all possible detail. Merely our goals has been to provide a framework into which relevant European studies could be incorporated and to stimulate the discussion regarding the further exploration and systematic study of these issues in education.

References

Atlas of the Future (2000) by Ian Pearson. Myriad Editions Ltd.

Blom, S.V. (1995) *Intellectuele vorming in Nederland en Frankrijk*. Groningen: Wolters-Noordhoff.

Bosker. R.J., B.P.M. Creemers & S. Stringfield (1999) *Enhancing Educational Excellence, Equity and Efficiency*. Dordrecht: Kluwer Academic Publishers.

Cummins, W.K. (1999) 'The InstitutionS of Education: Compare, Compare, Compare!' *Comparative Education Review* (43) 413-437.

Dronkers, J. (1998) 'Het betere is de vijand van het goede.' Pedagogische Studiën (43) 142-150.

Granheim, M. et al (1998) *Educational Goals: a Comparative Study*. Paris: OECD.

OECD (1992 and later) *Education at a Glance*. Paris, OECD.

OECD (1997) *Prepared for Life*. Paris, OECD.

PISA web site: http://oecd.org/els//pisa/

Veenstra, D.R., Dijkstra, A.B., Peschar, J.L. & Snijders, T.A.B. (1998) 'Scholen op rapport.' *Pedagogische Studien*, 121-134.

Waslander, S. (1999) *Koopmanschap en Burgerschap*. Assen, Van Gorcum.

Waslander, S. & M. Thrupp (1995) 'Choice, competetion and segregation. An empirical analysis of a New Zealand secondary school market 1990-1993'. *Journal of Educational Policy* (10)1-26.

Part 1

State

2

World Class Schools: Some Preliminary Findings from the International School Effectiveness Research Project

David Reynolds, Bert Creemers,
Charles Teddlie & Sam Stringfield

1. Introduction: The Intellectual and Policy Context of ISERP

Recent years have seen a greatly enhanced interest within educational research in issues of a 'comparative' nature. In most fields, there is an enhanced internationalisation evident in the increasingly international attendance at the conferences of educational 'specialities' and in the acceptance of the importance of 'nation' as a contextual variable of importance.

The reasons for this internationalisation have been fully dealt with elsewhere (Reynolds and Farrell, 1996; Reynolds et al, 1994; Reynolds et al, 1999) but briefly can be related to the ease with which ideas, both practical and conceptual, can now be spread throughout the world by information technology, and to the pressures that are being put upon national educational systems to maximise pupil outcomes by searching out and utilising effective practices from anywhere in the world that they may exist.

In this situation, the pressure upon the discipline of comparative education to resource this increasingly internationalised discourse has been growing, yet the discipline itself has been seemingly on an intellectual plateau for perhaps two decades. Much of the discipline appears to be simply descriptive, with little attempt to generate any theoretical underpinnings. There have additionally been 'macro level' attempts to generate theoretical understandings but these appear to be without empirical foundation. When there are discussions about educational policies in this literature, there is usually an assumption that the policies have the effects that their policymakers assume, a very dangerous assumption to hold! Perhaps most importantly, the conventional absence of any dependent variable internationally, across countries, against which to assess the various influences of the independent variables, makes analysis of the causal factors that determine the nature of countries' educational systems very difficult.

There has been, of course, an additional body of knowledge to resource the international discussion of education increasingly taking place, and that is the cross national achievement surveys undertaken by the IEA and similar organisations, such as the recent Third International Mathematics and Science Study (TIMSS) (Keys, Harris and Fernandes, 1996). However, although they have the intellectual advantage of being able to compare countries on a common dependent variable or metric of achievement scores, the paradigm that the achievement surveys work within seems to be deficient in many important aspects:

1. these studies usually utilise cross-sectional samples of students, rather than following cohorts of students over time through longitudinal research designs;
2. the samples of students from countries are sometimes not representative of the entire populations of students in those countries, which is especially the case when specific geographic or political regions are chosen to represent an entire country;
3. operational definitions of sampling 'levels' may vary across countries; for example, what constitutes third grade in one country may not be the same in another;
4. materials may not be translated the same across countries, thus resulting in reliability and validity problems;
5. the cross-country reliability and validity of surveys and questionnaires may be suspect, since the constructs that they measure may be different in divergent cultural contexts; for example, Purves (1992) concluded that written composition must be interpreted within a cultural context, not as a general cognitive ability;
6. there are difficulties in designing tests, which adequately sample the curricula delivered in multiple countries.

Other criticisms of these international educational surveys address a different set of issues related to a perceived need for more 'contextually aware and sensitive' investigations of the processes at work in differentially effective schools. These criticisms include the following:

1. there are few 'data rich' descriptions of the school and classroom processes associated with more effective (and less effective) schooling in international studies, partly as a result of the use of questionnaires to gauge classroom processes rather than observations, no doubt because of cost considerations;
2. there is often a lack of information on non-educational factors (e.g. socio-economic status of students' families; community type in which the school is located) that may affect the methods whereby individual schools attempt to effectively educate their students;
3. there is often a lack of information on the affective or social outcomes of the schooling process;
4. there are few examples of international studies that successfully link 'country factors' (e.g. educational policies enacted at the national level, unique aspects of national educational systems) with the effectiveness of schools or with what factors appear to be effective within schools.

This, then, was the context in the fields of comparative and international studies within which the International School Effectiveness Research Project (ISERP) was founded in 1991. It is important to note that not all the motivation for undertaking this project related to perceived deficiencies in the research base of comparative education paradigms, since the intellectual state of affairs in school effectiveness research also was a contributory factor.

Three sets of factors from the effectiveness community had an influence. Firstly, the 1990's had for the first time seen research findings which suggested that the effective schools 'correlates' or 'factors' might be somewhat different in different geographical contexts, with the Dutch educational research community, particularly, being unable to replicate more than a handful of the 'classic' school or classroom factors from the American 'five factor' theories of educational effectiveness (see Scheerens and Bosker, 1997 for a summary). Particularly interesting and potentially important was the failure of Dutch empirical research to show the importance of the leadership of the Principal in creating effective schools (van de Grift, 1990), in marked contrast to the importance of this role and of the role occupants shown from American research (Levine and Lezotte, 1990). The apparent 'context specificity' of school effectiveness factors suggested an interesting future direction for research, which would involve varying social context systematically between countries in order to see which factors universally 'travelled', and which factors did not but required particular cultural and social contexts to be potentiated in their effects.

Secondly, there was a clear need to generate theory, since the variation in 'what worked', if it could be explained and theoretically modelled, would force the field towards the development of more complex and multifaceted accounts than the 'one size fits all' mentality that had hitherto existed in the field. Useful contributions were already being made in the area of theory in the early 1990's (Creemers and Scheerens, 1989; Creemers, 1992) but there was a need to take them further.

Thirdly, it had increasingly become clear that the importance of comparative international research is that only these studies could tap the full range in school and classroom quality, and therefore in potential school and classroom effects. Within any country the range of school factors in terms of 'quantity' variables (such as size, financial resources, quality of buildings) and in terms of 'quality' factors (such as press for achievement) was likely to be much smaller than the variation in such factors across countries.

2. The Design of ISERP

ISERP eventually came to comprise nine countries, split across three broad regions: the United States and Canada, Australia, Hong Kong and Taiwan, and the Netherlands, Norway, the United Kingdom and Ireland. Each country selected either six or twelve primary (or elementary) schools, with these schools selected to be of high, average or low 'effectiveness', based upon either prior data on schools' intakes and outcomes or on nomination by those with close knowledge of the schools such as inspectors, advisers and the like. Half of the schools were selected from low socio-economic status communities and half from those of middle socio-economic status.

The basic methodology of the study was to follow a cohort of children aged seven through their schools for two years, the age being chosen to maximise the chance of ensuring that school effects did not masquerade as intake effects and because children in many societies of the world, such as Norway, did not begin their education until age seven. Mathematics was the dependent variable on which the relative progress of children and societies was to be measured, selected because it was more 'culture free' than any other measure given its similarity as a body of knowledge across cultures.

The ISERP study broke new ground in many areas. For student outcomes it utilised measures of children's social outcomes in the different countries, such as measures of attitudes to education, self perceived ability in school and attitudes to teachers. Most innovative of all, the research included direct observation of teachers in different contexts in different countries, with the use of an adapted version of Robert Slavin's QAIT classroom observation system designed to measure quality of teaching, appropriateness of teaching, the teacher's use of incentives and the teacher's time use (Schaffer, 1994), to generate descriptions that were qualitatively rich on classrooms. The research design was also based upon the use of 'mixed' methods, both quantitative and qualitative. Immersion in the schools and cultures of different countries was to be undertaken by the 'core' research team, to understand the cultural 'taken for granted' that might be the explanation for country differences in the educational processes that appeared to 'work'. Rich case studies of schools were also undertaken.

To summarise, there was therefore one major research question of the study:

Which factors may be universally associated with student academic and social outcomes across countries, which factors may be restricted to a certain cultural context, and why?

ISERP therefore involved trying to understand the effects of societal (country) differences on the ways whereby schools become effective. Since the design involved case studies, it was meant to allow for a better understanding of 'why' country differences in effective school characteristics might exist.

3. Some Preliminary Findings from ISERP

Full analysis of this very large database will be published shortly (Reynolds et al, in press), so all we can do here is to relate to some of the principal findings:

- although we were not sampled to be a 'country versus country' study of achievement differences, the relative position of the nine countries on the mathematics tests utilised was quite similar to the position shown in most of the international surveys to date (see Reynolds and Farrell, 1996, for a review), with Pacific Rim societies showing higher achievement scores than Anglo Saxon societies such as the United Kingdom or European societies such as The Netherlands;

- it is clear that there are interesting variations between countries in the reliability of their education systems, with some evidencing 'low variance' and some, predominantly Anglo Saxon societies, showing variability in terms of the variance explained by schools;
- there is variation between countries in the extent that social class factors in pupil backgrounds affect their achievement in school, with some societies particularly of the Pacific Rim ensuring that schools distanced individuals from their backgrounds more than others;
- interestingly, in virtually all countries the effect of pupils' time in school is to weaken the relationship between pupils' achievement and their parental, ethnic and social class backgrounds, over the two years for which we followed our children. One should have no doubt that these findings indicate the power of schooling to combat disadvantage - they tell us, as has the school effectiveness research tradition, (Teddlie and Reynolds, 1999) that schools can make a difference;
- there are a number of universals, which appear to be associated with schools being effective, with some being connected to classroom teaching and some being connected to the organisation of schools. At classroom level, across all countries the 'usual gang of suspects' that have formed the foundations of the teacher effectiveness tradition - such as questioning, structure, expectations etc., - are precisely the factors that discriminate the ineffective schools from others that are more effective across all our countries.

4. Some Policy Recommendations Based On Our Analyses

We now think it is useful to spell out some recommendations for educational practice based upon our preliminary analyses of our data. We think that four recommendations can be made:

- *World Class Schools Need Strong Systems Not People*

In many of the Anglo Saxon societies that we studied, there has been a strong emphasis in State pronouncements and planning upon the need to reward and train exemplary individuals to improve educational outcomes from schools. In England and Wales, for example, there have been government attempts to reward such individuals with honours and to 'showcase' them as part of national educational discourse. In the United States, the lionising of successful individuals has involved similar kinds of reinforcement.

In other societies, such concern to reward individuals as individuals is largely absent because governments have built strong systems that are given to all educational leaders to function as foundations of their practice. Indeed, in those societies teacher education more generally has often incorporated 'instructional theory' and 'instructional practice' courses that aim to deliver a determined 'technology of practice' to all.

Strong systems of practice or technologies of practice have considerable advantages in promoting educational outcomes. Whereas relying on the 'strong people' or 'unusual persons' to staff educational systems restricts one to the number of persons who possess naturally the characteristics required to be exceptional, relying on systems to create such people expands the number of persons who are available to include all those who can be 'made' exceptional. Strong systems minimise the variance in the quality of education provided, whereas systems that rely on persons to create their own methods increase it. Given inevitably variable competence amongst persons, the result of the latter is likely to be variance in the quality of schooling and teaching provided, according to how much educational 'strength' people have.

•   *World Class Schools Require Some Things to be Taken for Granted*
In each country that we have studied, there are beliefs regarding children, teaching and schools that form a basis for the development of educational practices amongst educational professionals across schools. The elements of these and the consistency with which they are held are very different from country to country. In Pacific Rim societies, for example, or in Norway there are values that virtually all educational professionals share about 'what should happen' in a classroom or a school. In part, of course, such cohesion reflects the very nature of the society itself, with its shared values of desired educational practice derived from Confucian traditions in the case of the Pacific Rim and from a strong national community in the case of Norway.

But it is clear that educational interventions can mould these cohesive values also, rather than just reflect them. Most elementary school teachers in Taiwan, for example, received training from nine institutions whose faculty come from only three major universities. Educational meetings to determine national policy include the major educational players, and changes can be rapidly conveyed to teachers who share the general national values about which educational values are important and which practices appropriate. There is, of course, variation among educational professionals in their practice, but it appears to be concerned with the degree of implementation of the particular practice rather than being based upon varying definitions about the purposes of teaching and the goals of the educational system in the first place.

Whereas some societies have this shared set of understandings about what schools should be doing, and particularly Norway, Taiwan and Hong Kong spring to mind here, Anglo Saxon countries evidenced huge variation in what is seen as appropriate practice, reflecting unresolved values debates at national level about what the purpose of education is, and what therefore 'good practice' is. In such situations, children in the various age phases of schooling may be the losers. They may be exposed to variation in practice because teachers have different sets of goals, and may be exposed to variation in the quality of the implementation of the practice by the different sets of teachers with the different sets of goals, making schools and classrooms unpredictable and lacking in consistency, constancy and cohesion.

The creation of World Class Schools clearly, then, requires agreement upon goals amongst educationalists as educationalists, if not as individuals. There seems to be little useful purpose to be served by a continued professional debate about values that is present in a number of societies that we have studied until the educational system can effectively deliver any of the values, which it cannot do at present because it has ineffective and varied 'means' that have been produced by the inability of the system to have clarity of mission and focus 'down' on delivery.

- *World Class Schools Require Technologies of Practice*

We noted above that there were interesting differences between countries in the extent to which children's achievements were associated with their parents' social backgrounds. In the United States and United Kingdom, children's mathematics achievement was strongly related to such factors as parental occupation and parental education. By contrast, in certain societies such as Taiwan and Hong Kong the relationship was weaker.

It is easy to see how this paradox may be explained, since the Anglo Saxon societies have largely permitted teachers to self determine much of their practice. In this setting, stereotypic pictures of how children are influenced by their parents that form part of nationally based value systems, and vulgar perceptions of children from lower social classes as from 'rough, feckless and unschoolworthy' homes can easily be reflected in classroom practices that discriminate against such children. Put simply, if there is an absence of a 'core' shared technology of practice transmitted through programmes of professional education, then the 'hole' will be filled by practices that are determined by the personal views of teachers and Principals.

The alternative, and some societies evidence this, is to ensure that professional education gives all teachers a technology that is to be applied uniformly and evenly to all children independent of any background factors that may exist. In such countries as Taiwan, therefore, all teachers receive the 'technology' of their profession through instructional theory courses that bring to all trainees the world's great knowledge bases about effective instruction, intervention programmes, novel approaches such as metacognitive strategies, and the like. The attempt is made to, in a structured fashion, fill the 'circle' of professional practice that would be largely filled by a process of self-invention or 'do-it-yourself' in other societies.

The specification of a teaching technology is also associated with a clearly specified professional ideology that minimises the chance of children from disadvantaged homes being educated by discriminating practices. In Taiwan, for example, the belief is inculcated that all children can learn, that the school should educate all children whether their background is advantaged or disadvantaged, and that education is the right of all. Correspondingly, there is a total absence of discussion about children's family backgrounds, since they are not seen as relevant to the job of the school, since the role of the school is to educate all children independently of the background they come from.

- *Educational Borrowing May Be Useful, If Practised With Care*

We noted above that policymakers have increasingly begun to look across the globe in search of policies and practices that might work in their own schools. Much of this search may be in simple desperation of further increments in school quality coming from enhanced understanding by the educators within the policymakers' own societies. Some of it may also be due to the genuine realisation that societies other than one's own may have useful initiatives, policies and processes that might be worthy 'try outs' in their own societies.

Whatever the reason for the internationalisation, policymakers should be reassured by the findings of our study, since it is clear that 'what is necessary for schools to work' is very similar conceptually in different countries. The classroom, the Principal, the relations between staff members and the other factors that make schools 'effective' or 'ineffective' across the globe are, then, an established technology of practice conceptually that should be drawn on without fear of irrelevance, or contextual irrelevance, by policymakers.

However, policymakers' capacity to validly use studies such as ours with the confidence that the same concepts discriminate between good and less good practice internationally should not be confused with their borrowing of the detail of school practices. As an example, although the Principal appears as a key factor in determining 'what works' across the globe, the precise way in which an effective Principal is effective in a Taiwanese context (by being quite vertical in orientation) and in a Norwegian context (by being quite horizontal or lateral) are very different. Policy borrowing from country to country may be useful but should therefore be practised with caution when it comes to the details.

5. The Implications of the Findings for Researchers

For researchers, the ISERP study has validated for those of us involved in it the value of comparative study, for three reasons. Firstly, we have simply seen in other societies a variety of educational practices at classroom and school levels that would not have been seen had the core research team stayed within their own societies. In Pacific Rim societies, for example, the majority of lesson time is filled with what has been called 'whole class interactive' instruction, in which relatively short lessons of forty minutes are filled with fast, emotionally intense presentations from teachers, with accompanying very high levels of involvement with pupils. This model of teaching, which is also found within a European context in societies such as Switzerland, is now of course the subject of considerable debate within United Kingdom schools.

In Norway, as a contrast, there is no formal assessment of children through the entire phase of their elementary/primary education from the age of seven, a marked contrast to the United Kingdom practice of formal assessment and associated publication of results. In Pacific Rim societies again, one can see micro level educational practices such as teachers teaching from a stage at the front of the class some six inches high (to help those at the back of the class to see), pupils marching to assembly through corridors in which loudspeakers play music (to ensure a relaxed attitude) and pupils starting the afternoon session of school with a 'sleeping' lesson (to deal with the fatigue brought about by the frantic pace of the school and the heat/humidity of the climate). Put simply, comparative investigation shows an enhanced range of what appears to be educationally possible.

The benefits from comparative investigation are more than simply a knowledge of educational factors that might of course be utilised in programmes of experimentation in one's own country. They are, secondly, that one is made aware of educational philosophies that are radically different from one's own, or those of the government of one's own country. In Norway, for example, there is a strong commitment to the child as an 'active citizen', and to what are called 'democratic values' that have no British or American equivalents. In Pacific Rim societies like Taiwan, there is a philosophy that the role of the school is to ensure that all children learn, and that a strong 'technology' of practice should be employed to ensure that children are not dependent on their family background. Such societies are very concerned about the use of practices to improve the achievement of their trailing edge of pupils, therefore, and are rather less concerned with the education of the 'gifted and talented' than are the societies of the United Kingdom and United States.

There is a third reason for comparative investigation that is probably even more important than the two above, concerning the possibility that within the right kind of comparative framework one can move beyond looking at the practices of other societies and actually so empathise with other societies that one can look back at one's own society with the benefit of their perspective. Such 'acculturation' is what happened to many of us in ISERP when we were confronted with, and may have identified with, Pacific Rim educational systems. Looking back at the British system through their 'lens', one wonders at the utility of the combination of the very complex technology of practice that is evident in British primary education, for example, with methods of teacher education that are premised on the importance of teachers 'discovering', or at the least playing an active role in learning about, the appropriate methods to use. To a Taiwanese educationist, this celebrates the desires of teachers for their long term developmental needs above the needs of children to receive a reliable, consistent, predictable and competently provided experience as they pass through their schools.

The use of another culture's 'lens' adopted through the intervisitation programme to better understand the limitations and strengths of one's own educational practice also applies at the level of educational philosophy as well as educational practice. As an example, those of us involved in the British ISERP team would have historically viewed our primary education practice as loosely 'progressive' and indeed would have thought that in many senses it was the envy of the world. The encouragement of children to learn on their own rather than simply being instructed, the new sets of social outcomes that the system is widely argued to concentrate upon and the reduced emphasis upon the testing of knowledge acquisition have been widely argued to be the hallmarks of progressive practice in the British system.

Seen from a Pacific Rim perspective, however, the characteristics of the British system would be seen as regressive, not progressive. Transferring the burden of learning to pupils would be seen as maximising both social class influences and variation between pupils within Taiwanese educational culture, since pupils' learning gains would depend on what they brought to the learning situation in terms of achievement levels and backgrounds. Removing the 'constant' of the teacher would be seen as further maximising individual variation in knowledge gain. Avoiding the testing of basic skills could be seen as maximising the chances of children who have missed acquiring particular knowledge bases being left without them, through the absence of short term feedback loops that alert school authorities that certain children have not learned.

It remains a great pity that comparative education in general, and the international achievement surveys in particular, have not shown consistent improvement in the quality of the data gathered, and in the insights derived from that data, over the last twenty years. In the absence of an intellectually vibrant comparative education community, the increasing tendency of educational research to be cross-national or international in focus will not be resourced, and the sub-disciplines of education may make the kind of intellectual and practical errors that comparative education could have warned them about.

Within comparative education, it is perhaps the large scale cross-national achievement surveys like ISERP that have most to offer, were they to improve in quality. These surveys are well known by educational researchers and policymakers, and command attention because of the themes they address. For all their faults, they have a common dependent variable and therefore, in theory, can handle the explanation of the effects of different patterns of independent variables. They include material on the focal concerns of educational research - schools and, to a more limited extent, classrooms. From our own experience, the quality of this work would improve if it, to summarise:

- utilised multiple methodologies and strategies of data collection;
- focused upon classrooms more, utilising observation of children's whole school days;
- adopted multiple outcomes;
- was sensitive to the variation between countries in their basic educational discourses;
- ensured that the factors studied were representative of the likely causal factors across all countries;
- utilised cohort studies that kept researchers in touch with the same children over time;
- utilised intervisitations across countries to understand educational phenomena better.

Our recommendation for comparative education is therefore that there should be more studies like ISERP, but which build on the lessons of the ISERP.

6. Conclusions: Towards Cautious Experimentation

The ISERP study has begun to generate its material on educational systems, nested within cultures, and to begin its speculations about which factors may travel across contexts, and which are potentiated within contexts, at precisely the time when such issues are generating controversy within comparative education.

On the one side are those who think that educational practices are manifestations of broader cultural patterns, values and styles of discourse that exist at societal level. Seen from this perspective, whole class interactive teaching in French classrooms, for example, can be seen as related to the French philosophic love of discourse. Supporting this view is the evidence from studies such as the IEA Classroom Environment study that once other wider cultural and social factors are accounted for, teacher behaviours themselves add little explanatory variance (Anderson et al, 1989).

Another perspective, which we would support, is to argue that the educational policies and processes of different societies are variable responses to cultural and structural situations and therefore have a degree of independence and potential transferability across contexts. Seen from this perspective, methods that are regarded as effective such as whole class interactive teaching or the rapid feedback to teachers produced by the short loops of repeated testing may be utilised in different cultural contexts with good chances of effectiveness independent of cultural context.

One suspects that the answer to these disciplinary controversies is unlikely to lie in the conduct of further studies of the ISERP variety, whatever their utility in terms of pioneering new methodologies and in terms of new insights. What may be needed is for cautious experimentation to take place, in which certain methods from certain contexts are experimentally 'tried out' within other different contexts, using methods where judged by the national research base the detail of the method seems likely to generate a positive effect in the country doing the experimentation. As the 'implanted' methods interact with societal structures and cultures one may see either educational potency or adverse effects, the precise nature of which will depend upon the systemic/cultural interaction. From this process, in turn, one can gain a deeper understanding of the nature of the cultures of different societies, the values of their inhabitants and their styles of discourse, as the methods variably interact with them. In comparative education, as maybe in education more generally, the way to understand something as complex as the educational system may be to try to change it.

References

Anderson, L.W., Ryan, D.W. and Shapiro, B.J., (1989). *The IEA Classroom Environment Study*. Oxford Pergamon Press.

Creemers, B.P.M. and Scheerens, J. (Eds) (1989). Developments in school effectiveness research. A special issue of *International Journal of Educational Research*, 13(7), 685-825.

Creemers, B. (1992). School effectiveness and effective instruction - the need for a further relationship. In Bashi, J. and Sass, Z. (Eds), *School Effectiveness and Improvement*, Jerusalem, Hebrew University Press.

Keys, W., Harris, S. and Fernandes, C. (1996). *Third International Mathematics and Science Study, First National Report*, Part 1. Slough, National Foundation for Educational Research.

Levine, D.U. and Lezotte, L.W. (1990). *Unusually effective schools: A review and analysis of research and practice.* Madison, WI: The National Center for Effective Schools Research and Development.

Purves, A.C. (1992). *The IEA Study of Written Composition II: Education and Performance in Fourteen Countries.* Oxford, Pergamon Press.

Reynolds, D., Creemers, B.P.M., Stringfield, S., Teddlie, C., Schaffer, E. and Nesselrodt, P., (1994). *Advances in School Effectiveness Research and Practice.* Oxford, Pergamon Press.

Reynolds, D. and Farrell, S. (1996). *Worlds Apart? - A Review of International Studies of Educational Achievement Involving England.* London, HMSO for OFSTED.

Reynolds, D., Creemers, B.P.M., Stringfield S, and Teddlie C. (1999) 'Creating A New Methodology for Comparative Educational Research: The Contribution of the International School Effectiveness Research Project (ISERP)' in R. Alexander (Ed) *Learning From Comparing, Volume One.* Wallingford: Symposium Books, pp135-148.

Reynolds, D., Creemers, B.P.M., Stringfield, S. and Teddlie, C., (in press). *World Class Schools (The Final Report of the International School Effectiveness Research Project).*

Schaffer, G., (1994). The contributions of classroom observation to school effectiveness research. In Reynolds, D., Creemers, B. P. M, Nesselrodt, P., Schaffer, G., Stringfield, S. and Teddlie, C., *Advances in School Effectiveness Research and Practice. Oxford, Pergamon.*

Scheerens, J. and Bosker, R., (1997). *The Foundations of School Effectiveness.* Oxford, Pergamon Press.

Stevenson, H., (1992). Learning from Asian Schools. Scientific American, December, pp32-38.

Teddlie, C. and Reynolds, D. (1999) *The International Handbook of School Effectiveness Research.* London, Falmer Press.

Grift, W. van de, (1990). Educational leadership and academic achievement in secondary education. *School Effectiveness and School Improvement,* 1(1), 26-40.

3

Paying the Price for 'Deregulation': The Rise of External School Evaluation through Inspection

Hans-Georg Kotthoff

1. Introduction

The international changes and reforms towards increasingly decentralised and deregulated education systems have changed the relationship between central administration and the individual school radically, in that they have strengthened the autonomy of schools, in particular with regards to finances and organisational matters (OECD/CERI 1995; Wielemans, 1998). At the same time however, the increased freedom of the individual school has been counterbalanced and restricted again through a number of new state-controlled measures and regulations. In this context various forms of state-controlled external school evaluations that have been introduced in many European education systems have to be mentioned. Taking the radically reformed English school inspectorate Office for STandards in EDucation (OFSTED) as an example, this study focuses on the features and pros and cons of school inspections as one form of external evaluation that is likely to emerge in deregulated education systems. The central question in this context is whether the rise of external evaluation through inspection that is, at least in the European context, most striking in England[1] is a price too high to pay for the increased autonomy of schools or whether school inspections are a worthwhile activity because they do lead to school improvement as OFSTED claims self-confidently in its logo 'improvement through inspection'.

This study which is part of a larger international research project on school evaluation in England, the Netherlands, Sweden and Germany is based on the analysis of official documents and regulations, as well as case study material and a series of interviews with experts which were conducted between October 1997 and June 1998[2]. The present paper intends to deal with the inspection system in England primarily and therefore makes references to the other research countries only when the developments in England are assessed from an international comparative perspective[3]. Although the following remarks presuppose the knowledge of the situation in England, the politico-educational background of the reform of the school inspectorate will be described briefly (2) in order to support the readers' understanding of the changed role of the school inspectors in the English educational system. This is followed by an analysis of the organisation and function of the inspectorate (3) and the inspection procedures (4) before the pros and cons of external evaluation through inspection are discussed and evaluated by comparing them with developments in other European education systems (5). The paper concludes with a summary and a discussion of the findings and draws conclusions about future developments of the English school inspection system (6).

2. The politico-educational context of the reform of the English school inspectorate

Until the Education (Schools) Act (DfE, 1992) of 1992 school inspections in England were conducted by Her Majesty's Inspectorate (HMI) and local inspectorates. HMI's history, which can be traced back at least until 1839, operated on a national level (Brighouse 1995, Lawton & Gordon 1987). Their main tasks were to check the quality of education in state-run schools, to report on the effectiveness of the educational policies of the government, to give advice to the Department of Education and to develop strategies for the improvement of the school system. The local inspectorates were assigned to the Local Education Authorities (LEAs) and had apart from their controlling function primarily an advising role. Although many LEAs used the formal terms inspector and inspection, they were far from having a systematic strategy for the evaluation of and reporting on the quality and effectiveness of their schools. Moreover, empirical studies at the end of the eighties showed that the LEAs inspected their schools relatively seldom and arbitrarily (Stillman, 1989; Audit Commission, 1989). The altogether small number of 300-500 HMI school inspections per year and especially the fact that the work of the LEA inspectors and their inspection criteria lacked transparency caused repeatedly harsh criticism at the end of the eighties and the beginning of the nineties (Wilcox & Gray, 1996:28) and made discussions over a changed role of the local and national school inspectorates inevitable.

Three reasons in particular can be given for these discussions. First, the politico-educational climate had changed decisively under the Thatcher government since 1979. Catchwords of these reform efforts during the eighties were market, competition and choice as well as accountability and standards. These tendencies which are on first sight contradictory were put on a legal basis through the passing of the Education Reform Act (DES 1988) in 1988. The increasing autonomy of schools which became apparent in the Act through the strengthening of the Governing Bodies, the introduction of open enrolment and the Local Management of Schools (LMS) as well as the establishment of so-called grant-maintained schools (GMS) which had been released from LEA-control indicated on the one hand the intention of the then Conservative Government to establish competition between individual schools under market conditions (Kotthoff 1994). The introduction of the National Curriculum and the related extremely elaborate national assessment and reporting system as well as the permanently rising number of so-called quasi-autonomous non-governmental organisations[4] (QUANGOs) on the other hand represented the attempt to increase the accountability of the schools towards the state and the parents. In hindsight it is, therefore not surprising that in this dense network of complementary central and decentral forces eventually also the barely transparent work of the state-financed school inspectorates came increasingly under pressure.

A second reason for the new organisation of the school inspection system was the declining trust of the Conservative Government in the teaching profession and the ability and the will of the (pre-dominantly Labour-controlled) LEAs to exercise their supervisory duties over the schools rigorously. Thus, it can be said while schools became more autonomous in financial and organisational respects, the Government's trust in the so-called educational establishment declined. An outward expression of this mistrust was amongst other indicators the first ever National Curriculum in England, which was introduced in 1988. Many teachers feared that their long-standing and valued autonomy in curricular and teaching matters was severely threatened. In many schools there were serious reservations towards the introduction of a national curriculum which, for the first time, not only prescribed the teaching content and objectives but also the standards which a pupil should usually achieve at certain points in time during his school career. Obligatory external tests and pupil assessment by teachers were prescribed for all pupils at the end of certain key stages throughout the period of compulsory schooling (ages 7, 11, 14, 16). The results of these tests were and still are collected, assembled in league tables and widely circulated through the press.

The Education Reform Act had placed extensive legal requirements on each school and the government needed to know now if and how all schools were complying with the law. This was even truer since the Conservative government had imposed a strict accountability to the parents upon itself. John Major's Citizen Charter from 1991 (Cabinet Office, 1991) according to which all public services have to work transparently and are accountable to the public also included the promise to raise standards and to strengthen the rights of parents to know about the state of the education system. The intended complete information of the parents about the state of education could, according to the government, not be achieved through a few hundred HMIs and barely co-ordinated local inspectorates. While HMI had conducted only a few hundred formal inspections at the beginning of the nineties, it was now envisaged that it would inspect and report on all 25,000 public schools once every four years. Due to staff shortages and a lack of conceptual frameworks for school inspections the local inspectorates too were stretched too far to cope with the scope of this huge task, especially since the inspection of schools was not necessarily at the centre of their activities:

Some seeing themselves mainly as advisers to teachers, concerned with curriculum development and in-service training, and devoting as little as 15% of their time to inspection [...]. The stark truth, which was highlighted in the Parliamentary debates on the 1992 Act, was that the institutions and authorities responsible for the education of our young people, the country's richest resource, were virtually unaccountable. (Perry, 1995:39)

The third reason for the re-organisation and expansion of the school inspectorate was therefore the necessity to satisfy the strengthened right of the parents to know about the state of the education system. The new school inspectorate was consequently under intense public pressure from its very beginning.

3. The organisation and function of the new English school inspectorate: OFSTED

The Office for Standards in Education was set up in September 1992 through the Education (Schools) Act (DFE 1992) as a non-ministerial government department. Its general task is to improve the standards and quality of education in schools through regular and independent inspections, public reporting and advice to the Department for Education and Employment (DfEE). Its specific task is to set up an effective school inspection system and to make sure that all state schools in England will be inspected every six years[5]. Thus, OFSTED has effectively taken over the responsibilities of the former LEA inspectorates as well as Her Majesty's Inspectorate. Since the Education (Schools) Act in 1992 OFSTED has been led by the so-called Her Majesty's Chief Inspector of Schools in England (HMCI). He is appointed for five years and is obliged by law to inform the government in his annual report about the quality of education, the educational standards achieved, the efficient management of schools' finances and the spiritual, moral, social and cultural development of pupils (cf. OFSTED 1995a).

While the number of administrative staff in OFSTED has risen to 300 employees, the number of HMIs, who form OFSTED's professional arm, has decreased to ca. 200 colleagues. However, HMIs' tasks have changed considerably: while they inspected schools themselves in the past, they are now conducting only a small number of inspections concerning special topics and problems (e.g. Drug Education in Schools, OFSTED 1997a). In spite of this, their importance altogether has rather increased because they are now playing the central role in OFSTED's three most important functions: the recruitment and training of new inspectors, the quality control of private contractors who employ the inspectors and the continuous supervision and quality development of the school inspections.

Ad 1. Only those inspectors who are accredited by OFSTED are allowed to conduct school inspections. For their accreditation the inspectors have to successfully complete a course lasting several days as well as long-distance learning tasks and a final written exam. On top of that applicants are expected to have recent teaching practice and work experience in senior management positions (headship or deputy headship). In the first application round which was initiated in 1992 through advertisements in various papers and journals several thousand highly qualified applicants (e.g. a quarter of all deputy headteachers in the country, headteachers, LEA inspectors) applied for the advertised posts. That this initially very high quality of the applicants declined in the following years, is indicated by the fact that the failing rate rose to 50%. In the meantime OFSTED has recruited 6,500 so-called accredited inspectors. However, an inspection team can only be led by a registered inspector (RgI) who has proved in practice that he can prepare and conduct an inspection. This requires primarily leadership qualities, extensive knowledge of the inspection process and the ability to convey the results of the inspection orally and in writing to different addressees. Usually the RgIs are appointed for three years, but their accreditation can be terminated or extended prematurely. After having trained and appointed ca. 2,500 RgIs, OFSTED can in future concentrate on the further education and in-service training of the RgIs and team members. Finally, each inspection team has to be joined by a so-called lay inspector who, as a representative of the general public, has no direct relationship with the education system.

Ad 2. While in the past the schools to be inspected chose two RgIs from a list which was drawn up by OFSTED and invited the chosen RgIs to make an offer for the inspection of their school, private contractors are now applying to OFSTED for the advertised school inspections and distribute them after a successful bid amongst their RgIs and team members. The intention of this revised bidding procedure is to guarantee the independence and objectivity of the inspectors and to avoid schools choosing inspectors who are known and/or favourable to them. The ca. 250 contractors who are momentarily under contract with OFSTED vary considerably in size from small one-man-businesses to multi-million commercial companies. Similarly, the composition of the contractors varies from 5-15 individual inspectors who work in a team and only share the considerable administrative workload to commercial educational consultants and to LEAs who try to increase their budget through inspection work. OFSTED controls the quality of their contractors through various, cleverly thought-out mechanisms and explicit criteria and standards. Since January 1998 all contractors have to satisfy the so-called quality assurance standard by proving that the quality of their inspections, their inspection reports and the training of their inspectors achieve a high standard. Only those contractors who satisfy OFSTED's quality assurance standards will in future be allowed to bid for advertised inspections.

Ad 3. Controlling the quality of school inspections is probably OFSTED's most important function. This takes place on several levels. Firstly, HMI will also in future take part in selected school inspections in order to control and supervise the work of the RgIs and their inspection team in schools. Secondly, RgIs' inspection reports are permanently controlled and assessed through OFSTED's Inspection Quality Monitoring and Development Team (IQMD) according to exact criteria (e.g. validity, reliability, objectivity and comprehensibility). Thirdly, OFSTED supervises each contractor's in-service training arrangements for their inspectors as well as the overall efficiency of the company and its financial solvency. Through these manifold mechanisms OFSTED hopes to assure and develop the quality of the, as from now, privatised inspection system.

4. The inspection process

OFSTED informs the school to be inspected three to twelve months before the planned inspection and then starts negotiating with the school in question about the exact inspection date and the object of the inspection. At the same time the headteacher is asked to provide extensive information about his school, including number of pupils, staff, socio-economic environment of the school etc. This self-made school portrait serves as first information for the RgIs and also influences the invitation of tenders, which OFSTED then sends to all contractors. The contract is given to that contractor who, according to the strict criterion value for money, makes the cheapest and qualitatively best inspection offer. OFSTED informs the school about the chosen RgI who from then on takes full and also legal responsibility for the entire inspection process including the publication of the inspection report.

Before the inspection the RgI visits the school in question to get a first impression of the school. The school on the other hand has to provide the RgI with extensive documentary material (school and staff development plans, extra-curricular activities etc.). Additionally, a meeting between the responsible RgI and the pupils' parents, but without the participation of the staff has to be arranged by the school's governing body in order to find out the parents' impressions and worries about the schools. Finally, the RgI can send a questionnaire to the parents to get hold of additional information. Apart from the documentary material that the school has to provide, the responsible RgI also uses information and data for his preparation that has been collected by OFSTED. In this context the so-called PICSIs (Pre-Inspection School Indicator) are particularly useful because they allow the RgI to analyse the pupils' achievement in comparison to local and national results. During this preparatory phase there is finally a meeting between the inspection team, the senior management, the governing body and the teachers.

The inspection, which lasts approximately one week depending on the size of the school, is conducted according to strict guidelines outlined in the so-called Framework for Inspection (OFSTED 1995a) and in the Handbook for Inspection (OFSTED 1995b) which explains these guidelines in greater detail. The handbook is published in three different editions for primary, secondary and special needs schools and contains, apart from a code of conduct for inspectors, explicit directives for the carrying out of the entire inspection process. Apart from lesson observations which should take up at least 60% of the entire inspection time, inspectors examine pupils' written work, talk with teachers, pupils and other people who are actively involved in the life of the school. The aim of the inspection is to arrive at a comprehensive judgement on the quality of the school. Four central aspects of each school are analysed with the help of the inspection guidelines:

[...] the quality of education provided by the school; the educational standards achieved in the school; whether the financial resources made available to the school are managed efficiently; and the spiritual, moral, social and cultural development of pupils at the school (OFSTED 1995b: 8).

At the end of the inspection the headteacher and his senior management are given a short verbal feedback on the results of the inspection which is based on a first analysis of the generated data. The purpose of this meeting is to give the school the opportunity to comment on the main results of the inspection and to correct factual inaccuracies. However, the inspectors' judgements are not negotiable. If the inspectors are unanimously of the opinion that the school does not fulfil their standards, the RgI has to inform the headteacher about this decision before his departure with the following standard phrasing:

I am of the opinion that special measures are required in relation to this school because it is failing (or likely to fail) to give its pupils an acceptable standard of education (OFSTED 1995b: 38).

If this assessment is confirmed through HMCI the school is put into special measures according to the Education Act of 1993 (DFE 1993). This means in concrete terms that the school will be supervised and looked after by OFSTED's School Improvement Team until HMI, after one or several follow-up inspections, reaches the conclusion that the school does not require any more special measures. If the hope for improvement does not happen the management of the school is taken over by a so-called Education Association. If this measure is not successful either, the school will be closed.

Since September 1997 schools that are in many respects unsatisfactory but, according to the inspectors, nevertheless provide their pupils with an acceptable standard of education fall into the category 'schools with serious weaknesses' (OFSTED 1997b: 20). This judgement which has to appear in the final inspection report also leads to a regular supervision through OFSTED's School Improvement Team.

The responsible RgI has to present the written inspection report within five weeks after the completion of the inspection. Copies of the entire report and a summary of the report are sent to the school, the governing body, OFSTED and the responsible LEA. The school is obliged to make the report available to all their parents as well as to the general public. The main results of the inspection and the resulting key issues for action form the basis of the so-called action plan which the governing body of the school has to draw up within 40 days after the publication of the inspection report. The action plan contains objectives, deadlines, and criteria for the successful achievement of the objectives and lays down responsibilities. The action plan, too, must be sent to all parents, the staff, OFSTED and the LEA in charge. In each annual report to the parents progress in the realisation of the plan must be documented.

5. The pros and cons of school evaluation through inspection: A critique in comparative perspective

Before we place the developments in England in a wider European context and evaluate them from an international comparative perspective it seems advisable to identify the inherent strengths and weaknesses of the described OFSTED inspection system first. The following critique is based on an analysis of the inspection guidelines and case study material as well as the results of a participant observation during which the author was given the opportunity to accompany an HMI-inspection team[6].

A critical appreciation of the described inspection process must first of all stress the high degree of transparency and objectivity of the entire procedure. Through the obligatory use of so-called lesson observation forms for example, OFSTED tries to standardise the recording and assessment of the lessons. The inspectors are not only obliged to make detailed comments on the objectives, contents and the course of the lesson they also have to evaluate (the results of) the lesson according to the criteria: teaching, response, attainment and progress on a seven point scale (cf. OFSTED 1997:42). Another advantage of the described procedure is that many aspects of school life are taken into account: the inspectors do not only analyse the standards of academic achievement and the quality of teaching, but also other important factors and areas of the school such as the behaviour and the moral development of the pupils, the state of the school buildings as well as the effective management of resources. As a result of this wide range of generated data the inspectors get a rather detailed impression of the school inspected. Especially informative are in this context the conversations and interviews with selected members of the teaching and non-teaching staff and the pupils. In confidential interviews and in the absence of the headteacher representatives of these different groups can speak quite openly about internal school developments, which allows inspectors to find out the opinions of all persons that constitute a school and to detect possible contradictions between the written aims of the school and the everyday practice. Finally, first independent empirical studies (i.e. not commissioned by OFSTED) on the effects of inspections on secondary schools indicate that particularly the preparations for an inspection which take up to one year have led to internal school development processes (Ouston, Fidler & Earley, 1996).

Supplementing these general observations with further research evidence from our own case study material the following characteristics of the current inspection process have to be added to the list of positive features. Firstly, the case study material seems to suggest that HMI-inspectors handle the inspection instruments very competently and confidently and generally make an extremely professional impression during the lesson observations, their conversations with members of the staff and in their internal consultations. Given the fact that HMIs belong traditionally to the experienced and very well trained professionals of the English education system who usually look back to long active teaching and headteaching careers, this does not come as a surprise. It should be noted however, that through the privatisation of the inspection system under OFSTED, the involvement of HMI-inspectors in the actual inspection work is increasingly becoming an exception rather than the norm. Secondly, OFSTED-inspections seem to expose serious deficiencies and weaknesses of individual schools that might otherwise have gone undetected and unchanged. Thus, it was only when the case study school was confronted with its poor inspection results that the serious mismanagement of the former headteacher became evident and that it was forced to have a critical look at the identified problems and to formulate an action plan to tackle them. Thirdly it needs to be stressed that through the inspection, the school in the case study came under the focus of attention of OFSTED's School Improvement Team and the responsible LEA which, by putting the school into special measures, initiated a number of school development processes (Kotthoff, 1997).

On the other hand, the case study material does also suggest that the inspectors, because of their tight time schedule, frequently do not observe whole lessons but leave lessons prematurely to see as many lessons as possible. While the lesson plan might be assessed without having seen the entire lesson a judgement on the results of the lesson (progress etc.) which is also requested from the inspectors seems to be rather problematic. Closely related to this problem is the often criticised fact that many teachers do not get any feedback at the end of a lesson observation (cf. Dean 1995, Brimblecombe et. al., 1995). In their endeavours to observe as many teachers as possible inspectors seem to be under intense time pressure and have hardly enough time to study the teachers' detailed weekly and individual lesson plans in detail. For teachers who usually prepare high-stakes OFSTED inspection for weeks if not months (an additional burden that influences their daily schoolwork considerably) this is a frustrating, rather than a motivating experience. The feeling to have invested a lot of time in the preparation of the inspection week, of which both, teachers and inspectors know very well that it does not reflect the normal everyday school work, is, according to the results of the case study, another frustrating experience for the teachers (Kotthoff 1997).

Further research evidence on the effects of inspections on individual schools and internal school development processes after inspections revealed initial feelings of shock and bitterness among the teachers after devastating inspection results ('post-inspection-blues') and the inability and helplessness of the governing body to take up the inspection reports' explicit key issues for action productively (Brimblecombe et al., 1995, Hargreaves, 1995, Sandbrook, 1996). These studies also suggest that the effects a school inspection has on individual members of the staff depend largely on their status and position within the school hierarchy. While, for example, the publication of the inspection criteria through the two documents Framework for the Inspection of Schools (OFSTED 1995a) and the Handbook for Inspection (OFSTED 1995b) was widely welcomed especially by headteachers and members of the senior management teams as very useful instruments for school development (Earley, 1996:19), the inspection experiences and reactions of teachers who do not belong to the senior management are distinctly less positive. First empirical research studies on this topic revealed the experience of stress before and after the inspection and the massive disturbance of the ordinary school work as the main targets of teachers' criticism (Brimblecombe et al., 1996).

Judging the rise of external school evaluation through inspection in England from an international comparative perspective one has to bear in mind that school inspections serve different functions in different educational settings. Thus, they have to be seen as an integral part of an overall concept of measures and strategies that individual education systems employ to safeguard the quality of their schools. An exemplary, brief look at recent debates on the strategies of quality control and assurance in two other European education systems that traditionally share a similar 'top-down' distribution of educational responsibility which is altogether different from the English tradition may serve to illustrate this point.

In Germany, for example, there is no tradition to evaluate the quality of the school as whole. Until recently, quality evaluation was almost exclusively focused on the individual student or teacher, so much so that an OECD study on school evaluation in seven OECD countries could conveniently use the German example to characterise one extreme end of a wide spectrum of national approaches to school evaluation, England exemplifying the other:

[...] the degree to which schools themselves are evaluated as units varies, and this report intentionally considers a spectrum of national approaches, from Germany - which does not formally assess the performance of its schools at all - to England - where schools are not only evaluated through inspection, examination results and other indicators, but are publicly compared. (OECD/CERI 1995b: 18)

Taking the education system of Nordrhein-Westfalen (NRW), Germany's biggest state in terms of population, as an example, the idea of evaluating the quality of an individual schools as a unit by looking at its 'output' has only been discussed since the mid-90s in the wake of the debate on the pros and cons of extended school autonomy (Bildungskommission NRW 1995). Although it is widely accepted that an increase in the autonomy of schools requires a new system of quality control and assurance it seems highly unlikely that the new system of quality control will be primarily based on external and output-orientated forms of school evaluation because the cultural barriers are too powerful for a change in this direction:

It is their [the school supervision officers'] trust in the quality of the regulations and their belief in the closeness of adherence to them by the teachers, which make the concept of external assessment and evaluation so alien in the German situation. (Hopes, 1997:169)

At present it looks therefore as if the traditional and well-established German 'input-control' of educational quality through state-controlled teacher training courses, detailed curricula and syllabi, the official authorisation of textbooks, the structuring of the timetable and the teaching time devoted to various subjects and the school inspectorate (Schulaufsicht) which supervises the teachers' adherence to these regulations is likely to persist.

However, in spite of the strong belief in input-control through regulations, one irreversible result of the debate on increasing 'autonomy' for German schools is, that the traditional and taken-for-granted belief in the comparability of individual schools is once and for all gone. In the German State of Bremen the realisation and dropping of this false assumption has already led to more general regulations and an increased emphasis on school evaluation and assessment:

[...] a comparability of educational qualifications has been taken for granted. The growing recognition that this is a myth and the increased responsibility and autonomy of the individual school, which is now given more freedom to make its own way within a framework of rather general regulation, have attached new importance to the questions of assessment and evaluation. (Quoted in Hopes, 1997:170)

This increased importance of school evaluation and assessment is reflected in numerous measures and steps that a number of German States have recently taken, or are about to take, to supplement the traditional 'input-control' with new forms of 'output-control' like the introduction of standards for the completion of the lower secondary level, the regulation of examination standards for the graduation from the upper secondary level (Abitur), the testing of pupil achievement through criterion-referenced tests for different age groups in German, maths and the first foreign language and the regular participation in international comparative studies of student achievement (e.g. TIMSS, PISA).

The new emphasis on school evaluation will also most certainly lead to a re-organisation of the inspectorate and a changed role for the school inspectors. But, whatever the outcome of the present debate may be, a system of quality control and assurance that is primarily relying on full-inspections of individual schools seems at present to be the most unlikely outcome of the reform of the school inspectorate in Germany. With regard to NRW, this assumption is supported by official announcements and documents from the Ministry for School and Further Education on the future of school evaluation in NRW (Ministerium für Schule und Weiterbildung, 1998a,b, c) and first practical experiments with different forms of school evaluation commissioned by the Ministry (Ministerium für Schule und Weiterbildung et al. 1998) which seem to suggest that quality control in NRW will rely heavily on internal school evaluation. This assumption is secondly supported by the fact that some German States like Bremen, Hessen and Hamburg have already moved in this direction and changed their legislation accordingly.

Another interesting case to look at in this context is the Swedish education system because for many years, the control of education was, similarly to Germany, heavily centralised and regulated. The State authorities played a central role in the steering of the system through relatively detailed regulations, curricula and through national budget allocations. In contrast to Germany however, processes of decentralisation and deregulation started already in the 80s and quickly gained momentum. The present distribution of responsibilities in the Swedish education system is that the Parliament should control the education system by defining national objectives (steering by goals), while the national and local education authorities (municipalities) are responsible for ensuring that local initiatives correspond with these national goals and achieve the necessary results (Eurydice, 1997).

For our purposes it is interesting to examine the changes in the system of school evaluation in general and the role of the school inspectorate in particular that went along with these processes of decentralisation and deregulation. According to the already quoted comparative OECD study on school evaluation, 'the Swedish experience of external evaluation through inspection has been, over the last two or three decades, very limited, and restricted to regional boards carrying out the enforcement of national regulations' (OECD/CERI, 1995b: 125). In the wake of decentralisation the National Board of Education and the regional boards were abolished in 1990 and replaced by a new National Agency for Education (Skolverket). Its foremost responsibilities include the national monitoring, evaluating and supervision of all school activities, and central development work within the school sector. The National Agency submits annual reports and budget proposals to the government. In addition, at three-year intervals or longer it is to provide the Government with a comprehensive picture of the education system together with data for the long-term national development of the education system (Skolverket, 1996).

In line with the new steering mechanisms (distance steering) the Agency refined itself from the very beginning to national system evaluation. This strong emphasis of the National Agency on its national evaluation task and its very reserved supervision and consultation of individual schools was, according to Eikenbusch (1995), from the beginning quite controversial among many schools which felt neglected. The growing criticism led 1994 to a reorganisation of the National Agency in which 12 new regional offices were established to strengthen the link between Skolverket and the municipalities and schools around the country (Skolverket 1994). While the National Agency is still concentrating primarily on national system evaluation, it is nowadays the responsibility of the municipalities to ensure that Swedish schools uphold equivalent standards all over the country. In theory, school evaluation is supposed to work like this:

Each municipality is required to set out the general objectives for its schools in a school plan, adopted by the municipal council. The municipality is obliged to monitor and evaluate the school plan and to provide the State with reports on facts and circumstances of relevance for the evaluation of educational activities. In addition, every school has to devise a work plan, based on the curriculum and local priorities. The work plan is also to be monitored and evaluated. (Eurydice, 1997:10)

The experiences and results that are collected at school and municipality level should then be the basis for a sound nation-wide external system evaluation performed by the National Agency.

In practice however, this decentralised system of school evaluation does not work properly yet because, due to the lack of national guidelines on school evaluation which was already criticised in the OECD's review of Swedish education policies (OECD, 1995:200). The municipalities employ very different forms and strategies of quality control and assurance, making the compilation of the generated data on a national level rather problematic. In addition, the Swedish Ministry has criticised the fact that some municipalities are not cooperating properly with the State because they have not yet realised that decentralisation and the increased freedom for school autonomy comes along with the duty to be accountable for their work (Swedish Ministry of Education and Science, 1997). The quite haphazard evaluation practices of some municipalities was therefore strongly criticised in the Ministry's National Development Plan on 'Quality and Equivalence':

Some municipalities have also built up systems for systematically following up and evaluating school activities. However, it is still the case that municipal monitoring in this area is often imperfect, and this is shown by the fact that the National Agency receives far too many complaints concerning unsatisfactory conditions which should have been identified and remedied by the municipalities themselves. The Government regards with great seriousness the shortcomings in municipal steering and the consequences arising as a result for the activities and thus the pupils. (Op.cit: 10/11)

The careful (re)centralisation and the strengthening of the inspection task of the National Agency, which has been evident since 1994, have gradually reduced the perceived lack of supervision. At present it seems as if this trend towards an increasing centralisation of quality control and assurance on the one hand and an increasing decentralisation and autonomy of the school or municipality on the other hand is going to continue and might even lead to the establishment of a national inspectorate, as the following quotation from the National Development Plan suggests:

The Government believes that formal supervision should continue to be an important part of the work of the National Agency. The work carried out by the National Agency will be supplemented by the quality assessment which it is intended shall take place through the state educational inspectorate to be attached to the National Agency. (Op.cit: 11)

To sum up, our brief look at current developments and trends in quality control and assurance in three different European education systems suggests that in the wake of decentralisation and deregulation the important role of school inspectorates in safeguarding the quality of schools is not only taken for granted but seems to become more important as the international trend towards increasing school autonomy of schools accelerates. In some cases, most notably in Sweden, this has even led to plans to establish a new national inspectorate although there is traditionally 'no formal inspectorate tradition or function in Sweden' (OECD, 1995:200). Thus, processes of deregulation and decentralisation in education systems may not be what they seem to be at first sight because there is a price to be paid for deregulation and increased powers at the periphery of the education system. Rather than giving up its influence and control function, one could argue, that the State extends its power base because the new forms of output control through evaluation are arguably even more effective than the old bureaucratic forms of state-control through detailed regulations. In the long term there is therefore the real danger that individual schools will be watched more closely than ever before if the current reforms towards greater school autonomy are not taken seriously or carried through.

While the growing importance of school inspectorates in quality control and assurance seems to be an international trend, the function of each individual inspectorate and the inspection model used is in line with the specific cultural traditions of the education system in general and with its complementary strategies and mechanisms of quality control in particular. Thus, the traditionally strong trust of the German school inspectorate in the quality of the regulations and its belief in the teachers' close adherence to them seem to make the whole concept of external school evaluation through inspection rather inappropriate, if not superfluous. In the case of the Swedish education system which has had, as the OECD study (OECD/CERI, 1995b) suggested, a very limited experience of inspection over the last two or three decades, the barriers against external evaluation through inspection are almost equally strong. At present, it seems as if the Swedish education system is still in search of a sound system of school evaluation that is appropriate for their newly decentralised and deregulated education system. Finally, the importance of the educational context - which is in the English case characterised by a long tradition in school inspection and an increasingly dominant market principle in education - also helps to explain the rather unique features of the English inspection system. From a comparative point of view, the English system is characterised by its extraordinarily strong emphasis on external control and accountability of the individual school. Whether this will stay under the New Labour government remains to be seen.

6. Discussion and outlook

Turning back to our initial question: are external evaluations through school inspections a price too high to pay for the increased autonomy of schools or are they a worthwhile activity because they really lead to school improvement'. While positive internal school development processes which were initiated through an OFSTED-inspection can easily be identified in individual schools (Kotthoff, 1997) the question on the influence of external evaluations on the public school system in general cannot be answered so easily. Only 500 of all inspected schools fall into the category 'failing schools' and enjoy therefore the intensive supervision and consultation of OFSTED's School Improvement Team. In all the other schools, internal school development processes are for two reasons, at least questionable because firstly since the lengthening of the inspection cycle to six years (OFSTED, 1997b: 5) a lot of time passes before the school is re-inspected. Secondly, those schools that are neither very good nor very bad (i.e. the vast majority of all schools) have got nothing to win or to lose through an OFSTED inspection. In view of the huge costs for one inspection (on average ca. 30 000 pounds for the inspection of an average-sized secondary school) it is indeed comprehensible when critics ask whether such an expenditure of limited financial means stands in reasonable proportion to the expected return for relatively few schools (Earley, 1996).

However, most recent developments indicate that OFSTED is striving for a new balance between controlling and advising schools. Firstly, OFSTED's School Improvement Team has grown steadily ever since its foundation and represents now, with 40 HMIs, OFSTED's second biggest department. Secondly, by establishing a second category for weak schools (schools with serious weaknesses) a further group of 14% of all schools is put under supervision of OFSTED's School Improvement Team. Thirdly, OFSTED's new guidelines for the inspection of schools that came into force in September 1997 indicate that school improvement is supposed to play a central role in the second inspection cycle that began in September 1997 in the case of secondary schools:

When a school is inspected for the second time, as well as evaluating and reporting on its current standards and provision, inspectors must assess, report on and grade:
a. The school's progress i.e. the extent to which it has changed, for better or worse, or the extent to which it has sustained earlier excellence. This includes how effectively it responded, through its action plan, to the previous inspection.
b. Whether the school has the capacity, that is the strategy and systems in place to secure improvement or maintain high standards (OFSTED, 1997b: 5).

Finally, the often criticised lack of feedback to individual teachers following a lesson observation from an inspector has also been resolved in the new inspection guidelines by turning the inspector's feedback to the teacher which was until now voluntary on the part of the inspectors into a duty. The aim is to help the teachers concerned to recognise their strengths and weaknesses and thus to support their further improvement:

Inspectors are required to offer oral feedback on the quality of teaching to every qualified teacher and all others involved in the school's teaching programme during, at the end of or as soon as practicable after an inspection. Teachers must be left in no doubt about the strengths and weaknesses of their work as observed by inspectors, and any issues to which they should attend (op. cit.: 4).

In spite of the described changes and developments which, as we have seen, moves the English system of school evaluation through inspection closer to developments in other European countries, further corrections and changes of the inspection procedure will be necessary to achieve more profound effects of inspections on internal school development. In principle, the question remains whether the inspection process as a whole should not be tailored more to the individual school and teacher in order to be able to help them in their specific situation. Such an approach could also help to prevent the 'OFSTED model of a good school', which is hidden behind the inspection criteria, from dominating the English school system at the expense of the traditional highly valued variety. However, the individualisation of the inspection procedure suggested here stands in clear contradiction to the (at the moment) politically desired strict comparability of schools.

Internal school development, which is initiated through external evaluations, requires in addition that the inspections are integrated in a continuous school development process. The achieved sensible balance between control on the one hand and support or advice on the other which, until now was unfortunately only valid for the failing schools, could serve as an example in this context. To achieve this balance, expensive external evaluations through inspections would have to be completed and supported through internal school self-evaluations. If the LEAs were strengthened again financially and given more staff they could play an important role in initiating school self-evaluations and in consulting their schools.

Finally, one could ask critically whether the private contractors who carry out the bulk of all school inspections are really interested in processes of internal school development. In the face of rapidly decreasing profit margins in recent years due to the strong competition on the inspection market it is more likely that the individual consultation of teachers - which OFSTED will be demanding in future - will be regarded as an unpleasant duty because it is time consuming and therefore expensive.

In view of the present political and educational climate in England in which accountability and standards are regarded as the main pillars of the education system it seems certain that inspections are here to stay. That this is true, irrespective of the political party in power, is documented in Labour's first White Paper which was published in July 1997 under the title Excellence in Education and which also emphasises the need for external evaluations of schools, and recently also LEAs, through inspections (DFEE 1997a: 30f.). The Standards and Framework Bill (DFEE 1997b) which was presented to Parliament in December 1997 represents a further confirmation of the adopted course. At the same time however, the bill stresses the LEAs' duty to support internal evaluation, school development and consultation. Taking account of these most recent changes, it seems that other countries which are presently experimenting with deregulation policies and evaluation strategies could gain something from studying the English education system which seems to be heading to a new network of complementary internal and external advice and control mechanisms. Finally, the current efforts of various European education systems to establish a sound system of school evaluation should be guided by the principle 'to get it right first time' because it could save a lot of money in times of severely restricted public sector spending and, most importantly, it might help to secure the support of the teachers who are indispensable in any evaluation system. This is particularly important for countries like Germany, where teachers, due to a lack of tradition in the evaluation of educational quality, are quite sceptical about educational evaluation anyway.

References

Audit Commission, (1989). *Assuring Quality in Education*. London, HMSO.

Bildungskommission NRW, (1995). *Zukunft der Bildung-Schule der Zukunft*. Neuwied, Luchterhand.

Brighouse, T., (1995). The history of inspection. In T. Brighouse, B. Moon (Eds.), *School Inspection*. London, Pitman.

Brimblecombe, N., Ormston, M. and Shaw, M., (1995). Teachers' Perceptions of Inspections: a stressful experience. *Cambridge Journal of Education*, 25, 1, 53-61.

Brimblecombe, N., Ormston, M. and Shaw, M. (1996). Teachers' Perceptions of Inspections. In J. Ouston, B. Fidler, P. Earley (Eds.), *Ofsted Inspections: The Early Experience*. London, Fulton.

Cabinet Office, (1991). *The Citizen's Charter: Raising the Standard*. Cmnd. 1599. London, HMSO.

Dean, Joan, (1995). What Teachers and Headteachers think about inspection. *Cambridge Journal of Education*, 25,1, 45-52.

Department of Education and Science (DES), (1988). *Education Reform Act 1988*. London, HMSO.

DES, (1991). *The Parent's Charter: You and your Child's Education*. London, DES.

Department for Education (DFE), (1992). *Education (Schools) Act*. London, HMSO.

DFE, (1993). *Education Reform Act*. London, HMSO.

Department for Education and Employment (DFEE), (1996). *School Inspections Act*. London, HMSO.

DFEE, (1997a). *Excellence in Schools*. Cm 3681. London, HMSO.

DFEE, (1997b). *The Standards and Framework Bill*. London, HMSO.

Earley, P., (1996). School Improvement and Ofsted Inspection: the Research Evidence. In: P. Earley, B. Fidler, J. Ouston (Eds.), *Improvement through Inspection*, (pp. 11-22). London, Fulton.

Eikenbusch, G., (1995). Tendenzen und Entwicklungen der Schulaufsicht in Schweden. In Landesinstitut für Schule und Weiterbildung (Hg.). *Schulentwicklung und Qualitätssicherung in Schweden*. Bönen, Kettler.

Eurydice. (1997). *The Swedish Education System*: March 1997. Stockholm, Eurydice Swedish national unit.

Hargreaves, D.H., (1995). Inspection and School Improvement (pp. 117-125). In: *Cambridge Journal of Education*, 25, 1.

Hopes, C., (1997). *Assessing, evaluating and assuring quality in schools in the European Union*. Frankfurt/M., DIPF.

Kotthoff, H.G., (1994). *Curriculumentwicklung in England und Wales: Das National Curriculum zwischen 1976 und 1990*. Köln u.a., Böhlau.

Kotthoff, H.G., (1997): Schulinspektionen als Motor der Schulentwicklung' Englische Erfahrungen mit einem reformierten Schulinspektorat. Tertium Comparationes, *Journal für Internationale Bildungsforschung*, 3, 1, 10-27.

Kotthoff, H.G., (1998). Interim Report on the Research Project 'School Autonomy and School Evaluation: A German Approach to a European Theme'. In A.M. Kazamias, M.G. Spillane (Eds.): *Education and the Structuring of the European Space*. Athens, Seirios Editions.

Lawton, D. and Gordon, P., (1987). HMI. London, Routledge and Kegan Paul.

Ministerium für Schule und Weiterbildung des Landes NRW, (1998a). *Evaluation in der Schulpraxis: Beiträge zur Qualitätsentwicklung und Qualitätssicherung von Schule*. Frechen, Ritterbach.

Ministerium für Schule und Weiterbildung des Landes NRW, (1998b). *Qualitätsentwicklung und Qualitätssicherung: Aufgabenbeispiele Klasse 10*: Englisch. Frechen, Ritterbach.

Ministerium für Schule und Weiterbildung des Landes NRW, (1998c). *'Qualität als gemeinsame Aufgabe: Rahmenkonzept 'Qualitätsentwicklung und Qualitätssicherung schulischer Arbeit'*. Frechen, Ritterbach.

Ministerium für Schule und Weiterbildung des Landes NRW/ Landesinstitut für Schule und Weiterbildung (Hg.), (1998). *Schulentwicklung und Schulaufsicht - Qualitäts- entwicklung und Qualitätssicherung von Schule*. Bönen, Kettler.

Perry, P., (1995). The Formation of OFSTED. In T. Brighouse, B. Moon, (Eds.), *School Inspection*. London, Pitman.

OECD, (1995). *Reviews of National Policies for Education*. Sweden. Paris, OECD.

OECD/CERI. (1995a). *Decision-Making in 14 Education Systems*. Paris, OECD.

OECD/CERI. (1995b). *Schools under Scrutiny*. Paris, OECD.

OFSTED, (1995a). *Framework for the Inspection of Nursery, Primary, Middle, Secondary and Special Schools*. London, Ofsted.

OFSTED. (1995b). *The OFSTED Handbook: Guidance on the Inspection of Secondary Schools*. London, HMSO.

OFSTED. (1997a). *Drug Education in Schools*. London, HMSO.

OFSTED. (1997b). *Inspection and Re-inspection of Schools from Sept. 1997*. London, Ofsted.

Ouston, J., Fidler, B., and Earley, P., (1996). Secondary Schools' Responses to OFSTED: Improvement through Inspection' In J. Ouston et al. (1996). *Ofsted Inspections*: The Early Experience. London, Fulton.

Sandbrook, I., (1996). *Making Sense of Primary Inspection*. Buckingham, OUP.

Skolverket, (1994). *Skolverket har förändrat sin organisation*. Stockholm, Skolverket.

Skolverket, (1996). *The Swedish School System*. Stockholm, Skolverket.

Stillman, A.B., (1989). Institutional Evaluation and LEA Advisory Services. *Research Papers in Education*, 42 (2), 3-27.

Swedish Ministry of Education and Science, (1997). *Summary of the National Plan for Pre-School, School and Adult Education: Quality and Equivalence*. Stockholm.

Wielemans, W., (1998). Educational Policy in the Countries of the European Union. In A.M. Kazamias, M.G. Spillane (Eds.), *Education and the Structuring of the European Space*. Athens, Seirios Editions.

Wilcox, B. and Gray, J., (1996). *Inspecting Schools: Holding Schools to account and helping schools to improve*. Buckingham, OUP.

Notes

1 Although the inspection system considered here concern both England and Wales reference will be made only to England as the differences between England and Wales with regard to their inspection systems are so slight that it is not worth while dealing with them in the course of this article.
2 An outline of the research design of the underlying research project including a summary of interim findings are presented in an earlier publication (Kotthoff, 1998).
3 A detailed analysis and interpretation of school evaluation strategies in the Netherlands, Sweden and Germany is left to a later publication. In view of the manifold and frequent changes and reforms that have affected the English school inspectorate since my research visit to England in 1997 this paper does not attempt to keep up to date with the most recent development to the present day but rather provides a detailed insight into the state of affairs of the inspection system in the years 1997/98. From this it should be clear that any changes which have happened since then are not included in the present discussion. Parts of this paper are based on an earlier article published in 1997 (Kotthoff, 1997).
4 QUANGOs are formally independent from the government; they are, however funded by government money and run by government appointees. Examples for powerful QUANGOs in the English education system are the Funding Agency for Schools (FAS), the School Curriculum and Assessment Authority (SCAA) and the Office for Standards in Education (OFSTED). The growing number of QUANGOs has led to the concern that these operate merely as instruments of Government policy.
5 In September 1997 the inspection cycle was extended from originally four to six years (OFSTED 1997b).
6 Readers who are particularly interested in the case study material should refer to my earlier publication in which the case study is documented and analysed in greater detail (Kotthoff, 1997).

4

Curriculum Control in 'Deregulated' and Bureaucratic Educational Systems in Europe: The Cases of England and Greece

Stavros Moutsios*

1. Introduction: recent educational reforms and new modes of control

During the 1980s and early 1990s major educational reforms took place in countries such as the USA, Australia, New Zealand and England. A common denominator in those reforms was the economic exigencies to which the respective states responded by treating education as a tool to overcome economic crisis (Kennedy, 1995). Schools were held responsible for poorly meeting the needs of national economies, for being inadequate in equipping students with basic skills, and for providing a poor return on the money spent upon education. Terms such as school effectiveness, accountability, efficiency, excellence and value-added education emerged in public discourse to stress that reforms should target teachers' performance and students' attainment.

In particular, educational reform in the USA was officially initiated in the early 1980s when the Federal Government published *A Nation at Risk* (National Commission on Excellence in Education, 1983), a highly influential report written by distinguished federal and state policy-makers and business leaders. The document warned of an increased 'tide of mediocrity' in American education and stressed that schools were failing to supply the country with the skilled work force necessary for its economic competitiveness in the global context. The changes that followed were different in the various states of the USA but they were characterised by the same reform agenda, known as the 'three waves reform' (Bullock & Thomas, 1997).

During the first wave of reform (1983-1986) many states embarked upon such measures as increasing the teaching time for academic subjects, the establishment of higher graduation requirements in secondary schools, and an

* I am grateful to Bob Cowen, Reader in Comparative Education in the Institute of Education University of London, for reading and commenting on this paper.

increase in teacher salaries. The main feature of this period was the production by many states of curriculum frameworks and requirements of accountability through 'top-down' policy-making.

The second phase (1986-1990) had a 'bottom-up' approach in reform, meaning the widespread introduction of various schemes of school-site or school-based management (Hanson, 1991). Those schemes transferred decision-making powers for the day-to-day running of schools to headteachers and councils of parents and teachers. Management of budgets, staffing and resources became in most states the job of the schools, which were thus prompted to implement entrepreneurial ways of efficient self-governance.

The third phase of the reform (1990 onwards) included the introduction of open-enrolment and free choice in many states as well as pupil-based funding formulae for schools. Part of the last wave of the reform was also the national setting of curriculum frameworks and standards (U.S. Department of Education, 1994).

Australia during the 1980s also went through a similar reform process though, as in the USA, the federal character of the country meant that changes differed in pace and dissemination from state to state. The reform was also here justified by economic pressures. The document *Skills for Australia* (DEET, 1987), written and released by the Minister of Education John Dawkins, made clear that the reform should deal with the economic challenges that Australia was facing and should set national goals of performance. Important for this purpose was the role of the Australian Education Council which embarked upon collaboration with the federal government and the states to set up national curriculum statements and frameworks of accountability for schools (Louden & Browne, 1993; Carter, 1995).

Within these frameworks the states were to produce policy guidelines and schools were to develop plans for implementation. Measures were taken to reduce state bureaucracies and to devolve control over resource matters either to individual institutions or to local agencies (Chapman *et. al.*, 1996). In many cases, schools were given extensive decision-making powers to manage financial and curriculum resources such as school budgets, textbooks, student consumables, excursions and activities. In Victoria, for example, the reform was quite extensive, as the schools and particularly the headteachers were enabled to recruit the teaching staff. According to the official statements (Caldwell & Hayward, 1998), 'schools were provided with rigorous and world-leading curriculum and learning standards' and they 'were given operating autonomy and control of their resources so that they would be better placed to achieve [their] mission' (p. 79).

Similar changes occurred in New Zealand. Concerns about the ability of public education to contribute to the economic growth and competitiveness of the country were discussed within neo-liberal assumptions and market ideologies in the reform process, despite the fact that a Labour government was in office (Gordon, 1992). The reform was given momentum with the publication of the *Picot Report* (1988) and the official endorsement of its proposals by the government document *Tomorrow's Schools* (MoE, 1988). The new policy brought an extensive re-organisation of the system by giving major managerial responsibilities to schools and by introducing open enrolment of pupils. School boards and headteachers are now responsible for the management of human and financial resources (such as appointments and dismissals of teaching and non-teaching staff, maintenance of premises, operational expenses and consumables) whereas the 'role of the State government has become one of regulator, funder, owner, and purchaser: it reviews and audits the school system' (Bullock & Thomas, 1997, p. 53). However at the same time the curriculum has come under the control of the Ministry of Education, 'creating greater centralisation than at any point in the past' (Peters, 1995, p. 59). Indeed, the government introduced in 1991 a national framework of curriculum and assessment, which specifies principles, skills, learning areas, objectives and assessment procedures and it, is compulsory for all schools.

The above outlined reforms in the 1980s and early 1990s created two major changes. On the one hand, authority and financial resources were delegated to schools for their day-to-day needs and parents were given decision-making powers in school management. School-based management and budgeting were introduced to create competition among schools, to increase their performance and to facilitate parental choice in a kind of educational market. This move was called, by many authors, educational or school 'restructuring' (Lawton, 1992; O'Donoghue & Dimmock, 1998). School-based management, as Reavis and Griffith (1992) underline 'takes decentralisation one step further by, in effect, 'decentralising' decision making to each building' (p. 3). The main rationale is that hierarchies are flattened, bureaucracies are diminished and thus schools can be flexible and can control their strategies and practices - including the strategies of enhancing performance. On the other hand, those reforms were accompanied by the establishment or re-planning of national curriculum frameworks, which are mandatory for all schools. State appointed bodies have been assigned to set national goals, establish learning priorities and define requirements of accountability.

In Europe, the most striking similarities to the patterns described above were in England in the late 1980s. These changes are discussed below and compared with Greece, where a traditional bureaucratic organisation of schooling is still in place.

2. England and Greece: bi-dimensional and mono-dimensional patterns of educational control

In 1988, the Education Reform Act (ERA), the most fundamental educational legislation in England since 1944, transferred decision-making powers to parents (considered as customers), weakening decisively the responsibilities of Local Education Authorities (LEAs) and establishing an entrepreneurial style in the management of schools. In particular:
- The creation of the educational market is primarily based on parents' rights to choose the schools they prefer. This provision was gradually developed in the 1980 and 1986 Education Acts (DES, 1986; Tomlinson, 1993) and was

finally established in the 1988 Act (DES, 1988a). Open enrolment permits schools' governing bodies to admit pupils up to the limit of the physical capacity of their premises. Local authorities are unable to balance admissions amongst schools or to prevent poor or excessive rolls as in the past.

- Local Management of Schools (LMS) brought a fundamental alteration in the way that schools operate. Traditionally the LEAs received funding from central government and distributed it to schools. The LEAs decided the amount of money spent on staff employment, operational needs and curriculum resources and in general were responsible for all expenditure decisions. With the LMS the discretion over expenditure was transferred to individual schools. That is, the LEAs make available to schools a great amount of budget and their governing bodies decide its allocation to various needs.

- The LMS scheme extended decisively the powers of governors, which had already been increased by the 1986 (No. 2) Act. School governing bodies can now decide about appointing, disciplining and dismissing staff, curriculum resources, educational visits, premises costs etc. (DES 1988b).

- Schools were given the right to acquire the so-called Grant Maintained (GM) status, namely to opt-out from LEA control and be directly funded from the DfEE (Department for Education and Employment). In this way GM schools break all their relations with the local authorities and operate as independent institutions with complete managerial autonomy.

- The funding that schools receive depends upon the number of pupils that they receive on a pupil-based funding formula; funding is combined with the open enrolment of pupils. Therefore, the more pupils a school attracts, the more budget it has to spend. In these terms, schools have to compete in order to generate pupils and funds.

- Headteachers are given the managerial role of running a business within the framework of control retained by the governing body and become 'de facto employers of teachers' (Ball, 1994, p. 85).

- Schools establish 'external relations' with their local community, to manage open enrolment, marketing and the promotion of the institution. For example, schools can carry out market research to identify parental preferences, issue brochures to present themselves, rent their premises for other uses, sell printed material or seek sponsorship (The LMS Initiative, 1990).

- Schools under the LMS provisions are recommended to follow the objectives approach (system analysis) in their management plans by considering their inputs (such as enrolments and finance), their pedagogic practices and outputs (performance measurements). For this purpose schools are asked to specify *performance indicators*, amongst which are pupil assessment results, in order to monitor their effectiveness according to the initial plan (DES, 1988c; DES, 1989).

However, whereas the 1988 reform decentralised decision-making on school management issues it centralised curriculum decision-making with the introduction of the National Curriculum. A mixed system of control was established in which schools manage themselves in an entrepreneurial manner within the frame of a curriculum prescribed by the state.

It is suggested that the traditional distinction 'centralisation - decentralisation' cannot describe the new condition, since educational control is characterised by both a centralising and decentralising dimension. A novel pattern of educational control has thus emerged which is marked by both dimensions and for this reason it will be termed here *bi-dimensional*.

The *bi-dimensional* pattern of educational control indicates the re-classification of central/local responsibilities over 'who decides about what': the re-distribution of power between the centre and local agencies, the diminishing of intermediate levels of decision-making and schools competing to attract pupils. It refers to what is often called 'marketised' schooling, 'education in the market-place' or an 'educational quasi-market' (Whitty *et. al.*, 1998), but under a centralised curriculum. In other words, the *bi-dimensional* pattern represents the 'paradoxical' combination of a regulating central authority with self-managing institutions.

This English *bi-dimensional* pattern can be contrasted with the *mono-dimensional* pattern of Greece, where a traditional centralised organisation of both the curriculum and school management is still in place.

Bureaucratic educational control has been a traditional characteristic of the Greek system since its genesis and it was further developed during this century (Kazamias & Kassotakis, 1995). Though political and ideological changes were often reflected in the state bureaucracy (Samatas, 1995) no structural alterations were introduced to loosen up the strict bureaucratic control and thus the administrative machinery has remained largely impermeable to alternative practices. In education the effect was the continuation of the same structure in central/local power relations which entails a 'top-down', 'outside-inside' and hierarchical regulation in both curriculum and school management issues.

Schools are subject to the so-called Directorates and Offices of Education which distribute the centrally appointed teaching staff, exercise disciplinary action, allocate textbooks and curriculum resources, transmit statutory orders and circulars to schools and in general operate as local services of the official educational hierarchy (Lainas, 1989). The headteacher's duties are restricted to 'implementing the laws, statutory orders and circulars' and along with the *Teachers' Board* he/she is responsible for 'the better implementation of the educational policy and operation of the school' as well as 'for the implementation of the statutory curriculum and timetable' (MoE, 1985).

The Greek *mono-dimensional* pattern is an example of the traditional 'bureaucratic centralism' in which, according to Lauglo (1995), co-ordination is achieved by regulations issued centrally and by clear hierarchies, 'so that chains of authority for each service radiate downwards from its ministerial headquarters in the capital' (p. 6).

It is clear that whereas the two patterns differ in their mode of management control they intersect at their mode of curriculum control. Thus, the proposed distinction enables a more productive comparison of the two centralised curricula policies by highlighting *the way that the state regulates schools' pedagogic practice when different modes of management control are in place.*

3. State regulation of pedagogic practice in the two cases

The two curriculum control policies considered here derived from education reforms in the 1980s which foregrounded different educational aims. The reform project in Greece from the mid-70s and especially in the 1980s foregrounded principles of *external* and *internal* democratisation, equality, participation and democratic citizenship. In the same period, the rationale for reform in England was the international pressure for economic competitiveness and the whole project moved towards the enhancement of performance and efficiency, rules for competition and differentiation in the provision of schooling. In crude terms, whereas the reform criterion in Greece was *social/pedagogic*, in England it was *economic*.

Considering the differences in both the patterns of educational control and curricula aims, it is argued here that *while in the Greek mono-dimensional pattern there is an emphasis on the regulation of curriculum content and pedagogy, in the English bi-dimensional pattern the state emphasises the regulation of evaluation procedures.*

Taking the distinction of the three *message systems* offered by Bernstein (1975), curriculum *content* defines 'what counts as valid knowledge', *pedagogy* 'what counts as a valid transmission of knowledge' and *evaluation* 'what counts as a valid realisation of this knowledge on the part of the taught' (p. 85).

In pursuing the above argument, this section reviews the national curricula and monitorial policies (inspection) in Greece and England, drawing evidence from a comparative study between the two countries (Moutsios, 1998).

Greece
In Greece the management of schools rests heavily with the official hierarchy to the extent that schools lack sufficient responsibilities to manage their curriculum resources. Curriculum resources and in particular textbooks are designed and produced by agencies associated with the Ministry of Education. The *Pedagogical Institute* - a curriculum development body whose decisions are subject to ministerial approval - not only plans the statutory curriculum, it also constructs textbooks and curriculum resources (MoE, 1985, section 60) which schools are obliged to use within the hierarchical centralised mode of management control.

The Greek central authority regulates strongly content and pedagogy by using the textbooks as the main carriers of the curriculum into the classroom. Central curriculum planning, through the textbooks for both pupils and teachers, prescribes in detail what is valid knowledge and what is valid transmission of knowledge. Curriculum content is analysed from general statements down to specific themes and school time is specified from the level of the year down to the teaching hour. Prescription of what exactly should be taught is matched with when exactly it should be taught: the sequence and pace of the transmission of content is strongly regulated by the state. Any attempts by teachers to break this order are not considered legitimate, unless this shift is provided for within the statutory curriculum itself. In the same way, central curriculum planning prescribes in detail classroom pedagogy. Through their special textbooks teachers are given instructions on how to teach, for every subject, for every theme and for every teaching hour.

In contrast with the emphasis placed on the control of content and process, the control of what is learned is weak: tests are not externally devised, standardised or moderated and the criteria of evaluation are largely implicit and diffuse. Evaluation of pupils' performance is an affair internal to the classroom and no procedures are in place to monitor progress towards meeting standards and to allow for comparison between schools. Therefore, curriculum planning in Greece is interested more in making explicit what is to be taught and how it will be taught rather than what is learned in schools.

Accordingly, monitoring (inspection policy) in Greece consists in ensuring the conformity of teachers' pedagogic practice to the official content and process rather than in identifying its effectiveness in raising performance. School visits are characterised by a general and vague framework of inspection, focus on the individual teacher and aim at guiding the teacher in the implementation of the official curriculum content and pedagogy.

All monitorial activities are described in a set of duties which render the *school adviser* the agent of the official curriculum and *the* valid state pedagogy: the adviser directs, instructs, informs, makes sure that the content will be completed, demonstrates model ways of teaching and gives guidance on the use of curriculum resources (Law 1304/1982; PD 214/1984). This is because the advisers' role of 'guidance', as a transfer of governmental decisions to teachers and as monitoring of pedagogic practice, is actualised in a hierarchical mechanism in which the teacher's position is subordinate.

The school advisers are asked to report on what the state channels to schools rather on what is performed in them. In the absence of any explicit criteria of conduct and reporting, the monitorial activity is finally shaped by the single textbook. The duties of the adviser (planning, guidance and teaching exemplars) are circumscribed by the single teaching text, just as the same text circumscribes teachers' pedagogic practice. Thus, both the adviser and the teacher share a common text upon which the relationship between the 'instructor' and the 'instructed' is based. The same text is the framework of the whole apparatus of monitoring, which exists in a hierarchy (curriculum planners-advisers-teachers) of 'scientific-pedagogic guidance' on what, and how to teach.

The latest reform agenda foregrounds the responsiveness of the education system to the national economy and prioritises expansion and objectification of assessment procedures at the upper secondary level. Curriculum change in the compulsory phase is not yet part of the agenda but there are initiatives for re-introducing evaluation procedures. Officially: 'the basic problem of education and the educational process is the lasting lack of evaluation of teachers and educational practice for about 18 years' (MoE, 1997, section 2.6). A Body of

Permanent Evaluators will be established as a mechanism to assess schools, teachers and senior administrative staff. However, the intended evaluation, which is subject to strong reactions by the teacher unions, will seek to identify teachers' compliance to inputs rather than the performance of the school unit. This is because no parallel initiatives are being promoted for the alteration of the mono-dimensional bureaucratic pattern of control and the devolution of managerial powers to schools so that they regulate their practices. Earlier ministerial attempts to devolve financial responsibilities to local authorities met also massive teacher protests. In these conditions it is likely that the return to strong forms of evaluation, as a part of the changing reform criteria, will not mean the abstention of the central authority from strong content and processual regulation.

England

Central curriculum planning in England is heavily reliant on the assessment scheme to the extent that the National Curriculum and the assessment arrangements cannot be seen separately. The National Curriculum is built upon a linear scale of attainment targets, which, by using both external and internal testing, aims at rendering the outcomes of pedagogic practice publicly transparent and thus serving the educational market. Schools in their turn, albeit with wide managerial discretion, are obliged to implement the assessment arrangements and consequently demonstrate their compliance to the National Curriculum requirements and its performance expectations. In the framework of the *bi-dimensional* pattern of control, the assessment scheme becomes the main carrier of the National Curriculum to schools.

Indeed, the Education Reform Act created the conditions on the basis of which schools have managerial discretion to produce the results required by the National Curriculum. Their performance is judged by the parents/consumers who can select or reject a particular school through the policy of open enrolment. What makes the school's performance visible to the market is the various indicators available to the public amongst which the assessment results over the National Curriculum can be crucial for parents' decision. With respect to the National Curriculum, the performance results provide the most powerful indicator since they derive from a compulsory and universal assessment scheme and their publication allows for nation-wide comparisons. The national assessment is compulsory and rests on standard tasks and tests (*Standard Assessment Tasks*-SATs) and Teacher Assessment (TA). The results of the two assessments are juxtaposed and aggregated and are published in comparative performance tables ('league tables') which list each school's scores in the core subjects.

Initially, the requirements for publication of assessment results were introduced under the 1980 Act and concerned exclusively the results of O- and A-level examinations. The 1988 Reform Act however extended these requirements to all phases of education by giving the power to the Secretary of State to collect and publish information concerning schools' performance (DES, 1988a). Schools are now obliged, under the *Parents' Charter,* to report their performance in prospectuses and governors' annual reports to parents and publish scores of achievement in comparative tables alongside local and national averages (DES, 1992). A typical report to parents, according to Circular 1/95, should not only provide evidence about an individual pupil's progress but also comparative information about his/her performance and the averages of the school and the country (DfE, 1995a). Thus, parents can base their judgement either on school reports or on the league tables published on the media.

Evidently, the assessment scheme is the main means used by the central authority to regulate schools' pedagogic practice and a chief exemplar of the co-action of the two modes of educational control; the assessment scheme (imposed by the central mode of curriculum control) ensures that schools comply with the National Curriculum requirements since they have to make that visible to the market in which their entrepreneurial operation (decentralised mode of management control) forces them to compete.

The National Curriculum itself is centrally planned on the basis of the national assessment scheme. At a first glance, this is apparent by the new organisation of school years; English compulsory education is now divided in two 4 *Key Stages* which refer to the performance assessed, reported and published when pupils reach the age of 7, 11, 14 and 16. This division indicates that the main concern of central curriculum planning is the public demonstration of the acquisition of the pre-defined content at these time points, rather than the mere prescription of what is going to be taught in these ages.

In this sense, the National Curriculum operates as a set of national criteria of standards constructed by the central authority, which schools have considerable autonomy to work towards in order to optimise their position. Its focus is on defining a sequence of expected performances (*level descriptions*) (DfE, 1995b) not on a sequence of content or classroom activities, as in the Greek setting. Whenever there is direct control it has to do with the mandatory assessment procedures which reveal whether the national criteria are fulfilled. In this respect, the adopted version of curriculum planning is specific to the bi-dimensional pattern in that it allows for managerial autonomy for the organisation of content and pedagogy and controls directly the production of assessment results and their public juxtaposition with the national objectives.

Accordingly, the prime function of the new inspectorial scheme is to evaluate the overall performance of the whole school and make the outcome available for public judgement and choice.

The new arrangements were established by the 1992 Education (Schools) Act which created a non-ministerial government department, the Office for Standards in Education (OFSTED), to manage a national scheme of school inspection by independent inspectors (DfE, 1992). Now inspections are carried out by the so-called Registered Inspectors and teams that they set up - with the restriction to include a member with no previous professional experience in education ('lay inspector') (DfEE, 1996). Her Majesty's Chief Inspector (HMCI) is charged with promoting competition and efficiency by selecting Registered Inspectors on a value-for-money basis. OFSTED invites tenders on the inspection of particular schools and once a proposal is cost effective a contract is signed between the two parties. OFSTED in this way 'has the responsibility for opening up and regulating an inspection market' (Matthews, 1995, p. 70). Thus, the new monitorial scheme relies, not on a permanent inspectorial body, but on accredited individuals and their teams who bid for contracts to inspect specific schools.

Inspection aims at evaluating the school and exposing the pedagogic practice performed in it (its 'strengths and weaknesses') to the public (OFSTED, 1995). Improvement (in the sense of meeting the National Curriculum standards) is expected to be brought about by 'rigorous external evaluation' rather than by advising and guidance. To facilitate this process inspection operates on the basis of a published framework of explicit criteria of performance (OFSTED, 1994b). The inspectorial penetration of pedagogic practice is extensive and the evaluative criteria particularly detailed. Like the assessment scheme, inspectors seek to produce national performance data either by comparing the existing data with the observed outcomes or by juxtaposing these outcomes with the official level descriptions. In fact, the inspectorial teams go further than the national assessment scheme since their judgement is not restricted in the tests and tasks but it is extended to numerous other sources and instruments which reveal attainment outcomes.

In this way the 'mystery' is taken out of education, as the Secretary of State declared in 1991 (Wilcox & Gray, 1996), and the pedagogic practice of each school becomes visible to both the government and the public. It is characteristic that copies of the full reports for all those schools which have been inspected can be found on the Internet (OFSTED, 1998). The customers/parents are enabled to know which school is succeeding and which is failing to approach National Curriculum standards and can make their choices. Consequently, the school can be rewarded or rejected by parents' preferences and governmental funding.

Overall, the monitorial mechanism in England is concerned with recording the school's practices, making the school visible to the public and classifying it. Detailed prescriptions are not given only standards of performance. If these standards are not met *special measures* can be taken which may lead to the closure of the school. Inspection thus can bring about alignment to the official curriculum criteria through its evaluative function rather through procedures of guidance as in the Greek setting. State hierarchy in England (i.e. the appointed *Education Association*) is activated only as a result of an unfavourable evaluation (*special measures*) and its temporary presence in the school consists in a continuous evaluation until correction is brought or exclusion (closure of the school) is decided.

The market-based re-organisation of the English education system and the establishment of the modes of control described above were the result of the neoliberal political project of the 'New Right' which foregrounded the principle of 'free market/strong state'. Gable (1994) remarks that this principle involves a paradox: 'The state is to be simultaneously rolled back and rolled forward. Non-interventionist and decentralised in some areas the state is to be highly interventionist and centralised in others' (p. 36). Both these dimensions of control are not disputed by the Labour government elected in 1997 but they are placed on a different ideological basis. According to the so-called Third Way politics

(Giddens, 1998) 'social democrats must respond to the criticism that, lacking market discipline, state institutions become lazy and the services they deliver shoddy' (p. 75). Market-based solutions are thus supported - this time with the involvement of local communities and business agents - and the bi-dimensional leverage is retained. As the Prime Minister underlined in summarising government policy:

'Intervention is inverse proportion to success' is the philosophy underpinning our education reforms: Ministers have been given tough powers to intervene in the case of failing schools and education authorities, but they are increasing the autonomy of the majority doing a good job . . . In all areas, monitoring and inspection are playing a key role, as an incentive to higher standards and as a means of determining appropriate levels of intervention. A new pragmatism is growing between the public and private sectors. The emphasis must be on goals not rules, and monitoring achievements not processes (Blair, 1998, pp. 16-17).

The Labour Government is now abolishing Grant-Maintained schools (from September 1999) and replaces them by the so-called Foundation schools which retain the extended managerial autonomy of their predecessors but receive funding through their Local Authority (Waterman, 1998). LEAs are requested to delegate all schools-related expenditure to individual institutions ('100% delegation' policy) and are themselves subject to OFSTED inspections for their ability to raise standards and ensure value for money in the provision of services (DfEE, 1998). Except 'failing schools' inspections may identify 'failing LEAs' which, in that case, are placed under the discretionary power of the Secretary of State who is entitled to ask for special measures and even for the privatisation of their services.

4. A different economy of curriculum control

Focusing on the way the two states regulate schools' pedagogic practice it was demonstrated above that the two centralised curricula policies emphasise the control of different message systems. In the Greek mono-dimensional pattern the textbook-based planning and a set of accompanying measures, such as prescribed materials for pupils and teachers, detailed circulars and guidelines, timetables, teaching aids and monitorial activities, exemplify an emphasis on the control of content and process. In the English bi-dimensional pattern the assessment-based planning and resources, such as standard assessment tasks and tests, examining and marking agencies, performance indicators and league tables, records of evidence, frameworks for inspection, inspectorial schemes and their published reports, indicate the strong emphasis on evaluation.

Therefore, the Greek pattern gives rise to a mechanism of guidance while the English pattern prioritises a mechanism of assessment. Such a contrast is not simply an emphasis on an input control in Greece and an output control in England, but it entails regulation *through* guidance and *through* evaluation. For

this last issue, English commentators have suggested contradictory interpretations. Broadfoot (1983; 1996), for example, maintains that assessment for
'system control' in England has always been focusing on *product* and that the
1980s reform policies signified an increasing emphasis on *process* evaluation.
Neave (1988) remarked that state policy to keep the accountability of higher
education has moved from evaluation for system maintenance to evaluation for
strategic change, meaning a move from *a priori* to *a posteriori* evaluation, from
process to *product*. This shift of emphasis, which according to Whitty *et al.*
(1998) is applicable also to the compulsory phase, 'seeks to elicit how far goals
have been met, not by setting the prior conditions but by ascertaining the extent
to which overall targets have been reached through the evaluation of 'product'
(Neave, 1988, p. 9). The scrutiny of the National Curriculum planning and the
monitorial procedures showed that there is a clear official intention of stressing
the outcomes but also of causing changes in pedagogic practice through
evaluation. For example, though monitoring is an outcome-based assessment, the
detailed evaluation by OFSTED of a wide range of classroom practices carries the
potential to cause alterations to those practices. Foucault's analysis (1977) of the
examination as 'a means of control and a method of domination' has shown its
multiple regulative effects (i.e. correcting, training, categorising, normalising)
over the evaluated. An outcome-focused evaluation, from this point of view,
should not only be considered in its intention to encourage the production of
results but also in its potential to produce the desired changes in both content
and process and to alter previous practices.

From this perspective, the contrast between the Greek bureaucratic guidance
and the English evaluative mechanism reflects a different strategy of central
steering or in other words a different *economy* of curriculum control - in terms of
human, symbolic and financial resources made available to regulate pedagogic
practice. In this sense, terms such as 'deregulation' and claims of a post-modern
persuasion that education in many Anglophone countries 'can neither control
nor be controlled' due to a 'decentring of educational authority, control and
provision' (Usher & Edwards, 1994, pp. 211-212) cannot been sustained.
Clearly, the state in the bi-dimensional pattern still projects officially particular
pedagogic identities to respond to cultural changes and economic exigencies
(Bernstein, 1996) and the education system is still used to promote national
values and social careers (Green, 1997). The diversification of educational
activity in England (and the other countries mentioned above) concerns primarily
greater leeway of strategies in achieving pre-determined targets rather than a
deregulation in purposes and orientations. The weakening of bureaucratic power
- a pivotal rationale for the reforms - in school management entails the
strengthening of evaluation as an alternative means of regulation.

Moreover, authors who interpret the symbiotic relation of the two modes of
control in the bi-dimensional pattern as 'paradoxical' (Weiler, 1990; Cole, 1992;
Johnston, 1992), fail to recognise the use of evaluation as an alternative to the
mono-dimensional bureaucratic prescription as well as the analogous historical
tradition. The prioritisation of evaluation procedures should not be considered a
novel phenomenon. In England the role of assessment was from the beginning

crucial in controlling a largely voluntary and dispersed schooling. As Broadfoot noted: 'In recognising public examinations as *an alternative to a centrally directed* education system, many people also recognised the potential power of ... examinations to impose their own form of control' (Broadfoot, 1996, p. 204, italics added). Indeed, examination systems like the payment-by-results in the 19th century, the 11+, the O- and A-level in this century and the traditional inspection (HMI) constituted schemes of external evaluation which had powerful regulative effects on schools' pedagogic practice.

However, it is important to note that the current use of evaluation marks the new role of the state, after the re-classification of the central/local power relations and the creation of a competitive 'marketised' schooling, in England. In the past, assessment and monitoring, as alternatives to centralised prescription, were serving the need of the state to superintend schooling as they provided information to the central government about 'what was actually happening in schools'. Today, with a move to market principles in educational provision, evaluation serves primarily the operation of free choice and competition for standards, pupils and funds, by providing information, at the state's demand, to the parents/consumers. That is particularly evident in the analysis of both curriculums planning and monitoring in which evaluation and publication of results/reports are tightly connected. Through these procedures the state imposes an unprecedented visibility in the way schools operate and perform which allows for public comparison, classification and choice. The current use of assessment therefore signifies the shift to a state, which is an evaluator, an agent of information and a mediator between the autonomous institutions and the citizens/consumers.

New reform measures are now initiated in Greece and other European countries on the basis of criteria of effectiveness and supranational pressures for economic improvement. Whether the current shift in reform criteria would entail a shift to a bi-dimensional pattern of control, like that of England, is largely controversial. Green (1997), for example, recommends that educational researchers should be sceptical of claims that a global policy-shift is occurring with respect to educational 'marketisation' and outcome-related control because not enough evidence exists to support these claims. He notes that in many Eastern Europe and western continental countries issues concerning 'deregulation' and choice have been central in the debates about educational reform. However, as he remarks, most movements have been concerned with devolution of responsibility to regional and local levels rather than to institutions (France, Sweden), no serious moves there have been to abolish state bureaucracies and to introduce choice (Germany) and in eastern European states (Hungary, Poland, the former Czechoslovakia) strong educational bureaucracies are still in place. Finally, Green underlines that the economically advanced Anglophone countries have been particularly prone to neoliberal ideas of diversification and choice, as their educational systems were historically pluralistic, though he mistakenly attributes the recent moves only to 'New Right' governments. From this perspective it would be valid to assume that a general shift to a bi-dimensional pattern as that of England and its characteristic economy of curriculum control would presuppose a change in the role of the state and its power relations with the schools, apart from changes in the reform criteria and supranational pressures. Whether such changes would be accompanied by radical modification in the traditional educational structures or whether resistances of inherited modes of control would mix with new purposes (Cowen, 1996) is something to be seen and further researched.

References

Ball, S.J., (1994). *Education Reform: A Critical and Post*-structural Approach. Buckingham, Open University Press.

Beare, H. and Boyd, W.L. (Eds.), (1993). *Restructuring Schools: An International Perspective on the Movement to Transform the Control and Performance of Schools*. Washington D.C., The Falmer Press.

Bernstein, B., (1975). *Class, Codes and Control, Vol.3: Towards a Theory of Educational Transmission*. London, Routledge and Kegan Paul.

Bernstein, B., (1996). *Pedagogy, Symbolic Control and Identity: Theory, Research, Critique*. London, Taylor & Francis.

Blair, T., (1998). *The Third Way: New Politics for the New Century*. London, The Fabian Society.

Brighouse, T. and Moon, B. (Eds.), (1995). School Inspection. London, Pitman Publishing.

Broadfoot, P., (1983). Assessment Constraints on Curriculum Practice: A Comparative Study. In Hammersley, M. and Hargreaves, A., (Eds.), *Curriculum Practice*. London, The Falmer Press.

Broadfoot, P., (1996). *Education, Assessment and Society*. Buckingham, Open University Press.

Bullock, A. and Thomas, H., (1997). *Schools at the Centre: A Study of Decentralisation*. London, Routledge.

Caldwell, B.J. and Hayward, D.K., (1998). *The Future of Schools: Lessons from the Reform of Public Education*. London, The Falmer Press.

Carter, D.S.G., (1995). Curriculum Reform and the Neo-corporatist State in Australia. In Carter, D.S.G. and O'Neill, M.H.O., (Eds.), *International Perspectives on Educational Reform and Policy Implementation*. London, The Falmer Press.

Carter, D.S.G. and O'Neill, M.H.O. (Eds.), (1995). *International Perspectives on Educational Reform and Policy Implementation*. London, The Falmer Press.

Chapman, J., Dunstan, J. and Spicer, B., (1996). System Restructuring, School-based Management and the Achievement of Effectiveness in Australian Education. In Chapman, J.D., Boyd, W.L., Lander, R. and Reynolds, D., (Eds.), *The Reconstruction of Education: Quality, Equality and Control*. London, Cassell.

Chapman, J.D., Boyd, W.L., Lander, R. and Reynolds, D. (Eds.), (1996). *The Reconstruction of Education: Quality, Equality and Control*. London, Cassell.

Cole, M., (1992). Education in the Market-place: A Case of Contradiction. *Educational Review*, 44, 335-343.

Cowen, R., (1996). Last Past the Post: Comparative Education, Modernity and perhaps Post-Modernity. *Comparative Education, 32,* 151-170.

DEET, (1987). *Skills for Australia.* Canberra, AGPS.

DES, (1986). Circular No. (8/86)-Education (No. 2) Act 1986, 19 December. London, DES.

DES, (1988a). *Education Reform Act 1988.* London, HMSO.

DES, (1988b). *Education Reform Act: Local Management of Schools.* Circular No 7/88. London, DES.

DES, (1988c). *Local Management of Schools* - A Report to the Department of Education and Science by Coopers and Lybrand. London, DES.

DES, (1989). *Planning for School Development: Advice to Governors, Headteachers and Teachers.* London, HMSO.

DES, (1992). *The Parents' Charter: Publication of Information about School Performance in 1992,* Circular 7/92. London, DES.

DfE, (1992). *Education (Schools) Act 1992.* London, HMSO.

DfE, (1995a). *Reports on Pupils' Achievements in 1994/95,* Circular 1/95. London, DfE.

DfE, (1995b). *The National Curriculum.* London, HMSO.

DfEE, (1996). *School Inspections Act 1996.* London, HMSO.

DfEE, (1998) *Fair Funding: Improving Delegation to Schools.* London, DfEE.

Foucault, M., (1977). *Discipline and Punish: The Birth of the Prison.* London, Penguin Press.

Gamble, A., (1994). *The Free Economy and the Strong State:* The Politics of Thacherism (2nd ed.). London, Macmillan.

Giddens, A., (1998). *The Third Way: The Renewal of Social Democracy.* London, Polity Press.

Gordon, L., (1992). The New Zealand State and Educational Reforms: Competing Interests. *Comparative Education*, 28, 281-291.

Green, A., (1997). *Education, Globalisation and the Nation State.* London, Macmillan Press.

Hanson, M.E., (1991). Educational Restructuring in the USA: Movements of the 1980s. *Journal of Educational Administration, 29,* 30-38.

Johnston, J., (1992). Quality Assurance, School Self-management and the Contradictions of Control. *European Journal of Education, 27,* 165-175.

Kazamias, A.M. and Kassotakis, M. (Eds.), (1995). *Greek Education: Prospects of Reconstruction and Modernisation* [in Greek]. Athens, Serios.

Kennedy, K.J., (1995). An Analysis of the Policy Contexts of Recent Curriculum Reform Efforts in Australia, Great Britain and the United States. In Carter, D.S.G. and O'Neill, M.H.O., (Eds.), *International Perspectives on Educational Reform and Policy Implementation.* London, The Falmer Press.

Lainas, A., (1989). *Central-Local Relations and role of the Director of Education: A Study in Greece and England.* Unpublished PhD Thesis, Institute of Education University of London.

Lauglo, J., (1995). Forms of Decentralisation and their Implications for Education. *Comparative Education, 31,* 5-29.

Law 1304/1982 (F.E.K. 144A/7-12-1982) [in Greek].

Lawton, S.B. (1992) Why Restructure? An International Survey of the Roots of Reform. *Journal of Education Policy, 7,* 139-154.

Louden, L.W. and Browne, R.K. (1993). Developments in Education Policy in Australia: A Perspective on the 1980s. In Beare, H. and Boyd, W.L., (Eds.), *Restructuring Schools: An International Perspective on the Movement to Transform the Control and Performance of Schools.* Washington D.C., The Falmer Press.

Matthews, P., (1995). Aspects of Inspection, Improvement and OFSTED. In Brighouse, T. and Moon, B., (Eds.), *School Inspection.* London, Pitman Publishing.

MoE (Ministry of Education), (1985). *Law No 1566/85:* The Structure and *Operation of Primary and Secondary Education* [in Greek]. Athens, OEDB.

MoE, (1988). *Tomorrow's Schools: The Reform of Education Administration in New Zealand.* Wellington, Government Printer.

MoE, (1997). *Education 2000: For an Education of Open Orisons* [in Greek]. Athens, MoE.

Moutsios, S., (1998). *State Curriculum Control in England and Greece: A Comparative Study.* Unpublished PhD Thesis, University of London Institute of Education.

National Commission on Excellence in Education (1983). *A Nation At Risk: The Imperative for Educational Reform.* Washington, DC, U.S. Government Printing Office.

Neave, G., (1988). On the Cultivation of Quality, Efficiency and Enterprise: An Overview of Recent Trends in Higher Education in Western Europe, 1968-1988. *European Journal of Education, 23,* 7-23.

O'Donoghue, T.A. and Dimmock, C.A.J. (1998). *School Restructuring: International Perspectives.* London, Kogan Page.

OFSTED, (1994b). *Framework for the Inspection of Schools* (revised edition). London, HMSO.

OFSTED, (1995). *The OFSTED Handbook: Guidance on the Inspection of Nursery and Primary Schools.* London, HMSO.

OFSTED, (1998). Reports data base on the Internet: www.open.gov.uk/ofsted/repdb3.htm

PD (Presidential Decree) 214/1984 (F.E.K 77A/29-5-84) [in Greek].

Peters, M. (1995). Educational Reform and the Politics of the Curriculum in New Zealand. In Carter, D.S.G. and O'Neill, M.H.O., (Eds.), *International Perspectives on Educational Reform and Policy Implementation.* London, The Falmer Press.

Picot Report, (1988). *Administering for Excellence: Effective Administration in Education.* Report of the Taskforce to Review Education Administration. Wellington, Government Printer.

Reavis, C. and Griffith, H., (1992). *Restructuring Schools: Theory and Practice.* Lancaster, Pennsylvania, Technomic.

Samatas, M., (1995). The Greek Educational Bureaucratism: A Socio-Political Account of the Bureaucratised Greek Education. In Kazamias, A.M. and Kassotakis, M., (Eds.), *Greek Education: Prospects of Reconstruction and Modernisation* [in Greek]. Athens: Serios.

The LMS Initiative (1990). *Local Management of Schools: A Practical Guide.* London, CIPFA.

Tomlinson, J., (1993). *The Control of Education.* London, Cassell.

U.S. Department of Education, (1994). *Goals 2000: Educate America Act (Public Law 103-127, March 31).* Washington, DC, U.S. Government Printing Office.

Usher, R. and Edwards, R., (1994). *Postmodernism and Education.* London, Routledge.

Waterman, C., (1998). *The Education Acts 1998: A Concise Commentary.* London, Stationery Office.

Weiler, H.N., (1990). Comparative Perspectives on Educational Decentralization: An Exercise in Contradiction? *Educational Evaluation and Policy Analysis, 12,* 433-448.

Whitty, G., Power, S. and Halpin, D., (1998). *Devolution and Choice in Education: The School, the State and the Market.* Buckingham, Open University Press.

Wilcox, B. and Gray, J., (1996). *Inspecting Schools: Holding Schools to Account and Helping Schools to Improve.* Buckingham, Open University Press.

5

How Can an Educational System be Decentralised while Preserving its Unity? The Case of Russia and France

Henri Folliet & Jean-Michel Leclercq

1. Introduction

There is a very widely held opinion today that the world's future belongs not only to the market economy but also to what Von Hayek has already called the 'market society'. In this society, States have to let go of areas such as health care, security in the broad sense and education. Otherwise, as Von Hayek insisted, 'the extension of the role of the State will be detrimental to contractual, decentralised solutions and will favour coercive, centralised solutions' (Lepage, 1980 p. 433). It is well-known how enthusiastically American neo-Liberals such as Milton Friedman have taken up this thesis, particularly in order to denounce the inefficiency of state control (Lepage, 1978 p. 201). The only problem here is to know how and at what pace educational systems, particularly in countries which are being held back by an archaic form of centralism, would be able to submit to a demand for liberty which is presented as the new 'meaning of history'.

Here we will analyse two examples of countries which have been characterised by a centralised tradition for many years: Russia and France. In France, the State defines the national education policy and has extensive means of pursuing that policy, such as the organisation of curricula and examinations (Durand-Prinborgne, 1992 p. 177-181). In the former USSR, whose influence on the current situation in Russia should not be forgotten, an educational reform like the one that took place in 1984 had been halted by the central Party and Government authorities. Both countries have decided to move away from their initial model, but they have done so in different ways. For this reason they allow meaningful comparisons between the possible modalities that might be used to break with a centralised formula, and of their chances of success.

2. Centralism and unity of the educational system

When dealing with States which are said to be centralised, however, two precautions are required. First of all the concentration of powers is never total, but it is distributed, to varying degrees, across the geographical area between the representatives of the central authority, or between these representatives and other bodies which have more or less autonomous powers. Centralism can therefore take place in highly diverse configurations. On the other hand, it is not possible to see this situation in isolation from the historical processes which have resulted in these various configurations. That is because the political, economic and cultural meaning of these processes is not the same in all countries where a concentration of powers can be seen. The processes have not affected the functioning of society, or, in particular, the functioning of the educational systems in the same way in all these countries. The historical results of centralism, including its effects on the educational system, are therefore not perceived in the same way, for example, according to whether the system seems to be historically linked to an oppressive, authoritarian or even totalitarian regime, or whether it seems to be identified with the process of building a democratic national identity. Today, faced with a situation of centralism, these differences of interpretation can lead to radically different policies in terms of objectives - breaking with a hateful past or simply correcting ways of working which have become inefficient, in terms of strategies - deconcentration, decentralisation in the direction of local elected authorities or autonomous public establishments, privatisation, transfers of competence either accompanied by contractual commitments or not, or in terms of the pace of change - a 'sharp' break or prudent reforms.

Beyond these differences, however, it is possible to take the view that a centralised tradition inherently includes a specific perspective on the nature and functioning of the educational system. To the extent that the same policy is to be applied or the same regulations are to remain in force, such a system must have a certain unity or even uniformity. It is therefore remarkable that the *Dictonnaire encyclopédique de l'éducation et de la formation*

De Nathan, published in 1994, states in its article on the *Educational system* that the expression is mainly used to stress the unity of the system. Failing this, from a centralist perspective, State control can easily be considered to be stripped of its most essential effects. This is verifiable particularly with regard to equality in education, since in order to ensure such equality a network of identical or comparable establishments is required throughout the whole territory, and conditions of access must also be identical. There is an inevitable contrast in this connection with the systems, described as multipolar, which are in place in highly decentralised States like the United States of America or the United Kingdom. Even in the area of compulsory education, the types of establishment vary from one part of the geographical area to another, as do the conditions of access, which may be either free or selective.

As soon as one considers allowing a centralist model to evolve, the question will inevitably arise as to whether and how its unity can be preserved and whether, ultimately, an antithetical decision is being made between abandoning centralism and adopting a decentralised formula.

3. Processes of change in educational systems in Russia and France.

When one considers the possibility of avoiding the disadvantages of centralism without compromising the unity of the educational system, a comparison between the existing situation in Russia and France does not seem, at first sight, to be very relevant. In Russia the disappearance of the Soviet model led to the rejection of centralism, and by comparison the changes which have taken place or have been planned in France since the 1980s seem to be based on a much more modest inspiration and scope.

It is not inappropriate, however, to ask whether rather similar concerns may be identifiable in the two cases, if we look beyond this apparent contrast. Such concerns are linked, in particular, to ways of understanding the aims of education or the role of the State in education. At the same time they also provide an explanation for certain choices which are made and the difficulties which may be encountered as a result.

The decentralisation measures implemented in Russia and France should not, therefore, be considered as opposite processes. On the contrary, they deserve to be analysed as symptomatic illustrations of efforts to escape from an excessively rigid form of centralism without giving up some of its vital aspects. This is because most political decision-makers and the majority of people in society still consider that these are justified.

In brief, the same attempt has taken place, albeit driven forward with varying degrees of enthusiasm, to give the educational system a form of coherence that is more flexible and perhaps also more effective than the form of coherence in the system based on uniform, authoritarian regulations, whose shortcomings are now quite obvious.

Two opposite situations at first sight: At first sight, in terms of the renunciation of centralism, Russia and France give the impression of having made opposite choices.

In Russia (Leclerq, 1995), the Education Acts of 1992 and 1996 introduced a form of decentralisation which it would not be excessive to describe as radical. Under these laws, the Federal Minister of Education does still have the power to establish overall guidelines, for example concerning teaching structures, curricula and examinations. This authority, however, comes up against a double limitation.

On the one hand it is relative, because although the Federal legislation should apply throughout the whole territory, it actually only applies with the formal agreement of the subjects of the Federation, which are the regions, the municipalities and certain autonomous territories. That is why the Federal Minister of Education has to conclude agreements with these partners: so far he has only done this with half the regions; in the other ones there is therefore a legal vacuum which can almost paralyse his activities. On the other hand, the federal guidelines are only partial. Hence the curricula set out in these are only expected to cover between 50% and 60% of the pupils' actual timetables, while the rest remains subject to the discretion of local authorities and educational establishments, which have also been given greater autonomy. What is more, many areas of management are not mentioned in these guidelines: in particular these do not specify how education services should be organised on a regional or municipal level, nor what percentage of resources should be devoted to the education budget, which is mainly financed from local taxes. Under these conditions, many Russian and foreign observers consider it unsurprising that this extreme decentralisation leads to a risk of destabilisation and could result in a wide range of different, uncontrollable situations, although it was no doubt necessary to underline the break with Soviet practices.[1]

In comparison with this, the decentralisation (Durand-Prinborgne, 1992? p.181 ff.) which has taken place in France since the mid-1980s has been very slight. It has resulted in the transfer of certain competencies to the elected assemblies in the regions and départements, but this has mainly been in the area of construction and maintenance of school buildings. The monopoly of authority held by the Minister was therefore not removed, and the organisation and functional aspects of education are still under his authority. The only area in which it was possible to establish a partnership with the State was with regard to the training plans which are produced on a regional level. On the other hand, neither the creation of a Board of Directors in first-stage and second-stage secondary education establishments, nor the obligation, imposed by the 1989 Education Act, for every primary and secondary school to produce its own 'school charter' introduced any differences which were sufficiently perceptible to create the impression among the majority of observers that the system was actually being decentralised.

Otherwise, the predominant trend was towards deconcentration, which, instead of transferring competencies to non-State bodies, extended the responsibilities and scope for initiative by peripheral State departments at the regional or département level.

This accounts for the recurring theme of the need to continue decentralisation which is raised in many reports and large numbers of official declarations. The Government Minister of Education, who took up his post in June 1997, has clearly stated that he wishes to move in this direction and the report commissioned by him on 'The renewal of the national public education service: responsibility and democracy' is typical in this respect. It must be more appropriate, however, to focus much more on deconcentration than on decentralisation. This can be clearly seen from the decision taken in June 1998 with regard to the arrangements for the transfer of teachers, who are now covered by peripheral departments rather than by the Minister himself. It is, however, still impossible for the regions or départements to have a say in this matter, although they have wished to do so for some time (OECD, 1996, p. 262 and following).

In France, therefore, it seems as if every effort is being made in order to avoid the kind of disorganisation in the system which would result from an excessively radical decentralisation like the one taking place in Russia.

Similar concerns: The differences between these two strategies do not, however, make it impossible to see them as attempts to respond to concerns which bring together both the aims of education and the processes which are set in train in order to achieve them.

As regards the aims of education, the first impression might once again be that of a clear opposition, with, the desire to move from a 'unified, standardised, uniform education system to an education system where everyone has their own choice'[2] on one side and, on the other, the desire to continue the democratisation of education by focusing it more on students, as required by the 1989 Act.

It would, however, be appropriate in this connection to mention the convergence in terms of the importance attached to individualisation in the areas of planning and teaching. Above all, however, attention should be drawn to the need to harmonise the various stated ambitions, such as the desire to strengthen and develop democracy, to consolidate the national identity or to contribute towards economic prosperity, which are strongly emphasised in legislative texts in both countries. It is true that on a number of points it is necessary to see the possible overlaps between these in relative terms. They do, however, still testify to a similar strong desire to make education a factor for the transformation of individuals and society, based on the values and knowledge which it communicates. Most educational policies today have accepted this as their aim, but they have rarely done so with such clarity.

We are inclined to account for this in terms of the scope which is allowed for the role of the State in defining priorities and the way in which to achieve them. Once again it is necessary to take into account certain general trends towards strengthening the involvement of the State, at least in the area of fundamental decision-making, even when emphasis is placed on the need to disengage it from direct intervention. France and Russia are, however, clearly obvious cases in which the responsibilities of the State are only being reduced very slightly.

There is no need to demonstrate this with regard to France, where the lukewarm attitude towards decentralisation speaks for itself. In Russia, the new administrative and educational administration has no doubt resulted in the creation of decision-making centres other than the central authority, which have real autonomy in relation to it. Particularly in a federal context, however, the prerogatives still enjoyed by the State, *de jure* if not *de facto*, are still striking. It is responsible, in particular, for ensuring 'the existence and development of a common educational area in Russia[3] thanks to the introduction of 'State educational standards'[4]. It is no doubt the arrangements for working out these standards which are most symptomatic of the decision-making role which the State has retained. The 'National Centre for Standards and Evaluation in Education' pursues its activities in close collaboration with a specialised division of the Federal Ministry of Education. The planned partnership with the institutions involved in the various regions allows many exchanges of opinions to take place on proposals which come both from the periphery and from the centre, but the final decision is made by the central authority. It has even happened that different divisions of the Federal Ministry have issued standards without consulting the 'National Centre for Standards'. Hence there is a striking contrast with the procedures followed in other federal or decentralised systems such as the United States, where the 'standards' are mainly established by scientific associations of teachers from each discipline, or Spain, where the 'National Committee for the Quality of Education' produces accounts rather than standards.

This is what has made it possible to understand the recurrence of the same debates in France and Russia on the possibility of ensuring that the system is both united and diversified. In both cases, the State, which has been marked by centralisation over many years, and many social groups influenced by this tradition, would not be disposed to accept a fragmentation of the system into independent, competing parts, whether these are decision-making bodies or educational institutions. Due to the need to take into account the new requirements of society, however, and above all the users of the educational system, authoritarianism and monolithism are no longer appropriate.

The current French Minister of National Education, Research and Technology therefore considers it necessary to 'decentralise the system, break its rigidity in order to bring it closer to people', to know that 'equality is not egalitarianism', and to provide 'diversified pathways while keeping national aims in view' [5].

Hence there is no denying that, in many cases, France ends up with a need to break with the past which is very reminiscent of the situation in the new Russian Federation vis-à-vis the old Soviet world. Another factor that encourages parallels between the two attitudes is that many references to Soviet situations have always been made during the course of the processes taking place in France. A number of Ministers for National Education have compared themselves with the commander of the Red Army, due to the thousands of teachers under their command. Above all, however, numerous analyses over a long period have not hesitated to denounce the 'Sovietism' of education in France - which is not only a reference to the aspect of State control. Egalitarianism is another equally important factor, and for some people the ideal school in the Republic is not radically different from an official ideology which has been designed to be imposed upon everyone. It also should not be forgotten that many teachers, either individually or through their trade union organisations, have shown an interest or sympathy in schools in the Soviet bloc, above all because it seemed to them that they were working under similar conditions and with similar aims, despite certain failings which are more often attributed to transient errors than to fundamental weaknesses.

It is easy to point out the illusions on which these ideas are based. It is no doubt more important, however, to stress that they were largely facilitated by the sense of belonging to an administrative and teaching establishment which sometimes gave the impression that some collusion was taking place. This was particularly true with regard to the considerable degree of State involvement in a teaching system which was intended to be national in terms of the values which it proclaimed and the identical services which it claimed to provide throughout the whole territory. That is also why maintaining the unity and even the uniformity of the system was a primary aim. The acceptance of differences within it would have been an admission of failure. For this reason preference has been given to a hierarchy based on a selection process in which everyone is supposed to be equal and a form of elitism which is called a meritocracy for the same reason.

In France, the Republican ideal was therefore able to fit in with the system of recruitment of the 'Grandes Ecoles', and in the USSR the Socialist ideology was able to fit in with that of the universities.

The fundamental problem: It is necessary to establish to what extent these ways of seeing and doing things, these habits as Pierre Bourdieu called them, are deeply rooted among educational leaders, players in the sector and all those involved. These have constantly become more rigid, during a period of more than a century in France and over 70 years in the USSR, preceded by an equally autocratic Tsarist period.

When their legitimacy and appropriateness are called into question, as is the case today, they therefore come up against a new and fundamental problem, which is still at risk of being presented in terms which are too influenced by tradition to make it possible to envisage truly innovative solutions, failing which it will not be possible to face the real challenges involved in the situations. This problem is that of the idea of the unity of an educational system, at a time when its differentiation and diversification are based not only on the observation, but also on the choice of a principle.

As is attested by many reactions both in France and in Russia, reticence about accepting a very far-reaching decentralisation is based on the conviction that it would dismantle the system and take away from it the unity which is vital to allow it to function, and which it needs, for example, in order to meet demands of fairness or efficiency. This perspective is often disputed by referring to the many disparities which are not prevented by the most rigid forms of centralisation: the implementation of national regulations always necessitates relationships which are either heavy-handed or lax, the student populations of the establishments and their socio-economic environment complain about the inevitable differences in standards, and even if examinations and certificates are subject to national standards, they still are not absolutely identical.

These arguments, however, are rarely successful in disarming those in favour of centralisation. These people seek to justify their desire to maintain a unitary system by invoking the guarantees of democracy and fairness which it provides. These guarantees can, in turn, be disputed by claiming that they are likely to limit the freedom of choice which is so desirable. So is this a conflict of principles and ideologies, leading to a result that must by its nature be uncertain? This is very probably the case, since the essence of the question involves how the supply of education is conceived and how access to it is provided.

It must be pointed out, however, that the conflict is also linked to the concept of unity in an educational system.

4. The unity of an educational system

In general, the term unity can relate to two aspects of a system: the geographical homogeneity of its organisation, on the one hand, and its coherence on the other, i.e. the non-contradiction between the elements of which it is made up. Without insisting on our definitions, we would like to mention four types of coherence:

- *formal coherence:* namely the necessary non-contradiction, or compatibility between the various rules which govern the system at a given moment.
- *geographical coherence:* in the various geographical areas covered by the system, and at one time, the same rules cannot be applied to identical cases in a way which is not only different but contrary.
- *coherence in duration:* in a changing system, the change itself is governed by fixed rules.
- *functional coherence:* i.e. the non-contradictory complementarity between the various functions which contribute towards the efficiency of the system.

Although social systems, and in particular educational systems, cannot be considered as either machines or organisms, we still cannot expect them to be either perfectly geographically homogeneous or perfectly coherent.

All empirical observations confirm this. The more we refine the analysis of concrete realities, the more we observe geographical, social and cultural disparities etc. Although the structures, functional rules and aims are considered to be identical, what we tend to find in the geographical area in question is heterogeneity. The more we study the functioning of an educational system, the more we observe its malfunctions, the discrepancies between laws and reality, rules and application, aims and results, tensions and blockages, conflicts of interest and authority... in brief what are called 'problems'. Homogeneity and coherence have only ever been achieved to an approximate extent in the real world of educational systems.

With reference to the images of the machine or the organism, this approximate character can be understood by referring to the Aristotelian distinction between the essence and the accident or the principle of individuation, or to the inevitable margins of error which are inherent in all human thought and action. Scientific analysis, however, leads us to think that unity is not an objective characteristic or a 'natural' aspect of educational systems.

On the contrary, unity appears to be a necessary requirement for all educational policy, and to the extent that it is difficult to imagine an educational system without any educational policy, however difficult to see, since this is a necessary requirement for the existence of any educational system. This requirement in modern educational systems corresponds to a clear, dual social requirement. There is a requirement on the one hand for justice, as a necessary precondition for social cohesion, as expressed in particular by the concepts of fairness, equal opportunities and everyone's right to a high quality of education. There is also a requirement for efficiency, which is expressed in terms of the obligation to achieve results, meeting the educational needs of society and in terms of regulatory activity.

This requirement of unity cannot, however, be understood as a straightforward requirement for unification, with the aim of reducing heterogeneity and eliminating contradiction. In fact every educational policy tends to reconcile the need to unify - to preserve an existing unity or build a desired unity - with the need to diversify - to cultivate or develop diversity.

In every educational system and at every moment, this dual aim is characterised by the global social context, as it results from distant or recent history and as the various social players perceive it. Ideological assumptions, theoretical concepts and ethical principles are no doubt important factors in this perception, and thus in the way educational problems are approached. The problems themselves, however, are suffered rather than chosen; they arise at a specific time and demand a response, sometimes with some urgency. The solutions which are found are often based more on necessity - whether it is understood well or badly - than on a free choice by decision-makers. Problems and solutions can therefore vary from one system to another, and from one moment to another, but in every case there is a need to find the 'point of equilibrium' between the perceived need for unification and the perceived need for diversification, in a word to bring them into coherence, whether it is a case of organising school curricula, certification procedures, personnel training or management, distribution of resources, checking or evaluation systems etc.

It is usually when these very concrete problems arise and demand a solution that the problems of distributing competencies and responsibilities between the various categories of social players involved in the activities of educational systems will come to the fore. The question of modifying this method of distribution between existing decision-making centres, creating new ones etc. does not usually arise in the form of a simple, theoretical problem, but always in the form of a practical demand. And the response to the question owes more to necessity than to free choice, whether it involves bringing the decision-making centre closer to the 'grass roots' in order to take the diversity of local situations into account more effectively, whether it involves seeking convergence and compatibility between functions which have previously been autonomous - for example to meet the need for geographical or professional mobility, etc. This question certainly arises in different forms in highly centralised systems and in others, but the solutions which are chosen, however diverse they may be, always seem to be determined by what European terminology currently calls 'subsidiarity': the existing distribution of competencies is only altered if it seems to be necessary and likely to improve the efficiency of the system or its global or partial coherence.

Ultimately, therefore, the unity of educational systems seems to us to be the coherence which educational policies, which are themselves components of educational systems, seek to give them. This coherence is necessarily precarious, transitory and often approximate. It is, however, a form of coherence which is always demanded by modern societies. It is a form of coherence which is rarely entirely transparent, neither for citizens nor for decision-makers themselves, and which scientific research, particularly thanks to the comparative approach, can help to understand better.

In this context it is possible to ask whether those in favour of centralism may have a preference for an organic form of unity in terms of values and a mechanical form of unity in functional terms.

The reference values determine the culture of the system which is imaginable in terms of a living body constituting a planned whole, and which cannot be fragmented without destroying it. The education department is similar to a machine controlling a pyramidal organisation, deciding upon the alterations or improvements that have to be made in order to achieve the optimum yield.

The whole question is whether it is possible to make do with this type of representation of the unity which is attributable to an educational system. All the information which has been gathered concerning the way in which it is organised and operates should have made it clear long ago that using images which misrepresent realities and divert attention from the real problems will lead to an impossible degree of complexity.

It is necessary to move away from these first of all, to take the view that the unity of an educational system is not a characteristic which it initially owes to the plan on which it is created. This is not, therefore, a point of departure to which it is necessary to remain faithful, but a horizon which is approached without ever reaching it (Pocztar, 1989).

Under these conditions, and this is the second approach to be taken, an educational policy should not define, as its first priority, the need to impose an order and the unity that should result from it. Its primary responsibility, on the contrary, should be to introduce the ground rules for the deployment of initiatives by its partners which it should not restrict without depriving itself of its own object. To use an expression which is so often heard these days, what should be taking place here is a search for coherence. Of course the process should not involve the plans of decision-makers, which can unfortunately sometimes be accused of being contradictory, so much as those of their various partners, which are always more difficult to reconcile because they are inspired in many diverse ways.

That is also why, it must be repeated, in this type of context, a new concept of unity is required and the factors which it takes from previous ideas will form the basis for any possibility of accepting the prospect of decentralisation without denying its disadvantages, which are certainly not imaginary but which are also real in centralised systems.

It is also probable that the circumstances are likely to favour or hinder developments in this direction. From this perspective, Russia has been engulfed by a political, social and economic crisis which has forced it to review its decisions in ways that promote the emergence of hitherto unknown perspectives. France, on the other hand, which has escaped from far-reaching changes of this kind, is clearly encountering major difficulties in separating itself from its habits although it is aware of the change of direction that needs to take place.

Ultimately one might ask whether the relatively comfortable situation in France really is any better than the supposed chaos in Russia which is so often spoken against. Despite its very discouraging appearance, this situation could make it possible to gain experiences which are needed in the education system in order to relinquish visions rooted in the past and approach the present situation with confidence.

Our initial question was as follows: are renouncing the disadvantages of centralism and preserving the unity of an educational system two mutually exclusive requirements?

The views that we have set out here lead us to the hypothesis that this is less of a theoretical antithesis than a practical, strategic problem, whose solutions will probably never be either completely rational or perfectly satisfactory.

References

Durand-Prinborgne Cl., (1992). *Le droit de l'éducation.* Paris, Hachette.

Heyneman S.P., (1997). *Education and Social Stability in Russia, an Essay Compare* 27 (1).

Lepage H., (1978). *Demain le capitalisme,* Paris, Librairie Générale Française, p. 201.

Leclercq J.M., (1995). *La loi sur l M'éducation de la Fédération de Russie et les problèmes de son application,* Savoir (1) Jan-Mar 1995.

Lepage H., (1980). *Demain le libéralisme,* Paris, Librairie Générale Française, p. 433

(1996) *Russia's Educational System,* National Report of the Russian Federation, International Conference on Education, Geneva, 29-30 September 1996

(1996) Russia *Education in the transition,* Washington,World Bank.

OECD, (1998). *Examen des politiques nationales d'éducation, Fédération de Russie.* Paris, OECD.

OECD, (1996). *Examen des politiques nationales d'éducation France* Paris, OECD.

Pocztar J., (1989). *Analyse systémique de l'éducation.* Paris, Editions ESF

Notes

1 The following works have been consulted on the situation in Russia: Russia's Educational System (1996) National Report of the Russian Federation, International Conference on Education, Geneva, 29-30 September 1996- Russia Education in the transition (1996), Washington, World Bank-Examen des politiques nationales d'éducation, Fédération de Russie (1998), Paris, O.E.C.D.

Heyneman S.P. Education and Social Stability in Russia, an Essay

2 Russia's Educational System, Op. Cit. p. 5

3 Ibid. p. 7

4 Ibid. p. 5

5 Interview in the newspaper Le Monde, 22 April 1998

Part 2

Market

6

Universities, Markets, and the State: Higher Education Financing as a Laboratory of Change*

Hans N. Weiler

1. Introduction

There is a new game being played in European higher education. Some call the game 'deregulation', some call it a combination of greater autonomy and greater accountability, some call it a shift from input controls to output controls, and some call it simply 'passing the buck'. Whatever it is called, it certainly is different from the old game, which always looked a little like a state-owned version of 'Monopoly'. The new game is being played on different stages; it is being played on the stage of governance, on the stage of new programs of study and their accreditation, on the stage of new personnel regulations, and increasingly on the stage of new higher education legislation. Wherever the new game is being played, there are the same three players involved: the university, the state, and the market. And that is what makes it new. Because the old game was a pretty simple, straightforward and rather boring affair that was essentially limited to two players: the university and the state. And one always knew the outcome of the game: Both players claimed they won, but it was always the state that kept score.

Now there is a third player in the game, something called 'the market'. Nobody quite knows what a market is in higher education, but that doesn't keep anybody from talking about it. This construct of the market is an interesting new element in the discourse on higher education in Western Europe, and it is rapidly

* Prepared for delivery as the Lauwerys Memorial Lecture at the 18th CESE Conference of the Comparative Education Society in Europe (CESE), Groningen (Netherlands), July 9, 1998.
An earlier version of parts of this paper was presented at a workshop on higher education finance organized by the World Bank and the Soros Foundation (Budapest, June 1998).

spreading, with the tender care of the World Bank and the Soros Foundation, to Central and Eastern Europe. It is pretty clear that it won't spread into the United States, because there it has been around already for some time.

For Europe, the interesting question may not be so much why the market has recently moved into such a prominent position in the debate about higher education, but why it took so long. After all, we have known about markets at least since Adam Smith wrote 'The Wealth of Nations' over 200 years ago (1776). And we know how exasperated Adam Smith was when he incredulously took Colbert, the minister of Louis XIV, to task for daring 'to regulate (industry and commerce of a great country) upon the same model as the departments of a public office' (quoted in Lindblom 1977, 33). Somewhere along those 200 years, someone might have had the idea that there may be better ways to regulate higher education than 'upon the same model as the departments of a public office'. But apparently, until very recently, and with the exception of the U.S. and a few of its imitators, nobody did.

But now it seems to have happened. There is not only serious talk, but even some action in the direction of deregulating higher education, of performance-based models of resource allocation, of inter-institutional competition, of efficient management structures, of the development of specialised 'products' of higher education, even of 'privatisation'. And the arena of European, and even German, higher education, long a rather sleepy habitat, has all of a sudden become exciting, controversial, and lively.

Of the various stages on which, as I have said, the new game is being played in European higher education, there is one where it is being played with special intensity, and where it is particularly instructive to watch. This is the stage of financing in higher education, and this is the one on which this paper will focus. Because it is with regard to the question of financing that the new higher education discourse of the market becomes most tangible, most controversial, and thus most revealing (OECD 1990; Williams 1992).

I propose to organise my review of recent trends and developments in the governance and financing of higher education around a number of key issues that proceed somewhat loosely from a macro to a micro level, and will at the end, in a final section, raise a few broader themes in higher education policy that I regard as worth keeping in mind as one debates different options in financing and governance.

The macro/micro distinction in higher education financing is, by the way, not a particularly neat one, since many developments cut across all levels of the system; take, for example, the case of formula funding or parameter-based funding, which establishes principles and procedures both for the allocation of public resources to individual institutions and for the distribution of resources within each institution. Nonetheless, it may be useful to start with the broader view and work our way to some of the specifically institutional concerns.

As I see it, the twin goals in the current debate in Germany and among other OECD countries about the financing of higher education (and about the future shape of higher education more generally) have to do with autonomy and accountability. As institutions of higher education seek (or are pushed towards – it is not always clear which) greater autonomy from state control, there is a corresponding preoccupation with questions of accountability and transparency in the ways in which more autonomous institutions deal with their resources. Where once the state, through a tightly woven net of budgetary and other regulations, controlled or pre-empted a substantial part of a university's internal decision-making, policies of deregulation now confront the university with the task of designing, applying and enforcing its own groundrules for the internal allocation of resources. In the process, there is a transition from a system of control that operates 'ex ante', i.e., through a set of rules and regulations set up in advance, to a steering system that works largely 'ex post' and is based on allocating resources on the basis of performance. In other words: the overall tendency is from a situation where the resource situation of an institution is dependent on a given set of input parameters to a situation where output parameters are becoming more and more important. Line-item budgets, where a certain amount of money is in advance earmarked for a certain institutional purpose - e.g., the purchase of computers - are a key feature of controlling an institution 'ex ante' or through the specification of inputs; by contrast, providing a university with a lump sum budget and specifying the performance criteria by which it will be judged as to whether or not it has spent this budget wisely (and should therefore receive more the next time around) controls an institution 'ex post' or through its outputs.

This description may sound like a nicely professional and disinterested treatment of the transfer of responsibility for financial decision-making from the state to the universities. In actual fact, however, this transfer only thinly conceals a considerable state of emergency in the funding of higher education. In Germany and in most of the other OECD countries I know, at least part of the state's motivation for making institutions of higher education more autonomous in dealing with their financial futures has been the serious shrinking of public resources available for expanding systems of higher education. In this situation, it is very tempting for governments to transfer to the universities the increasingly unpleasant (and politically onerous) task of administering scarcity. In a review of changing financial policies in higher education in several Western European countries, the German HIS research service observes, somewhat tongue in cheek, that 'the radical transition from a supply-oriented allocation of resources to a competitive allocation occurs in all countries considered against the background of a severe curtailment of funds' (Schnitzer and Kazemzadeh 1995, 9).

Be that as it may, the overall and rather fundamental change in the general pattern of funding higher education has a number of specific facets, of which I consider the following eight as being both the most significant and, from the point of view of the experience of the OECD countries and my own experience, the ones most in need of a critical assessment.

2. Changing rationales in budgeting and resource allocation: From line-item budgets to block grants.

Of all the changes in higher education financing, none has probably been more

consequential than the change from line-item budgets towards global allocations or block grants, for the use of which the universities are to be responsible and accountable in an ex post manner. In the overall move towards greater autonomy by the institutions of higher education, this shift has probably been the single most important factor. Nowhere, however, has this change been accomplished in one giant and instantaneous step. Typically, this change has been, or is being, accomplished through a gradual series of consecutive steps, such as:
- allowing universities to use funds from unfilled staff positions for current operating expenditures in teaching and research, or
- making possible limited transfers between line items, or
- selecting a limited number of institutions for pilot projects to try out more encompassing schemes of block grants.

Where, as in the Netherlands, the change towards lump sum or block grant allocations has gone the farthest, it has been closely tied to a system of formulae on the basis of which the overall allocation has been determined (see below).

Without going into a great deal of technical detail here, I would like to point out a number of considerations that I have found useful as one moves in the direction of block grant funding:
Among the few advantages of line item funding is the fact that budget reductions on the part of the government become more easily visible and identifiable; budget cuts can be much more easily concealed in the allocation of block grants.
Implicitly or explicitly, block grant allocations are tied to an underlying contractual relationship between funding agency and recipient such that, in exchange for the grant, the recipient institution engages to perform a certain set of tasks in teaching and research, the satisfactory completion of which is the university's responsibility and on the basis of which it will be supported in the next budget cycle. This kind of contract has been one of the more interesting instances of negotiation between government and universities; in current discussions in a number of German states (e.g., Lower Saxony, Berlin), where the key term is 'Zielvereinbarung', universities and the state have negotiated a fairly explicit set of development targets which the universities are committed to achieve in return for (reasonably) secure multi-year funding prospects.
In the United States, the National Commission on Responsibilities for Financing Postsecondary Education has a few years ago spelled out a handy set of four conditions for the success of this kind of an autonomy-accountability relationship between funding agency and recipient institutions:
- Agree on the tasks that need to be accomplished;
- Ensure that the available resources are sufficient to complete the tasks successfully;
- Provide the enterprise (the university) with the authority it needs to be effective, and then let it do the job without interference; and
- Define a set of measurements to indicate how well the enterprise is doing relative to its goals, and follow up by tracking these measurements (as cited in Massy 1994, 6-7).

This set of groundrules already highlights the critical importance of performance measures and evaluation in making the transition to more global means of funding feasible. Here again an instructive debate on the nature and the measurement of desirable outcomes in higher education has begun in Germany, from completion rates in different programs of study to research productivity and from the employment record of graduates to the number of scholarly awards.

Block grant systems allow for an important facility especially for universities in a state of transition, namely, the achievement of cross-subsidies between programs, where savings in one program can be invested in the strengthening of another.

From the funding agency's point of view, one of the important elements in this reshaped or reshaping world of university funding could well be the retention of a central contingency pool of resources that can be used for such purposes as:

- special and particularly promising research programs;
- the support of graduate students on a competitive, cross-institutional basis;
- compensating an institution for overloads in teaching;
- bridging the time to anticipated retirements of faculty, thus making the early replacement of retiring faculty possible;
- investments in special teaching facilities, such as PC pools, or
- support of provisions for underrepresented groups, such as women students or faculty.

3. Formula funding: New parameters in resource allocation

As the pre-ordained structure of line-item budgets has begun to disappear, the need arises to find a basis on which to determine the new block grants or lump-sum allocations that universities are to receive under more open and autonomous funding arrangements. The search for this basis has led to a variety of 'formulas' which are used to compute the funds that a university is expected to need. In this development, the Netherlands and Denmark have played the role of pioneers among OECD countries, and anybody interested in the trials and errors encountered in this process should take a close look at their experience. Other countries have taken up the challenge, and my own state, the state of Brandenburg, is now experimenting with a model of formula funding of its own, as are any number of other states in Germany and countries in Europe. In reviewing these efforts, let me emphasise the following points and observations.

Initially and in its strictest sense, the formulae for funding higher education have focussed on input factors, i.e. on those indicators that represent the tasks universities are supposed to perform in teaching and research, and their estimated cost. By now, however, many funding formulae have a double face: they estimate input factors, but they also tend to specify performance measures that are considered to be particularly desirable outcomes of university efforts. To give an example: One of the most fundamental elements in any funding formula is the number of students. That is a straightforward input factor. By modifying or weighing this factor in such a way as to only count students within regular graduation time limits (that is, excluding those who take forever to finish their degrees), one adds an outcome or performance measure that reflects the university's ability to provide an effective teaching program.

One of the difficult questions in the business of designing formulae for funding is just how finely to tune them, and whether to concentrate on a few important indicators or include as many as possible. Here, the general wisdom seems to be to focus on the ones that really matter. This is easier on the input side, where one typically limits the formula to such things as:

- the number of students (possibly modified by limiting it to students within regular graduation time), as an indicator of the load and cost of teaching;
- the number of staff (academic and service), as an indicator of the cost incurred by their work; and
- space, as an indicator of the cost of maintenance.

The important point about these indicators, however, is that they need to be differentially weighed, depending for example on what discipline is involved, engineering and natural science subjects requiring substantially more cost in teaching and research than humanities and social sciences. It also makes sense to weigh the number of students differentially depending on whether the instructional capacity of a given institution (as determined by its staff and space) is underutilised or overutilised; the formula we are working on in Brandenburg envisages a statistical bonus for student numbers under conditions of overutilisation, and a malus or discount factor in case of underutilisation.

On the output side, the choice of a few key indicators to include in the formula becomes more difficult, especially since this also depends on what a given institution, by the nature of its institutional mission, considers particularly important: A heavily research-oriented university will value and weigh research productivity (as measured, for example, by the elaborate peer review procedures of the UFC in Britain) and the acquisition of research funding from the outside more highly, while a more teaching-oriented school will emphasise the quality of teaching and advising and the institution's success in bringing students to an early and high-quality completion of their degree. One of the important but as yet poorly developed outcome measures would clearly be both the occupational success and the satisfaction of an institution's graduates.

Some funding formulae – including the ones that I am struggling with at my institution right now – have an important and not adequately recognised structural deficit in that they disregard the rather simple management truth that institutions have funding needs that are independent of their size and the volume of their activities. Every university, no matter how small, needs a core admissions staff, a core personnel department, certain basic maintenance services, basic library resources, etc. The importance of this baseline estimate tends to be often overlooked when the logic of linear relations between size and funding needs prevails.

Funding formulas – and this is perhaps their most important function in shaping systems and institutions of higher education – serve as an important communication device: Their very composition sends a powerful message as to what is and is not considered important in a system or an institution of higher education. The relative weights given to teaching, community service, foreign student enrolment, scholarly awards, student-teacher ratio or number of women faculty all represent important value decisions for the system or the institution, and should be the result of a rather serious process of reflection and discussion.

Since so much controversy has emerged around the question of markets and democracy in higher education, and about their alleged incompatibility, I would like to pursue this question a little further. It is, of course, nonsense that markets and democracy are incompatible, in higher education as elsewhere. What is incompatible with a competitive and market orientation in higher education are the kinds of so-called democratic governance structures in universities that have, at least in German higher education, degenerated into mutual non-aggression pacts for the purpose of conflict-free and performance-independent resource allocation and of seeking and finding lowest common denominators among competing factional interests. In contrast, a rather worthwhile challenge to the internal democracy of academic institutions would be to specify the kinds of institutional priorities that would result in specific funding formulae. Wherever representative bodies of university governance start engaging in this kind of reflection on institutional values and profiles, both the causes of higher education and of democracy would be served well indeed.

4. Scholars and markets: The role of incentives

With its increasing emphasis on output or performance criteria, formula funding contains already a substantial element of incentives for contributing to the institution's mission, and of disincentives for not contributing.

I would like to add to this, however, by reporting on a particularly heated debate that is being conducted in Germany right now - a debate in which, not surprisingly, the experience of American higher education serves once again as a controversial benchmark. The issue is the determination of funds that should be placed at an individual faculty member's disposal for teaching and research and, furthermore and even more delicate, the determination of a professor's compensation. At present, both of these decisions are virtually unaffected by what a professor does, what a load he carries, or how he performs his tasks. The financial resources for his professorship are typically settled when he is appointed, and he has a right to receive them annually as long as the budget permits, regardless of load or performance. Similarly, professorial salaries are set by civil service guidelines and increase inexorably on the basis of only one criterion: advancing age – the only exception being a special raise available to counter an offer from another university. The current debate - fuelled by a recent resolution of the German Rectors' Conference - over changing this system with regard to both the financial resources at the professor's disposal and his salary in order to make it more incentive-oriented has all the drama of a war of religion, and may end up just as bloody. It highlights both the inherent difficulty of reform in higher education and the problems of bringing a modicum of market principles to bear upon academia.

On a much more minor scale, I wanted to relate an instructive example of making incentives work. I helped introduce this myself in my department at Stanford where we gave faculty members an 8% share in the overhead that the university charges on externally funded projects. Thus, for every $100,000 in sponsored research funds that a professor raised, he had $8.000 at his disposal for travel, added assistants, books, or other professional expenses. The effects were considerable.

Lastly, let me point out an important and often overlooked incentive that is entirely non-monetary, but in my experience extraordinarily effective. I am speaking of the devolution of decision-making, including financial decision-making, to lower levels of the organisation. Being involved in decisions in such a way that one's voice does make a difference serves as a powerful motivating factor in all organisations, but particularly in a highly professionalised organisation such as a university.

5. The search for new funds: Mobilising external resources

The growing shortage of public funds, combined with the desire for getting away from the state as the sole source of a university's funding, has contributed to an unprecedented preoccupation in German higher education with opening up additional and alternative sources of funding. This effort takes the form of seeking support from organised philanthropy through foundations, of a growing volume of contractual research and training programs for outside clients (for the coverage of both direct and indirect costs), of the sale of services such as language teaching or the use of libraries and data networks, the mobilisation of private individual and corporate donors to set up endowment funds for special projects (such as endowed chairs), programs of continuing education, and others. Having dealt with, and carefully observed, this process in both the US and Germany, I would like to offer the following observations.

It is important to realise that most externally obtained resources in higher education, with the exception of endowment funding, are of questionable longevity. They typically last for a number of years, and then disappear, leaving a promising program that was funded from these sources destitute or, just as badly, dependent on the institution's regular resources. Commitments by the state to pick up the support for activities that were started with external funds are, at least in my experience, notorious for being evaded (e.g., the experience of externally funded chairs ['Stiftungslehrstühle'] in Germany in comparison with endowed chairs in the US). This situation is especially serious where, as is often the case today, state funding only covers the basics of institutional cost, while everything dynamic and innovative about an institution comes out of outside funding. As such outside funding tends to disappear over time and may not be fully replaced, the institution is left with its status-quo-oriented basic framework and sees its innovative features disappear in the process.

A related risk has to do with the fact that external funds tend to carry hidden costs that sometimes even the more sophisticated calculation of indirect cost will miss. These hidden costs have to do with the gradual erosion of basic capabilities in libraries, equipment and physical plant. Some of these are opportunity costs for foregoing other valuable activities in favour of an outside contract. A particularly problematic policy is that of the German national science foundation, the Deutsche Forschungsgemeinschaft, which as a matter of policy makes research awards only on the condition that the recipient institution provides all of the basic outlay – space, equipment, basic staff, and adequate library facilities. In stark contrast to this philosophy, I think it is essential that external funds cover the full cost of the services they purchase and support, including both indirect costs and the cost of developing the institution's long-term capabilities, including the training of young researchers.

The most important and consequential problem with outside funding in higher education, however, is the risk it carries for sustaining the institution's mission and intellectual profile. Except in the rarest case, and protestations to the contrary from the involved parties notwithstanding, the seeking of outside support typically entails compromises between the institution's own priorities and the priorities of the outside funding agency. The attempt to balance market forces with the need for institutional coherence remains in most instances imperfect, and its imperfection causes the problem of a 'fragmentation of faculty allegiance' (Massy 1994, 32) between promising funding opportunities and institutional loyalties that is becoming a serious problem for a growing number of institutions of higher education.

6. Making users pay: Tuition and fees in higher education

Given the difficulties of not only obtaining outside funds, but also of dealing with their drawbacks once they are obtained, it is not surprising that the notion of charging users for the use of higher education is gaining ground. The number of countries in the OECD where some form of tuition is charged students of higher education is increasing, and the debate about introducing tuition in those countries that do not yet have fees is heating up. This is, once again, particularly true in Germany which has a long social democratic tradition of tuition-free higher education.

The arguments for and against fees are fairly straightforward. At a time of shrinking resources, tuition can be a significant source of new funding. Provided one makes sure that these resources do indeed remain at the university's disposal and do not serve to offset a portion of state funding so as to cure general fiscal ailments (not an easy condition to meet, I should emphasise), substantial financial benefits can accrue from collecting even (in comparison to, say, high-price US institutions) relatively modest fees. In this connection, it seems essential that students, parents and graduates have a major say in decisions about how tuition money is to be spent by the university.

Perhaps even more important in thinking about tuition fees is the prospect of creating more of a supply and demand dynamic in higher education. There is absolutely no question that in systems where there are fees, both universities and students behave differently. Universities tend to be more responsive to the interests and needs of fee-paying students who make a significant contribution to the financial well being of the institution and who also have the option of taking their tuition money elsewhere. By the same token, students and their families tend to pay a good deal more attention (including critical attention) to a university education, which costs them real money.

The main argument against tuition has been that it discriminates against students coming from economically disadvantaged groups, and that it tends to discourage those students from higher education altogether. There is some evidence from the United States that this is to some degree true, but there is also considerable evidence that this effect can be significantly moderated by appropriate programs of financial aid in connection with need-blind admission and affirmative action policies.

Those who argue against introducing tuition into higher education on social grounds also have to confront the argument, however, that there is nothing terribly social about a situation in which non-students who are working subsidise through their taxes the cost of university education for an upwardly mobile population of students who, by all accounts, tend to be rewarded quite generously for their degrees by significantly higher status and lifetime earnings.

In the end, the question of whether or not tuition in higher education can be justified hinges on the adequacy of the system of financial aid and its ability to compensate the effects of market-based tuition rates for students from disadvantaged groups. In this context, there is still much to be said for the original version of the Australian Higher Education Credit Scheme (HECS) – not the somewhat denatured version that has replaced it in the meantime – where needy students would pay both their fees and their living expenses out of a loan that is to be repaid through the tax system only if and when their later income exceeded a specified minimum income. A somewhat modified (and improved) version of this scheme has recently been proposed in Germany as well (Stifterverband und CHE, 1999).

7. Private initiatives in higher education: Panacea or dead end road?

All over the world, with the (perhaps overly) enthusiastic leadership of the World Bank, the notion of privatising higher education has in recent years picked up a momentum of its own. Having spent most of my academic life at a private university, I am following this development with both sympathy and some concern. There is indeed much to be said for challenging the monopoly of public forms of higher education in the many countries (including Germany) where such a monopoly effectively exists, but some critical remarks are in order to keep things in perspective and to make sure that an essentially good idea does not get defeated by its own exaggerated claims.

In most countries of the world, including the United States though possibly excluding Brunei, higher education institutions that are entirely or even predominantly funded from private sources are simply not feasible. Even the

United States that has arguably the most developed and successful system of private higher education has long moved to a hybrid situation where private institutions cover an ever increasing share of their costs from public funds – just as public universities draw increasingly on private sources of funding. Stanford and UC Berkeley provide an instructive pair in this regard.

What may well give the privatisation of higher education a bad name is the emergence of two rather peculiar types of institutions. First, there are institutions like the ones that have recently emerged in Germany and other Western European countries that pick for themselves one or two subjects that are particularly marketable among both prospective students and corporate sponsors (usually business management and informatics), then proceed to obtain substantial resources from both corporate sponsorship and tuition fees and, in addition, seek and receive significant state subsidies. If the (excellent) idea of more privatisation in higher education is to create more competition between different types of institutions, then there is no way for a fair competition to be held between these institutions and public institutions that can neither charge tuition nor market their much broader instructional spectrum, while having to maintain the full range of academic subjects over and above business and informatics. For competition to be meaningful, a level playing field is a prerequisite.

The other kind of newcomers in the animal kingdom of higher education are for-profit universities, of which one, the University of Phoenix, was very ably and instructively portrayed in an issue of The New Yorker some time ago (Traub 1997). I am not necessarily saying that there shouldn't be any institutions of higher education that are conducted for profit. What I am saying is that these institutions are unlikely to serve as the kind of catalyst that could help regenerate and mobilise our existing systems of public higher education.

Against the background of these somewhat problematic developments, we are likely to be more successful if we understand privatisation not necessarily as an alternative way of funding higher education, but as an organisational and structural alternative. To introduce, even under public or partly public funding arrangements, entrepreneurial or other private management structures into higher education strike me as an extremely worthwhile project. There are already enough examples within the overall framework of public higher education systems of running research institutes, language labs, or continuing education programs on a modified corporate model to demonstrate how much more flexibility, adaptability and innovation can thus be achieved.

8. Shaping the institution's profile: Steering and controlling in higher education

Financing in higher education, as I have said before is not just about money and accounting. It has a great deal to do with institutional purposes and with how they can be achieved. I happen to think that the sharpening, the cultivation of institutional purposes, the development of more specific and recognisable institutional profiles is one of the major challenges that lies ahead in German higher education. The time of the all-purpose, across-the-board university, where one could find everything but had a hard time finding excellence, is probably coming to an end. Institutions of higher education in Germany in the future will probably have a more limited, more carefully composed set of specialities, and will seek to excel in those. For this strategy to work, financing will have to play an absolutely critical part, especially in a system of allocating resources in which performance is a key determinant for funding decisions. Because if shaping and sustaining the institution's special profile is an important priority, then part of the funding formula needs to be not only the general quality of a unit's work (a department, an institute, a professor), but also the contribution which that unit makes to enhancing the university's special profile.

Let me illustrate this with the example that I know best, that of my own university. Viadrina European University was set up in 1991 to serve as an academic link between Germany and Poland, as a bridge across a particularly troubled border. It has opened up its programs of study to students from Central and Eastern Europe, mainly Poland, but also the Ukraine, Russia, the Czech Republic, with the result that it now has the largest percentage of foreign students of any German university, including over a thousand students from Poland alone. Building this bridge through teaching and research has become the special mission, the special profile of the Viadrina, and it is imperative that its limited resources be geared to sustaining this profile as much as possible. It does not work perfectly by any means, but those projects that do conform to this profile, and particularly to our cooperation with Poland through the Collegium Polonicum on the other side of the Oder river, have a priority claim on the university's resources, especially those resources that we receive from the European Union (EU).

9. Funds and fiefdoms: The internal distribution of resources

In talking earlier about the level where funding decisions are made in the relationship between the state and the individual university, I have spoken of a contractual kind of agreement by which institutional goals and priorities become the basis for a funding formula and a funding commitment by the state. At the next stage of the allocation process, the distribution of resources inside an institution, we face a similar problem, but with somewhat different players. The problem is at this level exacerbated by the existence of what I have called 'fiefdoms' inside the university – professorships, institutes, chairs – which have a tendency (a) to insist on the retention of previous funding commitments (invoking the principle of 'Besitzstandswahrung' or preservation of acquired property rights), and (b) to watch carefully over the maintenance of parity in the allocation of resources. Here, as at the level of resource allocation to entire institutions, the only answer to the problem seems to lie in carefully negotiated agreements in which the level of funding is a function of the recipient's responsibilities and performance. Those agreements are not easy to obtain, but they are easier to obtain if the agreement is openly and transparently negotiated so that, for every participant in the process looking at every other participant, the correspondence between performance and load parameters and funding commitments are understandable. Without that kind of transparency, there is very little chance to succeed in the effort to make the allocation of resources more performance-oriented.

10. Conclusion

Let me conclude by taking up once more the question of what all the talk about a stronger role of the market in higher education really means. Is it just some fashionable rhetoric designed to mobilise the legitimating (or at least fundraising) potential of corporate and managerial jargon? Or do we see, in this invocation of market models, a genuine change in policy in the direction of giving universities greater autonomy so they can compete more freely and aggressively in the markets for good students, good faculty, and good research funding? Or are we indeed on the threshold of a new paradigm of higher education, where Adam Smith finally catches up with Max Weber, and where the virtual monopoly of state authority over higher education is giving way to an accountable, but essentially autonomous model of higher education?

At first sight, one is tempted to conclude from this review of changes in financing: a little of all of the above. If indeed financing can serve as a crucial indicator, a bellwether for how serious systems of higher education are about their transition to market models, then this little review has shown that a beginning has certainly been made, that it's not all rhetoric, but also that there are still some major problems ahead, especially with regard to restructuring patterns of governance in accordance with the new modes of financing.

In one of the early and very influential contributions to thinking about markets in the context of making policy in modern democracies, Charles Lindblom (in his 1977 book on 'Politics and Markets') has a number of interesting things to say, including this:

A market is like a tool; designed to do certain jobs but unsuited for others. Not wholly familiar with what it can do, people often leave it in the drawer when they could use it. But then they also use it when they should not, like an amateur craftsman who carelessly uses his chisel as a screwdriver. (76)

That's about where we are in the reform discourse in European higher education: still trying to figure out what exactly to do with this powerful, but also somewhat risky tool, 'the market'.

References

Lindblom, C.E., (1977). *Politics and Markets: The World's Political-Economic Systems*. New York, Basic Books.

Massy, W.F., (1994). *Resource Allocation Reform in Higher Education*. Washington, National Association of College and University Business Officers (NACUBO).

OECD, (1990). *Financing Higher Education: Current Patterns*. Paris, OECD.

Schnitzer, K. and Kazemzadeh, F., (1995). *Formelgebundene Finanzzuweisung des Staates an die Hochschulen - Erfahrungen aus dem europäischen Ausland*. Hannover: HIS-Hochschul-Informations-System GmbH.

Stifterverband für die Deutsche Wissenschaft and Centrum für Hochschulentwicklung (1999). *InvestiF und GefoS - Modelle der individuellen und institutionellen Bildungsfinanzierung im Hochschulbereich*. Gütersloh and Essen, CHE and Stifterverband.

Traub, J., (1997). Drive Thru U.: Higher education for people who mean business. *The New Yorker*, October 20 and 27, 1997.

Williams, G., (1992). Finance and the organisational behaviour of higher education institutions. In E. Frackmann & P. Maassen, (Eds.), *Towards Excellence in European Higher Education in the 90's (Proceedings of the 11th European AIR Forum, Trier, August 27-30, 1989)*. Utrecht, Lemma, 69-95.

7

The State, Civil Society and Economies: The University and the Politics of Space

Robert Cowen

Thomas Jefferson, in creating the University of Virginia, wrote of his expectation that it would form 'the statesmen, legislators and judges on whom the common weal so much depends' (Peterson, 1977). Less fortunate perhaps was his expectation that American high schools would 'sort the geniuses from the rubbish'. Rather pointedly, he was determined that his new University in Virginia would contain no School of Divinity (Cunningham, 1987).

These three aspirations of Jefferson give the themes of this paper. The idea that the University would form statesmen and legislators and judges captures succinctly the powerful expected relation of the new University with the new political and civil society of the new American Republic. Raking geniuses from the rubbish, however harsh to the contemporary ear, establishes the clear point that Jefferson's view of American civil society was elitist, as befitted his formation as the owner of slaves and a plantation (Monticello) south of Washington. His antagonism to the power of established churches expresses not only views of the separation of the Church, the State, and education which found a way into the American Constitution but also one of the first breaks in the patterning of American higher education. The colleges of William and Mary, Dartmouth and Harvard were not only influenced by English and Scottish models of collegiate higher education. They also had produced ministers of religion (Brick, 1971).

Thus, starting from these anecdotes about Jefferson, I suggest that American higher education and its relations with the State, civil society and the economy changes dramatically, and fairly clearly, over time.

First, the early institutions of higher education were concerned with the formation of civil society – some ministers of religion, some lawyers, judges, and legislators. This was the creation of an American republic, politically and culturally, and a Republic able to rule itself and manage its public affairs.

Second, the insertion of the Land Grant college model into American higher education from 1862 onwards was an insertion of a relation with the economy. The Colleges, financed by Federal money, were to pursue the 'useful and mechanic arts' – which they did in the Plains States with the improvement of agriculture and wheat production; and in the southern States through their contribution to the planting and harvesting of cotton. In the mid-century period there was also a considerable expansion of other local colleges, often religious, as minority groups established their identity within American civil society. The struggle to establish black colleges and universities in the South is a poignant reminder that American civil society was flawed by a racist principle – legally so in education in the Southern States – at least until 1954.

Third, in the late nineteenth century the importation of the graduate school and the doctorate, into Johns Hopkins and the University of Chicago, and the subsequent expansion of the State University system from the 1920s, consolidated the awareness of civil society as a society of opportunity. There were links with the economy also. The State Universities provided the professional middle classes of America as its businesses and industrial complexity grew, and the 'Wisconsin idea' magnified the notion that the American University was a service agency for local, even State–wide, communities (Jencks and Riesman, 1968). The university's contribution to the formation of civil society and its contribution to local economies was to be direct.

Fourthly, what is interesting is that there is something missing. The Americans never developed specific institutions, like the French *grandes écoles* or the English Oxford and Cambridge (Oxbridge) into which the future political elite were selected and in which they were socialised in a separate and high culture. The academic study of French and English political elites, and their relation with educational routes, is relatively straightforward. C. Wright Mills had far greater difficulties in tracing the educational origins and educational pathways through which the American political elite is trained. Not least this is because of the deep suspicion, from the days of the American Revolution, of the (central) State. American higher education has never been dominated by State interests; in contrast to Europe where both Napoleon and von Humboldt with different degrees of subtlety expressed the interests of the State in the patternings of the university.

Fifthly, and the fifth layering in the history of American higher education, is the expansion and consolidation of the university system as a major industry in its own right after 1945. The Servicemen's Readjustment Act of 1945 (The G. I. Bill) was a statement of gratitude to veterans from the Armed Forces of the USA – but also an affirmation of a major principle of American civil society: the gradual opening up of access to education. However, just before and after 1957 and Sputnik, the political interests of the American State became clearly expressed in the patterns of higher education. Major Federal funds were located, as research money, in the universities. Their mandate included of course basic research, but in the crisis of the Cold War a great deal of research effort was placed in applied science and the potentials for technological and scientific 'victory' over the USSR (Clark, 1993). For the first time in American history, the (central) State itself became a major actor in shaping the American University.

Thus what we are seeing here is the construction, redefinition, and renegotiation over time, of the social space which American higher education and especially the University occupied.

Historically, following the Jeffersonian political project of anti-colonialism and Independence, the institutions of higher education reaffirm the nature of the new civil society. It will be republican, free of organised religious interests, and it will be elitist – as a minimum, blacks and women will be subordinate citizens. Later, the social space, which the university occupies, is redefined by Federal action. Through the Land Grant College movement, the university is inserted into the social space of the economy – it will contribute to the 'useful and mechanic arts' and make a direct contribution to the economic development of the regions of the USA, especially their industrial and agricultural capacities. Later still, from the end of the nineteenth century, the social space of the university is again redefined. Following the spread of the 'Wisconsin Idea' the university will not only make a general contribution to form the new professionals of the industrial age, but the 'community service' function redefines the responsibility of the university to include problem-solving for a scatter of communities. These problems may be economic, social or political, but the university must respond. Its social space is compressed – in the sense that any remaining 'Ivory Tower' philosophies are undermined. An alternative expression of the same proposition would be that its social space is expanded: it must undertake community-driven responsibilities.

Finally, the relative independence of the American University from the (central) State was sharply diminished from the 1950s. The social space of the American university was invaded by what even President Eisenhower called the business-industrial-military complex and its major research universities were geared up to deal with what was seen as a national crisis: the Cold War. Political connections between the State and the university system were now fully developed, though through the relatively subtle means of finance funding. McCarthyism did not develop into a cultural revolution (cf. the USSR of Stalin and the mid 1960s in Mao's China) which collapsed the internal social space of the university into the political shapes of the wider society. The American university retained its tenure and departmental systems, its academic trades union (the AAUP) and its insistence on its own intellectual freedoms and autonomy. It took the subtler attacks of political correctness in the 1980s and 1990s to undermine those – but those were problems of the relation of the university with American civil society rather than problems in direct political relations with the State.

I hope that by now the general line of argument of this paper is becoming clear, from this specific narrative about the development of higher education in the USA.

The argument in abstract form is that universities because of their genesis in medieval Europe at the interstices of the Church and the State contain an ideological and even an institutional dynamic; that dynamic is that they expand, epistemologically, to pull all knowledge within their purview. The knowledge may be sensitive e.g. knowledge-claims to analyse religion or politics. This ideological and epistemological tradition is respected in a range of institutional arrangements (the Professor, the Research Seminar, the department) and in contractual arrangements (tenure, 'academic freedom') and consultation mechanisms (Boards of Trustees or mechanisms to insulate financing from direct political consequences).

These institutional arrangements define systematically the social space of the university, which typically also is defended by ideologies of academic freedom. At the minimum, a sacred social space is claimed, and may even be established. At one extreme, this permits the accusation that the university is an 'ivory tower'. The university, even as 'an ivory tower', tends to increase its claims to social space – its epistemological self-justification is that it may examine, critically and through research, all of the cultural capital of society and indeed that it is its duty to change this capital (and not merely transmit it).

However, this claim to an expanding social space draws irritated opposition from those who dislike such hegemonic claims (such as the Church, and the more secretive sectors of industry and the military). The State may also insist on a voice in politically sensitive areas such as definitions of education or of history. The university's general expansionist claims may also draw occasional rebuke and redefinition as societies themselves are restructured and are redefined, under major historical influences.

In the case of the American university, its social space was altered by an insistence on the need to produce a variety of elites for civil society and the professions. Its social space was diminished and simultaneously expanded by the demands that it contribute to regional and industrial development. Its relations with the economy changed. Its social space was diminished as it was brought within the political project of the (central) State, which declared a political crisis. Thus the social space of the University was potentially expansionist (because of the knowledge claims of the university-in-itself) and therefore contested.

Thus the social space of the university alters over time and it does so through quite complex social processes. These social processes are always political and are finally expressed in public political form, as Laws or Reform Bills. The social space left to the university is always a consequence of the intersection of a triad of forces: the economic, typically expressed through industrialisation; the notion of civil society, most sharply expressed in time of revolution, post-war reconstruction and in escape from colonialism; and the State itself and the directness of its political emergency expressed as 'national need'.

Within this general argument and before moving on, I would like to remind you of the ways in which approximately similar points could have been drawn from narratives familiar to you. For instance, in France, the Napoleonic State interfered massively in the definition of the University. There was no especial economic motif. The university was not strongly linked to regional economic projects, The University was to form a national elite, very much within the Napoleonic conception (rather than the original Revolutionary conception) of the nation and an ordered civil society. In particular the Napoleonic *grandes écoles* were to form those legislators, judges, engineers and modern experts – including ultimately politicians – on whom the new Republic and Empire so much depended (Vaughan, 1969). The political interests of the State narrowed dramatically the social space of the University and on that social space, from Paris, major claims were also entered about the formation of citizens.

For instance, the English story of Oxbridge is also familiar. Oxbridge was used in the formation of leadership hierarchies appropriate for English civil society in the eighteenth and nineteenth centuries. The political claims on the social space of the university were also cheerfully accepted. There were two such claims. One was for the formation of the political elite of the nation; and the other was for the formation of the political elite of the Empire. The closure of the social space of the university was ideologically justified by both Locke and Newman – in the idea of the English gentleman. This idea not only defined the knowledge appropriate for a gentleman (and the University) but the social responsibilities of the gentleman and the political space between the university and the State – and their correct overlap.

Of course it is the case that in both England and France, later, economic claims were made on the social space of the university, in England as early as the 1860s. Efforts were made to re-balance the triad of economy, politics and civil society by creating universities useful to industry in the North. These efforts were not successful, at least not immediately, and it may be debated just when – or indeed, if - they became successful (Cowen, 1988).

As a third instance, the German case is remarkable. I am not thinking here of the destruction of the academic profession in the Nazi period, but of the up-dated nineteenth century university as this was outlined by von Humboldt. The claims entered on the university by von Humboldt were for the construction of civil society. The link between a conception of education (*Bildung*) and the research acts appropriate in a university (the creation of *Wissenschaften*) was beautifully articulated not merely because they were part of a coherent epistemological vision, but also because the concepts were linked to the formation of the State itself. The entry of those from the University into the running of civil society was through the State-Exam – and in a further remarkable vision the University, while dependent on the State was to be independent of it. The University was to be an enclave, protected by the State, and contributing to it by its independence. Thus the political interests of the State were to be served, but by an indirect and delicate articulation which left the University free to develop or to redefine its professoriat, its seminars, its research directions and its academic autonomy (Walters, 1996).

Of course, later, the German University towards the end of the nineteenth century made major contributions to the German economy and its social space was affected and redefined by this contribution. Even later its social space was massively invaded and became political and politicised. The shift is important, a part of a major tragedy in contemporary history, but the collapse of the mandarins is not the point of my analysis today.

Please notice how contextualised the story is so far. The American university, as it gets redefined in social space, gets redefined in American social space, even when part of the story covers the introduction of the doctorate, inspired by Germany. The various shifts in the definitions of the social space left to the university are strongly related to the politics, economy and the nature of American civil society. Similarly, part of the story of France is Napoleon and of Germany, von Humboldt; and the shifts in social space of the French and

German Universities occur against these initial (contemporary) definitions of the relations of the university to civil society, the economy and politics. The same is true of the English gentleman, distastefully distant from the Industrial Revolution, but happy with domestic and international political responsibilities and the serious games of Empire, war, conquest and balances of power. The shifting social space of Oxbridge, undermined and ultimately attacked by the new professionalism of London University and the new universities in the North linked to local industries, is an English and a separate Scottish story, which begins in the existence of a very few elite universities north and south of a national border within the UK.

These universities were nationally rooted, even though they were affected by events overseas, and they were rooted in a national economy, a national politics and specific versions of a civil society. Even when the theme of Empires (and the difficulties of running them) affected the universities, there was little doubt about their location. They were 'at home'; they were in domestic social space.

My final argument is that the idea I have so far developed no longer holds. I have been arguing that the shifting social space of national universities can be illustrated, precisely along the themes of this Conference – what is the relation between the State, civil society and the economy. I have suggested that we have a number of patterns. The patterns are different from each other (the American, the French, the German, and the English). They have different ideological roots; they have different trajectories, they produce different university systems. But the differences can be patterned. They are differences in the triad of relations of university to the State, civil society and the economy. The social space of universities increases or diminishes, reflects and accepts (or rejects) a range of demands made upon it by historical forces that in a full analysis could be outlined fairly fully.

However, I think the rules (of the real world and the assumptions in my analysis) have changed. We have – in Popper's terms - some black swans. Let me try and explain why my earlier analysis does not cover some new developments. I suggest that we are seeing a major new development – among several – which disturb the axioms on which my earlier analysis was based. There are three phenomena of great importance, which mean a new way of thinking is required.

First, universities are now not merely, as in Australia, Canada, the Netherlands, the UK and the USA, expected to compete within a national market and to behave at least for part of the time as if they were businesses. We are now seeing the creation of universities, which are in an international market and behave as such. The expansion of the Australian universities into Asia, particularly East Asia, construed as a market, is a case in point. Thus – although there was always elite mobility – we are now seeing the mass mobility of university students as consumers. Asian students come to Canada, Australia or Britain, but the universities of Canada, Britain and Australia also establish themselves, physically overseas, They build out-houses, as it were. Their finance, their students, their faculty and even their physical plant is now internationally mobile (de Wit, 1995).

This is an interesting development in that it can, at the very least, be classified as both a cultural and an economic change.

However the very loose vocabulary which is now starting to accrue around the terms 'internationalisation' and 'globalisation' is a source of intellectual vertigo. That is, analysis is becoming increasingly difficult as the vocabularies of internationalisation and globalisation are tending to be used as synonyms in conferences and in even written papers. Major efforts have been made to sort out the concept of internationalisation of higher education (Knight and de Wit, 1995) although some of the work on the globalisation (sic) of higher education seems to take on very similar meanings (Scott, 1998).

Nevertheless, the cultural change in the universities is that they import 'the international' – in the form of students, perhaps in the form of changed pedagogies and in the form of codes of practice designed to protect the 'overseas student' – into their academic cultures. The cultural change in the universities is also that – paradoxically - they import 'the international' by exporting their faculty overseas, with the faculty themselves becoming more skilled in understanding 'foreign' cultures or 'foreign languages'. In other words the 'foreign' is one way or another imported and, in course structures, in faculty experience, in pedagogic or examining modes, the university may think of itself as internationalised.

The economic change is that universities, as they import and export these people (their own faculty, incoming students, even their administrators), and even as they adapt their codes of practice to new ethics, may intentionally make money out of these transactions (Scott, 1998). In this sense, universities may be interpreted as having seen a market for their services. That market is part of a global economy in two senses. One version of the idea of 'the global economy' might stress the decreasing obstacles to the cross-national transfer of skilled persons, disciplinary and interdisciplinary knowledge for teaching purposes, and cutting edge research. Another version of the idea of 'the global economy' might stress that the global economy is no longer dominated by industry as a source of major wealth for nations, but by 'knowledge' – that is knowledge, created, organised and sold, in useful packages of biotechnology or information technology or materials science.

Thus universities can be players in both versions of the global economy. And they are (Blumenthal, Goodwin, Smith & Teichler, 1996). The cultural dynamic of their international academic relations affects their pedagogies, their examination systems, the skill profiles and experience of their faculties, and even their internal administrative structures (e.g. International Offices; or Deans of International Relations may be created). The global knowledge economy affects their research grants, their relations with overseas businesses (as well as domestic firms), and the skill profiles and experience profiles of the faculty, which they may wish to recruit (or encourage to retire).

Thus it is not especially useful here to invoke the conventional vocabulary which works well enough for looking inside particular countries and at certain kinds of recent educational reform. It is possible to stress that, for example, in Mrs Thatcher's England major reform efforts were undertaken on an extreme neo-liberal (or even neo-conservative!) vocabulary to construct a market in education: to let 'the invisible hand of the market' guide educational choice, create initiative, diversity, freedom and so on. The parallel ideological struggle to take control of concepts of 'quality', in rhetoric about accountability, total quality management, and 'effective' schools is one useful way to interpret particular moments of domestic educational reform – not only in contemporary England, but also Australia, Canada, New Zealand and so on.

However, to interpret the emerging role of the major contemporary research university and the social space which such universities, and other newer forms of university, occupy in such terms is probably to trivialise what is happening.

Certainly universities in many countries are now subject to domestic rules of 'performativity' (Cowen, 1996). Many of the rules are very domestic indeed, as technocrats make tactical choices about operational measures of quality, such as citation indices, or dispute delicate balances between quantitative and qualitative measures of performance. 'Quality' in academic production is emerging as whatever the domestic rule-system says it is – with predictable consequences for the destruction of the possibilities for work recognised as qualitatively excellent by specialist colleagues in other countries. However, what is happening to universities is even more interesting than this (on the assumption that sooner or later domestic rules for measuring quality and performance can be changed).

Universities are undergoing a change in form and they are now located in a new version of international space.

In form, universities are becoming virtual. Some universities exist only in cyberspace, such as Jones International University (www.jonesinternational.edu) and Western Governors University (www.wgu.edu). It is possible now to deliver teaching and learning over great distances through a variety of new media. These media of course include e-mail for responses to students' essays, themselves downloaded from e-mail; but also the possibility of delivering overseas lectures and even seminars which hitherto because of space-time distance could only be delivered in Harvard, or Berlin or Oxbridge. The university in its pedagogic relations is now free of its national space. These universities, not least in the mould of the Open University of the United Kingdom, are a transferable technology, and they are becoming massive. They instruct. They do not socialise. They deliver text and exercises and evaluation. They are, increasingly, mega-universities (Daniel, 1996).

However, these mega-universities also change their position in cultural and political space. Such universities and certainly the emerging pattern of virtual universities established by large corporations are not necessarily responsive to a specific local culture, nor even to some vision of an international culture. They do not serve the purpose of training local political elites, for example. Such tasks continue to be carried out by Harvard, Yale, the *grandes écoles*, the Universities of Oxford and Cambridge, Melbourne, McGill, Tokyo and so on.

Mega-universities increasingly exist in cyberspace, with some domestic infrastructures. Thus their cultural role is one of certification – in multiple locales beyond national borders – of a labour force which is thus, de facto, internationally certified. The certificate of qualification permits, in principle, international mobility, as the routes to the qualification and processes of gaining it are internationally transparent. Thus this is a qualification system which is part of an international marketplace in which entrepreneurial virtual mega-universities compete.

It is therefore possible to interpret this as another example of the 'invisible hand of the market' working. But again this is probably to miss a crucial point. In domestically based higher education institutions, such as junior colleges in the USA, the former monotechnics in the USSR, the IUTs in France, the Fachhochschulen in Germany, there was a context for the ambitions as well as the certifications offered. There were political, cultural and even civic identities delivered along with the formal qualification package. The shift in the form of some universities to mega-universities is not merely a reaction to a perceived market and economic opportunity; it is also a shift in higher education in the modalities of socialisation into cultures, including political cultures.

Such universities are now not merely part of an international economic market for students, where 'invisible hands' ensure competition. Such universities are loosely located in international space (cyberspace) and transmit cultural messages, which begin in domestic entrepreneurial, or domestic managerial institutional worlds. It is thus important that the cultural messages (as well as the quality of the qualification packages) offered by new forms of university be analysed.

The virtual-international and virtual-mega and emerging corporate universities are no longer responsive to the traditional triad – of politics and the economy and the civil society - of specific places. For the virtual international university there is no politics to respond to, except the irritations of political instability, which affect the market. For the virtual international university there is no economy to respond to, because 'the economy' is merely the demand of individual students for courses and 'the economy' has become the international market. And there is no State or politics for the virtual international university to respond to, except in the form of interference – from taxation or evaluation rules 'at home'. The university, politically, is rootless.

Of course this a practical policy problem. It is also for comparative educationists a fascinating illustration of cultural and political transmission through new forms of institution, in new social spaces and through new pedagogies.

We are seeing a new game in which it is not possible to trace the impact of the economy, civil society and politics on national university patterns. It is not possible to trace contested social space, as this expands and contracts, under shifting demands from the triad. The new international virtual universities do not exist in social space as we have understood it in comparative education (nationally, with an occasional international excursion). The virtual international universities inhabit a political space but one which we do not yet understand; they inhabit an economic space but one which is too rapidly reduced to the concept of market, and they serve no civil society.

Thus the phenomenon - of the changing political and social space of new forms of the university - is not interesting because it is economic; but because it is cultural. It is not interesting because it is an extension of domestic notions of the market or domestic notions of efficient educational reform; but because it is *terra incognita* in a sociological, cultural, political and comparative sense. At the moment we do not have the analytic perspectives to handle the issues, nor are we going to develop them if we continue to believe that all we are dealing with here is an interesting extra puzzle about markets and education, or some more kindly vision of the development finally of a universal world-wide civilisation. The world is not merely a market, and it is certainly not going to become a utopia in the present state of our knowledge.

References

Blumenthal, P., Goodwin, C., Smith, A. & Teichler, U. (Eds.), (1996). *Academic mobility in a changing world: regional and global trends.* London, Jessica Kingsley.

Brick, M., (1971). The University in the USA. In B. Holmes & D. Scanlon (Eds.), *Higher Education in a changing world: The World Yearbook of Education 1971/1972.* London, Evans Brothers Limited.

Clark, B.R. (Ed.), (1993). *The Research Foundations of Graduate Education: Germany, Britain, France, United States, Japan.* Berkeley, University of California Press.

Cowen, R., (1988). Relations between the university, research and industry. In Ministry of Education and Culture (Ed.). *Proceedings of the Second Anglo-Brazilian Seminar.* Brasilia, Ministry of Education and Culture.

Cowen, R. (Ed.), (1996). *The evaluation of higher education systems: The World Yearbook of Education 1996.* London, Kogan Page.

Cunningham, Jr. N.E., (1987). *In Pursuit of Reason: The Life of Thomas Jefferson.* New York, Ballantine Books.

Daniel, J.S., (1996). *Mega-universities and knowledge media: technology strategies for higher education.* London, Kogan Page.

De Wit, H. (Ed.), (1995). *Strategies for internationalisation of higher education: a comparative study of Australia, Canada, Europe and the United States of America.* Amsterdam, EAIE.

Jencks, C. & Riesman, D., (1968). *The Academic Revolution.* New York, Doubleday and Company. Inc..

Knight, J. & de Wit H., (1995). Strategies for internationalisation of higher education: historical and conceptual perspectives. In H de Wit, (Ed.). *Strategies for internationalisation of higher education: a comparative study of Australia, Canada, Europe and the United States of America.* Amsterdam, EAIE.

Peterson, M.D. (Ed.), (1977). *The Portable Thomas Jefferson.* Harmondsworth, England, Penguin Books.

Scott, P. (Ed.), (1998). *The globalization of higher education.* Buckingham, England, SRHE & Open University Press.

Vaughan, M., (1969). The Grandes Ecoles. In R. Wilkinson (Ed.) *Governing elites: studies in training and selection*. New York, Oxford University Press.
Walters, G.J. (Ed) (1996). *The tasks of truth*. Frankfurt-am Main: Peter Lang

8

Education Between State and Private Delivery: Civil Society as Equilibrium. The Dutch Case*

Anne Bert Dijkstra & Jaap Dronkers

1. The Dutch system of choice

Central to the Dutch arrangement of private deliverance of education is the constituted principle of 'freedom of education'. This principle has resulted in approximately 70 per cent of parents sending their children to schools established by private associations and managed by private school boards, yet fully funded by the central government. Given these characteristics of the system, the Dutch schooling arrangement is offering an 'experiment' in private production of education in a state controlled system, for almost a century, and including the entire education system. In this contribution, we will discuss some characteristics of the system of schooling in the Netherlands, as well as recent developments in this long-standing, nation-wide 'experiment' of state controlled, private deliverance of education.

Parental choice of a school for their children was one of the most important topics in the 19th century Netherlands. The political struggle between the liberal dominant class and the catholic and orthodox-protestant lower classes gave rise to Christian-democratic parties, which have held central political power since the start of the 20th century until the mid-1990s. This political struggle was not unique to the Netherlands but the unintended result of three interacting processes: the struggle between the state and the established churches in Continental Europe; the fight between the 18th century *ancient regime* (mostly with one state-church and suppressed religious minorities) and the 19th century liberal state (which claimed to be neutral to all churches); and the emergence of new social classes in the 19th century (skilled workers, craftsmen, labourers) which rejected the dominant classes, either liberal or conservative.[1] Nor was the outcome of these three interacting processes unique to the Netherlands: in several

* We wish to thank Wendy Naylor (University of Chicago) for her helpful comments to an earlier draft.

continental European societies (Austria, Belgium, France, some German *Länder*) these processes had more or less comparable results, with public and religious-subsidised school sectors offering parents a choice between schools of the same curriculum and usually under comparable financial costs for the parents.[2]

In the Netherlands, however, choice between religious and public schools was not only an educational choice: it was closely connected to other choices in life – voting, church activities, membership of clubs, unions, newspapers, etc. The choice between public and religious schools was linked to the choice between the catholic, orthodox-protestant and public sub-cultures – or 'pillars', as they were called in the Netherlands (Lijphart, 1968). A consequence of these religious grounds for the rise of subsidised schools was that parental choice on educational grounds (quality of schooling in public and religious schools) did not exist during the first half of the 20th century. Religious considerations and the belonging to a specific sub-culture were dominant with perhaps only some elite groups the exception to this rule.[3] Free parental choice of school was a religious choice. Since religious socialisation was seen as closely connected to education, this freedom of parents to choose a public or religious school under equal financial conditions was known as 'freedom of education', a concept which originally referred to one of the basic human rights formulated during the French Revolution.[4]

2. Religious schools in a secular society

From the middle of the 20th century onwards, the religious sub-structures or pillars in Dutch society broke down rapidly. In 1947 only 17 per cent of the population did not officially belong to any church; halfway the 1990s the proportion had increased to around 50 per cent. The same trend can be seen in the votes in favour of Christian-democratic parties in national elections: in 1948, 55 per cent; in 1998, less then 20 per cent of the vote. One might have expected this secularisation to result in a decline of the popularity of institutions such as religious schools that depend on religious affiliation for their recruitment. However, although such a decline occurred in a number of organisations and institutions (unions, journals, clubs, hospitals), it did not affect the educational system. In 1950, 73 per cent of all pupils in primary education were attending a non-public school; in 1993, 68 per cent.

How then can one explain the non-disappearance of religious education or the failure of public schools to attract the growing number of children of non-religious parents (cf. Dronkers, 1992)? This issue of legitimacy is also of interest to other societies with a growing number of religious schools and increasing pressure for subsidising, along with a not very active religious population. The Dutch situation therefore offers insight into the mechanisms of this increase in religious schools in not particularly religious societies. At least eight mechanisms can perhaps explain the existence of religious schools in Dutch society (for a detailed account, see Dijkstra, Dronkers and Hofman, 1997).

A first explanation may be the *financial differences* between school sectors. Dutch schools do not differ greatly in their fees. Religious schools charge certain extra fees, which are mostly used for extra-curricular activities. The choice of parents here can hardly be influenced by financial considerations. The irrelevance of financial criteria for choice during a school career is shown in various educational attainment studies (de Graaf, 1987). Financial differences are not a good explanation for the existence of religious schools.

Differences in *student intake* explain, on average, only one third of the outcome differences between schools. After controlling for the differences in student intake, the differences in effectiveness between public and religious schools are roughly the same as before controlling. Religious schools do not on average have a better-qualified student intake, so this second mechanism does not seem to offer a valid explanation for the attractiveness of religious schools.

The third explanation is the strong position of religious schools through *political protection* by the Christian-democratic party, by laws protecting 'freedom of education', and by the dense administrative network of the organisations of religious schools. This hypothesis has some validity. The central position of the Christian-democratic party on the Dutch political map till halfway the 1990s, made it possible to maintain the current school system and the religious schools within that system, despite the decreased religiousness. It was even possible to establish new religious schools in areas with only a low number of active church members. Nevertheless, the mechanism can't fully explain the flourishing private religious school sectors, because of the Dutch system enables parents to 'vote with their feet', despite all regulations and despite the strong formal position of religious schools.

Schools are financed according to the number of pupils enrolled, and the way to establish a new school is to find enough parents who will send their children to that new school. Several groups of parents (orthodox-protestant, Islamic, Hindu) have recently used this mechanism of 'voting with their feet' with success against the powerful, already established organisations of religious schools, and to found schools of their own religious preference. The question is therefore why irreligious parents did not use the same mechanism to increase the number of non-religious schools or the number of pupils attending them. It is hard to argue that these irreligious parents are less powerful or less numerous than the orthodox-protestant, Islamic or Hindu parents and their organisations. Irreligious parents are on average better educated and have more links with the established political parties than orthodox-protestant, Islamic or Hindu parents. One can conclude from this that irreligious parents no longer feel deterred by the religious socialisation of religious schools and thus do not see the need to change to non-religious schools. If this is true, this explanation by political protection is not sufficient to account for the continuing attractiveness of religious schools.

There exist slight differences in *educational administration* between public and religious schools (Hofman, 1993) and they can explain some of the outcome differences, despite the enforced financial equality and strong control by the state. It are not the formal differences in educational administration, but on the average the stronger informal relations between board and teachers in the religious schools which explains partly the better performance of their pupils and thus the attractiveness of religious schools for non-religious students and parents (Hofman *et al.*, 1996).

A fifth explanation is that irreligious parents prefer religious socialisation, because they still appreciate the *religious values* to which they no longer adhere. However, it is clear from longitudinal research that the number of adherents to religious values among Dutch adults is decreasing, which is in contrast to the stability of recruitment of religious schools. Only a minority of parents (about 30 per cent, depending on the local situation) mention religious reasons for choosing a religious school for their children. If the appreciation of religious values by irreligious parents offers an effective explanation of their choice of a religious school, the percentage of religious reasons should be higher. However, the valuesoriented character of religious schools leads them to stress secular, non-religious values as an important aspect of schooling in the broader sense (Germans would call this *Bildung* and the French *éducation*). Public schools with their neutral status tend to avoid discussion on value-oriented topics and stress instruction instead. Irreligious parents who prefer schooling to have a broad scope rather than a more narrow instructional purpose, thus choose the modern religious school for its breadth, which they consider an aspect of educational quality, rather than for religious values.

Neither protestant nor catholic churches have a major influence any longer on the curriculum of most religious schools, and religious education has decreased to the point where it simply gives factual information on various world views (Claassen, 1985; Roede, Peetsma and Riemersma, 1994). One good reason for this breakdown of religious socialisation is the scarcity of teachers who are religious and willing to undertake that religious socialisation. The lack of religious teachers in the Netherlands can be explained by the positive relationship between level of education and degree of traditional religiousness. A majority of pupils in religious schools have not an active religious background and their parents do not want them to be socialised into a religion they do not belong to.[5] But they do not object to cognitive information on various worldviews. There is a happy conjuncture between the impossibility of religious schools to provide religious socialisation and the small number of parents still wanting it. Thus, these schools offer as next best cognitive information on world views (which a teacher who is not religious can give as part of cultural socialisation, although it is often still known under the old curriculum title of religious education), and non-religious parents can accept information on world views as part of cultural socialisation (despite its old-fashioned title). The forced neutrality of public schools and the secular values-oriented character of religious schools explain partly the attractiveness of the private religious sector.

A sixth explanation of the attractiveness of religious schools in a less religious society is their mild *educational conservatism* (on average), compared to the more progressive (on average) tendency of public schools.

There are several reasons for this mild educational conservatism of religious schools. First, the board of public schools is the council of the municipality. These councils will favour educational experiments for political reasons (not necessarily bad ones) because education is one of the major instruments of policy makers to promote desirable developments. Boards of religious school have less direct connections with policy makers (although they are often in some indirect way connected with the more moderate political parties), and represent more parents (mostly indirectly). So they will feel less need for educational experiments for political reasons. Second, public schools have less opportunity to escape pressure from national government because they cannot use 'freedom of education' as a shield to protect themselves. Religious schools can only be obliged to conform to educational experiments if they are forced to by a national law which declares the educational experiment a quality condition necessary to qualify for subsidising. In all other cases, religious schools can only participate in educational experiments on a voluntary basis. Third, public school teachers are more often members of the more progressive union of teachers, which tends to support educational experiments, while religious-school teachers usually belong to the more moderate or conservative unions, which tend to favour the status quo.

As in most European societies, regular attendance of religious services even among church members is low in the Netherlands. The catholic and protestant churches are not communities in which a majority parents and pupils of religious schools participate on a regular basis. Since the *religious community* is the ultimate explanation of the positive effects on educational attainment in Catholic schools in the United States (as suggested by Coleman and Hoffer, 1987), one would not expect output differences between public, catholic and protestant schools in the Netherlands as a result of this mechanism.

However, Dutch research contains evidence of such positive effects of catholic and protestant schools on secondary education (for a review, see Dijkstra, 1992). These differences, all adjusted for the composition of their students, were found in terms of educational outcomes (drop out, degrees, attainment, etc). If this community of churches would be an important explanation of the varied appeal of different religious schools, one might expect the secularisation and the decrease in religiousness of the Dutch society has reduced the difference in educational outcome between public and religious schools.

Another explanation is the positive effect of a deliberate choice by parents and teachers of an 'unconventional' as compared with a traditional choice, which will increase the possibility of this 'unconventional' school becoming a community in which pupils perform better. Depending on the deliberate educational choice of the parents and the following self-selection, both religious and public school can become a community with shared values in which pupils perform better. The *deliberate educational choice* of parents and teachers of a specific school will increase the chances that this school will become an educational community in which pupils will perform better.

De Jong and Roeleveld (1989) found that religious, and especially catholic, secondary schools for junior and senior general education in Amsterdam obtained better results than comparable public schools. In the highly secularised city of Amsterdam, attending a public school is the 'conventional' situation and the choice of a catholic school 'unconventional'. Roeleveld and Dronkers (1994) found that schools in districts in neither which nor public, protestant or catholic schools attracted a majority of the students, the effectiveness of schools, also after controlling for student composition, was the highest. In these districts without a majority is no 'conventional' school choice and thus the parental choice is more deliberate. In districts in which public, protestant or catholic schools had either a very small part (<20%) or a very large part (>60%) of all pupils, the effectiveness of these schools was lower. In these district the 'conventional' school choice is most common and thus the parental choice is more traditional. Other results support this deliberate educational choice explanation. The positive effects of religious schools are found only in the 1970s and 1980s, when the church was no longer a significant community. However, during the 1950s, when the catholic church was still a powerful community, no positive effects of religious schools were found (Dronkers, 1989). Dijkstra (1992) did not find any greater effectiveness of a special group of orthodox-protestant primary schools when compared to the average Dutch school during the 1980s, despite the fact that these schools belonged to one well-organised orthodox-protestant church in which a large majority of the parents were active. There is also no other indication that when churches were more powerful in the Netherlands, religious schools had better outcomes than public schools. At that time, the choice of a religious or public school was not made on educational but on religious grounds. It was therefore not an indication of a particular dedication to education but that of belonging to a sub-culture. Public or religious schools were not forced to compete for pupils because religion dictated the choice of parents and teachers.

After the breakdown in the 1960s of the church as an important community, religious schools were forced to compete for pupils, because they could no longer rely on their recruitment along religious lines. The deliberate educational choice of parents and teachers became important for schools. Religious schools were on average better equipped for this competition for pupils because of their history (during the 19th century, Dutch religious schools won the struggle partly on the pupil market) and because of their religious administration (more flexibility than local government; Hofman, 1993). Perhaps public schools also lost this battle because their leading advocates expected the religious school sector to break down automatically as a consequence of the growing secularisation and the decrease in religiousness of Dutch society.[6]

3. Private deliverance and inequality

As already indicated, the equal funding of private and public schools has promoted the diminution of prestigious elite schools outside the state-subsidised sector. The equal financial resources of religious and public schools have prevented a creaming-off of the most able students by either the public or the religious schools. Before the 1970s, the choice of a religious or public school was not made on educational but on religious grounds. As a consequence the existence of parental choice didn't increase educational inequality in Dutch society.

The educational differences between religious and public schools are recent and could be the start of a new form of inequality, despite all other efforts of the Dutch administration to diminish unequal educational opportunities. Differences between parents in their knowledge of school effectiveness, which correlates with their own educational level, can perhaps be seen as the basis of this new form of inequality (cf. Dijkstra & Jungbluth, 1997). The importance of deliberate choice of parents to promote the educational opportunities of their children can explain the persistence of religious educational systems in the Netherlands as well in other European societies despite all secularisation. However, even in an educational system without a religious and a public sector this knowledge of school effectiveness by parents can operate.

Islamic schools working in the context of Dutch educational laws are a new form of religious school, although their number is not yet very large. The reasons for wanting an Islamic school are comparable to those given by protestants and Catholics during the 'school struggle' in the 19th century. Since the laws are based on those reasons, it is difficult to refuse the establishment of Islamic schools in the long run. There are three main problems with establishing such schools: the mobilisation of parents, religious and cultural differences among Islamic parents, and the lack of qualified Islamic teachers. Another argument against Islamic schools is that segregation will hamper the integration of Islamic children into Dutch society. The strongest opposition to Islamic schools on the basis of integration comes from advocates of public rather than protestant and catholic schools, since the integration of all religious groups into one school has always been the ideal of public schools.

On the whole, thus far there are no indications that private schools do produce more educational inequality then public schools, as long as these religious schools are treated in the same way by the state as the public schools and as long as the religious schools are not allowed to collect extra resources for their schools (see also section IV).

4. Recent developments

Freedom of choice has been embedded in the constitution since 1917 and has not changed since then. This is not to say that there is no movement in the changing of the autonomy of schools and the conditions under which religious and public schools must operate.

There have been attempts by more orthodox Protestants and Catholics to revive their schools by reintroducing a more serious religious curriculum. In general, this orthodox attempt has failed (for catholic more than for orthodox-protestants, because the latter succeeded in establishing orthodox schools with a national organisation of their own), since parents preferred the less strictly religious schools, in accordance with their less religious beliefs. However, the orthodox attempt has not produced any movement of parents towards public schools and has not been supported by the national organisations for catholic and protestant schools (lobby groups directed at the central government). Nor has this attempt been supported by major political, social or cultural organisations. Any debate on the religious content of education in nonpublic schools tends to fall on deaf ears, because most parents are not interested in this topic and politically it did not produce any gains.

Another debate focuses on the degree of autonomy of schools or school clusters, generally on the proposal to increase this autonomy. One aspect of the debate is to improve the accountability of schools, including that towards parents. This debate on autonomy does not, however, affect the freedom of school choice but instead will encourage it. Another aspect of the debate is the financial accountability of schools. There is a move towards a lumpsum system that is equal for both religious and public schools. This autonomy movement might promote the position of religious schools, who are already familiar with some autonomy, whereas public schools are not (they are administrated by the municipalities, usually in a more bureaucratic way). It is questionable whether, despite all lip service, municipalities will really give more autonomy to their schools, since they would be losing an important tool of their power.

There is also some debate about a change in the governance of public schools. Municipal councils now govern them. Proposals are being made for this to be carried out by special independent education councils or committees, more or less independent of the municipal councils. The Christian-democrat party opposes the proposals because they fear this change could diminish the perceived educational advantages of religious schools. They argue that a change in the government of public schools in the direction of more religious institutions is against the constitution, because the government would no longer provide public education. Another fear of religious school advocates is that such a change would free the hand of the municipalities. They could then act as arbiter between public and religious schools, promote common activities for them under the auspices of the municipalities, and issue regulations (not by national law) which might tie religious schools.

Advocates of public schools have long contested this movement, foreseeing government by local municipality councils as the symbol of the public nature of their schools. Perhaps they still hoped for the collapse of the religious school in an irreligious society. They are now moving away from their opposition to the change and conceding more possibilities for municipalities to co-ordinate religious and public schools in their communities.

Especially in secondary education, there is a trend to promote large regional school clusters governed by one board. Some believe that this may help to break down the distinctions between public and religious education because mergers cannot be made within one sector. This is a covert aim or an afterthought rather than a politically stated objective. However, given the political strength of Christiandemocrat parties and their roots in the local communities, there is little likelihood of it actually happening. The fused school clusters which have been formed until now follow the boundaries of the public and religious schools with some blurring of the distinction between protestant and catholic schools (the establishment of Christian schools).

With the secularisation of Dutch society, the question arises how these developments relate to the scale of private schooling in Dutch education. For this 'paradox' of the existence of large religious school sectors in a predominantly secular society, several explanations are available (for an overview, see Dijkstra, Dronkers & Hofman, 1997). One of these explanations emphasises the existence of a growing disparity between the supply and demand of schooling. In this view, institutions, which were established by the religious sectors, are simply outliving their religious foundation. Nevertheless, sheltered by a powerful coalition of special interest groups around private schools and their political alliances, and backed up by the dominant interpretation of the constitution, the current system seems effectively resistant against the effects of secularisation in society.

Recent developments, however, suggest that this resistance is losing ground. Especially noticeable was a report published by the Dutch Educational Council (the so-called Onderwijsraad, a powerful advisory council to the national government) which might become the marker of an important change in the current system of choice. The Educational Council, commonly seen as an important 'watchdog' regarding the current system of freedom of schooling, is proposing the adjustment of the educational system to the new social realities of Dutch society. In effect, the report radically re-interprets the design of the system of choice in education (Onderwijsraad, 1996; Leune, 1996). The Council argues no longer taking the religious charter of the school into account in the planning of the educational establishment, but to base this solely on a quantitative criterion. The main result of this will probably be an end of the relatively favourable position of the current, recognised private religious school sectors in the foundation and maintaining of schools.

Although the arrangement based on religious heterogeneity seemed unassailable during the time that the major Christian Democrat party were at the core of government, this discussion acquired a political translation in 1993, when the Christian Democrats were not part of the government coalition for the first time since years. The new coalition parties requested to the government to present proposals which would enable the adaptation of the schools to the supposed changing educational wishes of the parents. The Education Secretary reacted to this request by appointing a committee of experts, which published a report after a little over six months which contained a large amount of suggestions for the adaptation of the relationship between the educational consumer and the schools. The appointment of the governmental committee was cause for the interest groups of the large private schooling sectors to appoint their own committee. The report that was published by this committee had as its main conclusion that there were no large discrepancies between supply and demand in schooling, which would prompt adaptation of the establishment.

In line with the suggestions of the governmental committee, the Dutch Parliamentary Under-secretary for Education requested the Educational Council in the spring of 1995 to advise on the way in which the role of religious direction of the school could be put into the perspective of the school planning. The proposal by the government for the adaptation of the mechanisms of gearing educational supply and demand to one another could then be prepared, based on the advise of the Educational Council. Accompanied by two legal preliminary studies, the Educational Council released the requested proposal at the beginning of 1996 (Onderwijsraad, 1996).

Although the Educational Council (Onderwijsraad, 1996: 95) puts the existence of discrepancies between the supply of schools and educational preferences of parents into perspective in its proposal, it recognises a cause for drastic adaptation of the school planning, unlike the opinion of the advice committee of the private organisations. The Council, in doing so, goes further than the governmental committee, who put the issue of direction into perspective, especially where it concerns educational diversity, and suggests founding and maintaining schools solely on the basis of a numerical criterion. Essence of the criterion on the basis of which a private school may be founded will then be that a legal person, who can demonstrate the need for a school over a number of years with a sufficient number of parental signatures, will be eligible for state funding. There are no limitations on the nature of the school or the interested party in any way in the proposal of the Educational Council, only the number of pupils that is needed for foundation and the necessity of a legal person. This person needs to verify that he is acting on behalf of parents. He or she can do so by submitting parental testimonies.

At the end of 1996, the Parliamentary Under-secretary for Education published a memo, in which the proposal of the Educational Council is largely followed (Netelenbos, 1997). The purpose of the memo was to ascertain to what extent there would be parliamentary support for the State Secretary's proposals. If this is the case, the cabinet will later present a bill, which will bring the adaptation of the Dutch system of choice to a conclusion. The essence of these proposals is that the religious denomination of the school will no longer play any part in school funding. Furthermore, the religiously based exceptions in decisions regarding the funding from the state chest will be cancelled in this proposal.

The main reason for the proposed adaptation is to tune the teaching activities more to the parental wishes, although arguments in the field of retrenchment should not be left out, be it, that they are rarely mentioned. In practice, this will not so much mean the foundation of new schools. In the current system, the denomination of the school also plays a part in the funding of a school who wishes to change its religious direction, when, for example, the student population has changed its identity. This also holds for schools of different denominations that wish to merge. In a system in which religion is no longer a criterion for state funding, it is becoming easier to realise parental preferences through adaptation of the school's religious charter (Netelenbos, 1997: 11-14). So, by providing for diversity along other dimensions than the religious or philosophical lines, according to parental demands, it is hoped that the system would allow for more of a linkage between changing parental preferences and the teaching activities. Furthermore, the system would be more consistent, no longer having as its rationale the religious diversity which Dutch society no longer exhibits.

With the adaptation of the educational infrastructure based on religion to a solely demand-driven system, the evolution of the current religiously based system to an otherwise structured system, based on other than religious preferences, be they ideological, pedagogical, educational or based on any other diversity, could lie ahead.

By basing the founding and closing down of schools on a quantitative criterion, and having school boards satisfying themselves that there is parental support for the school's identity (another element from the proposals of the

Educational Council), the balance between educational consumers and suppliers is thought to tip in favour of the first. By increasing the sensitivity of the system to the wishes of the educational consumer, the role of control through supply and demand is supposed to be strengthened. Thus, the Educational Council's advice can be considered a plea for the enlargement of market forces in education through a regulation of educational supplies that is more demand-driven.

Regarded in the field of education and world view this would mean, that the educational supply is no longer sorted on the basis of denomination and the ideological diversity behind it, but that, now more than ever, the actual need defines the composition of the supply of schools. Different to a division of the stream of pupils based on religious diversity and a pre-programmed system of schools for the religious mainstreams, the decreased importance of religion and the enlargement of cultural diversity is reason to rid the organisation of the supply of as many impediments as possible, in order to create maximal freedom to whom ever manages to mobilise sufficient support for a school of the proposed identity, at least that is the idea.

The school, however, is not only responsible for the passing on of culture, but is also a selective and reproductive instrument. Prestige, power and possessions have been unequally distributed in society, and educational achievements play an important part in the acquisition of these. Getting ahead in the labour market and the division of chances in life are highly influenced by scholastic achievements, which closely corresponds to socio-economic background. Education, therefore, is an important instrument for the justification and reproduction of the inequality of power, social status and income. The school, through this, becomes a scene of battle of social groups centred on securing their position within the hierarchy of status of enlarging their part in the division of scarce means (see for example Bowles & Gintis, 1976). This means that not only is education a market where buyers and suppliers together decide on the setting of the transferral of standards and values, but also an arena, in which social groups meet to battle for the scarce social means.

This gives rise to the question what implications the intended enlargement of the freedom of educational consumers in the Netherlands will have for the arena in which social groups meet face to face in the competition for scarce means. What does enlargement of educational freedom mean for the reproduction of social inequality? (cf. Dijkstra & Jungbluth, 1997).

5. Discussion

The developments outlined earlier make the Dutch experiment interesting because of, among other things, the question why parents in a secularised society do not favour education that is managed by the government on behalf of that society, but favour education managed by private organisations. This preference seems also to be demonstrable in other modern societies, and it is growing. There seem to be complementary explanations available, as discussed above. Schools run by private non-profit organisations will eventually, in equal circumstances have more chances to have a more effective management and a social network around those schools, than schools that are run by local or national governments. These explanations cannot be seen as separate from the problems governments have to effectively produce and allocate in the long term quasi-collective goods in the areas of education, the arts and social services. Particularly the two-sided character of these quasi-collective goods is important in this. These are goods that neither the market nor the state is able to produce and allocate both efficiently as well as effectively. Private non-profit organisations seem to be able to deal better with the two-sided character of these quasi-collective goods than private, profit seeking organisations or public organisations, so that the former can produce quasi-collective goods, under equal circumstances, more effectively and efficiently than the state or profit organisations.

What does this mean for the future of the Dutch system of choice? The most likely development seems to be that it continues to exist, but in a transformed shape. The ideological and religious legitimisation of private non-profit organisations will move more and more to the background. This will happen, however, without the legitimisation being publicly renounced by all, because religion and ideology still form the building blocks of society. In those cases where that religious legitimisation will be abandoned, it will be traded in for one that will refer to the efficiency of the education offered. This efficiency does not need to relate only to school results, but also to the measure in which the school offers protection against the dangers of modern society. The legitimisation of this efficiency will probably be rather multiform: ranging from ideological attention to a certain didactics, and from a religious identity to a certain social-cultural composition of the student population. Because private non-profit organisations may offer this efficiency in providing adequate surroundings more easily, there will not be a movement in the direction of an increase in education managed by local or national government. On the contrary, schools that are at the moment being managed by a local or national government, will increasingly try to transform into schools managed by private non-profit organisations, or something resembling this. In short, the most likely development of public and denominational education is a transformation to a type of denominational-neutral education.

The role of the national and local government has become rather important in all of this. Regarding the optimal production and allocation of the quasi-collective good, which because of its nature cannot be left fully to the free market, the government is given the role of allocator of the collectively financed costs of the initial education, of guard of the quality of the initial education, and of determiner of the scale and the duration of the initial education. These roles are not new to the Dutch government: it has fulfilled these roles since the education legislation of the Batavian Republic. But the role of administrator of education is, because of the anticipated transformation, transferred to private non-profit organisations.

This transformation of private production of education based on religious and ideological organisations to a system based on private non-profit organisations is also problematical. Private delivery of education by non-profit organisations does not automatically lead to an economically efficient organisation of education. A situation with too many small schools under the responsibility of too many private non-profit organisations leads via one with a large number of small schools to scale inefficiencies and therefore to an expensive educational system and economic inefficiency. On the other hand, large non-profit organisations, which each manage many large schools, will no longer be very efficient, because frequent and intensive contacts with the internal sections in the school, and with external authorities, will diminish. The cause of this is the necessary increase of bureaucracy and legal rigmarole. The chances to form a functional community in and around the school will also diminish. Therefore, it will remain the task of the government, as provider of the collective means for education, to continually find the balance between efficiency and effectiveness.

Private non-profit organisations have another classical drawback: they may fall into the hands of a certain elite in society. The managerial control of education may, in such a situation, become an uncontrollable instrument of power. The current 'denominalisation' of education is a good illustration of just such a situation: there is a close bond between administrators of denominational education and the (Christian-democratic) political party that took up a central position in Dutch political relations for a long time. This classical drawback of private non-profit organisations makes permanent action of the national government necessary, to prevent unproductive power concentrations in education. If the transformations of education systems toward a more private production of education take place too quietly, or are dominated by rhetoric and symbolism, this disadvantage will work out more seriously. Solutions, handing power of administration over to parents or schools, will also have to indicate which groups will have to receive this power to administrate, in situations where parents or schools do not have adequate power to administrate or market positions at their disposal. Given the inequality between schools and parents, it in unlikely that these will always manage to summon the force to administrate.

References

Archer, M.S. (1984). *Social Origins of Educational Systems*. London/Beverly Hills: Sage.

Box, L., Dronkers, J., Molenaar, M. and Mulder, J. de. (1977). *Vrijheid van onderwijs*. Nijmegen: Link.

Bowles, S. & Gintis, H. (1976). *Schooling in Capitalist America. Educational Reform and Contradictions of Economic life,* London: Routledge & Kagan Paul.

Claassen, A.W.M. (1985). *Schipperen tussen school en kerk*. Nijmegen: Dekker and van de Vegt.

Coleman, J.S. and Hoffer, T. (1987). *Public and Religious High Schools. The impact of communities*. New York: Basic Books.

Dijkstra, A.B. (1992). *De religieuze factor. Onderwijskansen en godsdienst*. Nijmegen: ITS.

Dijkstra, A.B. and Jungbluth, P. (1997). The institutionalization of social segmentation? Segregation of schooling in the Netherlands. Paper presented to the 33th World Congress of the International Institute of Sociology, Cologne, July 7-11.

Dijkstra, A.B., Dronkers, J. and Hofman, R.H. (Eds.)(1997): *Verzuiling in het onderwijs*. Groningen: Wolters-Noordhoff.

Dronkers, J. (1989). Schoolkenmerken en individuele prestaties, in P. Vogel et al. (eds.), *De school: keuzen en kansen*. Muiderberg: Coutinho.

Dronkers, J. (1992). Blijvende organisatorische onderwijsverzuiling ondanks secularisering. *Beleid and Maatschappij, 19,* 227237.

Dronkers, J. and Hillege, S. (1995). De besturen van studentencorpora en de toegang tot de Nederlandse elites. *Amsterdams Sociologisch Tijdschrift, 21,* 3764.

de Graaf, P.M. (1987). *De invloed van financiële en culturele hulpbronnen in onderwijsloopbanen*. Nijmegen: ITS.

Hofman, R.H. (1993). *Effectief schoolbestuur.* Groningen: RION.

Hofman, R.H., Hofman, W.H.A., Guldemond, H. and Dijkstra, A.B. (1996). Variation in effectiveness between private and public schools. *Educational Research and Evaluation, 2,* 366-394.

Jong, U. de, and Roeleveld, J. (1989). Public and religious secondary schools in Amsterdam, in B.F.M. Bakker, J. Dronkers and G.W. Meijnen (eds.), *Educational Opportunities in the Welfare State*. Nijmegen: ITS.

Leune, J.M.G. (1996). The meaning of government legislation and funding for primary and secondary schools with a religious character in the Netherlands. Paper for a colloquium on 'The ambiguous embrace of government'. Rotterdam, November 22-24.

Lijphart, A. (1968). *The Politics of Accommodation: Pluralism and democracy in the Netherlands.* Berkeley: University of California Press.

Netelenbos, T. (1997). *De identiteit van de school in een pluriforme samenleving.* Den Haag: OCW.

Onderwijsraad (1996). *Advies Richtingvrij en richtingbepalend.* Den Haag: Onderwijsraad.

Roede, E., Peetsma, T. and Riemersma, F. (1994). *Betrokkenheid bij godsdienstonderwijs.* Amsterdam: Universiteit van Amsterdam.

Roeleveld, J. and Dronkers, J. (1994). Bijzondere of buitengewone scholen?' *Mens en Maatschappij, 69,* 85108.

Vreeburg, B. A. N. M. 1993. *Identiteit en het verschil.* Zoetermeer: De Horstink.

Notes

1 Of course, these three processes did not have equal importance in different societies.
2 For good reasons, these processes had a quite different effect in the United Kingdom (Archer, 1984). The United States has never experienced these long conflicts over school between the state and the church or the ancient regime and the liberal state.

3   It can be shown that during the first half of the 20th century, children from elite catholic families had a preference for public universities and non-Catholic student organizations, despite the existence of a Dutch catholic university and the small distances within the Netherlands (Dronkers & Hillege, 1995). An explanation of this phenomenon is that they saw catholic organizations and universities as serving their more humble, upwardlymobile catholic brothers, and as a means of controlling them.

4   Originally, the concept of freedom of education referred to the freedom to teach without church approval, contrary to the situation of the ancient regime. Later, it came to mean freedom of persons and juridical bodies to establish and maintain schools of different denominations under equal conditions to public schools maintained by the liberal state (Box, Dronkers, Molenaar and de Mulder, 1977).

5   Vreeburg (1993:140) estimate that in 1986 at Catholic secondary schools 45% of the pupils have no religion, 31% of the pupils goes to church once a month or more and 51% sometimes visit a church. In Protestant schools 53% have no religion, 31% goes to church once a month or more and 42% sometimes visit a church.

6   The only exception to this danger of being a 'conventional' school comes from the municipal gymnasiums (classical grammar schools). Although they are mostly public schools, municipal gymnasiums can avoid becoming 'conventional' schools because of their long history, their unique position as the pinnacle of the hierarchy of secondary school types (which means a more selective entrance selection), and their strong relations with local and national elites.

9

Capacity Building for Market Orientation in Higher Education: Experiences in Vietnam and Kenya

Bram de Hoop and Wim Jan T. Renkema

1. Introduction

Throughout the world, institutes for higher education are in turmoil. With the collapse of the Soviet Union in 1991, ending the Cold War period, globalisation has started in earnest. Universities increasingly have to compete with new actors on the market for training and knowledge development and the traditional roles of universities are being redefined. The current position of universities in developing countries is quite difficult, as they are struggling with increasing student enrolment figures against dwindling financial support from the government. Higher education is nevertheless still considered of paramount importance to the social and economic development. Universities in developing countries often are perceived as leading institutions of the nations concerned and are expected to play a key role in national development (World Bank, 1997). How can such institutes of learning and research keep in tune with the needs and demands of society? Although both international organisations and bilateral agencies are increasingly shifting their attention to basic education (IIEP, 1995), the higher education sector remains an important educational level for investments and technical cooperation by donor agencies (World Bank, 1994). This paper discusses how universities in developing countries can be supported in meeting market demands.

The first section discusses 'capacity building' as an emerging concept in development assistance. The MHO programme, a Dutch programme for assistance to institutes of higher education in developing countries, is shortly introduced. Moreover, a number of important global trends in addressing market demands related to university research and education are discussed here.

The second section present two cases: Moi University in Kenya, and Can Tho University in Vietnam. A similar structure for each case-description is followed.

The external environment of the institute is described, its current position and the contribution of the MHO programme to its development. The third section compares the two cases above and discusses the specific lessons that can be learned. It is argued here that the guiding principle for the development of universities in the South should be a response to local market demands.

2. The university's functions: education and research

Call for market orientation to support capacity building in higher education: The last 10 years have brought an increasing focus on the strengthening of educational organisations to address local market needs. Within the context of development assistance this strengthening of an organisation, aiming at building up sustainable capabilities, mostly is referred to as 'institution building', or 'capacity building'. In a recent review of literature and ideas on institution building as a development assistance method it was concluded that 'it is not possible to agree on clear and simple definitions of the term institution building' (Moore et. al., 1994). However, substantial agreement exists that the core concern of institution building activities is to improve the long-term effectiveness of formal organisations. Institution building, as a distinct strategy for development cooperation is relatively new, and donors, executing organisation and recipient institutes are only starting to understand its dynamics. There is nevertheless a growing awareness that building capacities in formal organisation will require and evoke processes of change (Tung et. al., 1997).

An important change in institution building exercises in higher education is the call for addressing market opportunities. This implies that any university should become more autonomous for developing its own education and research programmes as long as this serves market opportunities and needs. For some universities it implies more awareness of parental choice and preferred study areas by students. Any university should increasingly listen to employers: what capacities should their graduates have, and what kind of research would benefit local companies. The local market of universities in developing countries is especially important, as they can not, for the most part, compete with universities of northern countries on the international market for students and research. Developing universities should be given the means and control to either diversify or specialise education and research programmes in line with local market demands. They should be given the opportunity to develop their own indicators of success for their main tasks: education and research. A number of global trends in higher education and research are relevant for universities that are moving towards a market orientation. These trends are described in section 1.2 (education) and 1.3 (research).

Universities and education: The first major function of the university is to train professionals to take up positions in society. The university is expected to give the highest level of education, as the last stage in the formal education system. To a certain extent the 'teaching' function of a particular university depends on the realm of disciplines and subject it offers. During the last century, the classical broad academic institute, offering degrees in all scientific fields, has been complemented with institutes that focus on specific areas of expertise such as agriculture and technology. In addition, the higher education sector has been expanded to included non-university institutes. The way in which these institutes for higher education are preparing students for their future life is currently subject of major changes. Three trends, intimately related to each other, can be distinguished:

i.   Increasing tendency to link the education of graduates to their occupational future;
ii. A shift from teaching to learning;
iii. A redefined notion of 'curriculum'.

(i) The occupational future of students

The global shift to a market-driven economy, in which flexibility and employability are important individual assets, has resulted in important changes in the way students are prepared for their professional life. Reporting on the educational effects of the change from a planned economy to a market-driven economy, Heyneman indicates that 'in market economies, occupational future is uncertain, and individuals must be prepared to move across many possible vocations and economic sectors. But when the economy is planned, technology changes are planned. The content of skill training then could be treated as a relative certainty, thus justifying priority on information acquisition rather than problem solving (Heyneman, 1998).

Today's societies are primarily in need of people who can use their knowledge in new and unanticipated circumstances, who are creative, and who can solve problems. The definition of 'intelligence' is expanding into other than cognitive domains, and social, communication and emotional skills of people are increasingly valued. Emphasising knowledge acquisition and the retention of provided information becomes futile, as the pace in which knowledge is changing is accelerating. Therefore, a willingness and capability to learn and to continue learning throughout life are more important characteristics of graduates.

Commenting on the link between the labour market and the 'teaching' function of the university, Cabal remarks that 'the student's preparation for a profession should not be reduced to merely satisfying demands in work organisation and distribution (...). A student's education should not consists of projects of projects tailored simply to fit the size of the job, dispensing his or her spiritual, intellectual and moral development' (Cabal, 1993). Although in many universities the mere preparation of students for the labour market is considered as a threat to a more liberal academic education, it is clear that the relationship between employment and education is becoming more and more direct. Universities are expanding from offering only general academic education, to also including professionally oriented and vocational differentiations in their curricula. Universities are critically reviewing the extent to which the education they are offering is relevant for the labour market. Increasingly, occupational profiles are developed and contacts with employers and alumni are kept.

Many universities in developing countries have the problem that its graduates can not find employment. The economic crisis in many countries has resulted in mass unemployment, even among those who have advanced degrees. It is clear that the external environment is having an important impact on the way these universities can contribute to producing the necessary human resources that possess relevant skills.

(ii) An emerging shift from teaching to learning
The changing employment profiles of university graduates requires universities to be increasingly innovative in their education. If the output society is demanding from universities, in terms of graduates, is changing drastically, an important question becomes how to facilitate the learning of students. In recent years, a shift from teaching to learning is taking place in higher education (Barr et. al., 1995). It may in this respect be more appropriate to talk of the 'learning' function of a university. According to Barr and Tagg, the shift from teaching to learning is not less than a paradigm shift. This indicates that the shift is profound, comprehensive and irreversible. Under the teaching paradigm, institutes of higher education exist to provide instruction, whereas under the learning paradigm they exist to produce learning. This shift has various aspects. Only three are mentioned here: a focus on learning, a new role for university teachers and a different concept of 'knowledge'.

Under the teaching paradigm, the main purpose of the university is to transfer knowledge from teacher to students. However, under the learning paradigm, the university is to elicit student discovery and the construction of knowledge. The ambition of the university becomes to create learning environments, using a wide array of methods to produce the learning of students. Learning through projects, job-related assignments, problem-based learning and the use of information and communication technology are examples of methods that can be used to create a powerful learning environment within the university. The student and his or her own learning becomes the central concern for the university, rather than the teacher's instruction. This also means that there is more concern with the quality of exiting students, rather than with the quality of entering students.

Related to this focus on learning is a new role for the university teacher. Rather than delivering one type of instruction, often lecturing, he or she is to facilitate learning. In order to facilitate learning, a university teacher has to become a designer of learning methods and environments. Under the teaching paradigm, any expert can teach. Yet, under the learning paradigm, facilitating learning is a challenging and complex task. Teachers' focus on selection and classification is replaced by the wish to develop every student's competencies and talents.

'Knowledge' is conceived quite differently under the two paradigms. Under the new paradigm, the creation of knowledge takes place at the individual level. Knowledge is constructed, and shaped by the individual. In other words knowledge cannot exist without personal interpretation. It is created by individuals, when they attach meanings attached to their experiences (Box, 1991). This implies that knowledge is not simply transferable and is not part and parcel of a scientific publication, a lecture, or a textbook.

(iii) A redefined notion of 'curriculum'
As a consequence of the above changes, a different concept of the 'curriculum' is emerging. The 'curriculum' used to be understood as an educational planning document in which all the courses of a given educational programme would be listed. The order and exact content of all these courses would be described in detail, including indications of subject matter, through an enumeration of definitions, concepts and theories. This concept is increasingly being replaced by a much wider one. The curriculum becomes then the whole of educational reality as aimed for in a department or faculty. It encompasses the whole educational cycle of formulation of occupational profiles, qualifications of the graduate, objectives, teaching/learning activities, and evaluation and assessment. This shift implies that curriculum development is no longer the production of a bulky, written document, but rather the continuous process of quality improvement.

For universities in developing countries the above changes are difficult but unavoidable. Impediments for change can be found in the difficult position universities find themselves in, prohibiting them from hiring qualified staff, investing in staff development, infrastructure and materials. Yet, the difficulty of change should not be underestimated. The current practice of teaching and learning in many universities in developing countries is one in which passive students are exposed to lecturer-experts who channel down their knowledge, often by means of monologues. Both lecturers and students are so much used to this educational practice, and often hardly have been exposed to alternatives, that the process of change towards a university education that is relevant and empowering will be long and difficult. Programmes for capacity building in higher education will have to reflect how to assist universities in making this change.

Universities and research: Traditionally, the second task of universities is the construction of new knowledge elements by conducting research for the public good. Today, research remains important as one of the pillars for strengthening capacities, and is often decisive for the prestige of the university as a whole (Cabal, 1993). Similar to education, research at universities can be heavily influenced by the external market environment of the university. For universities in developing countries research is often rudimentary because of a lack of resources. However, global trends affect both universities in developing and industrialised countries, in a similar way. Research at universities experienced considerable change over the last decades. The most important change is that many research fields shifted from fundamental research, or the production of new data and concepts, to combining generic knowledge elements and suiting them to different contexts (Gibbons, 1998). This change can be attributed to the following trends:

i.   Knowledge has become more easily accessible;
ii. There is increasing competition and commercialisation in research;
iii. Demands for research outcomes are changing.

(i) Increased accessibility of knowledge

Through rapid developments in information and communication technology (ICT) and the standardisation of technical systems and even services through the International Standards Organisation (ISO), highly specialised knowledge, once the traditional domain of universities, is becoming easily accessible. For universities in developing countries the picture is more complex. Before long, science in these countries was practically non-existent as the means were simply not available for researchers to enter into dialogue with their peers (Latour, 1987). More often than not a scientist in a developing country was the only expert in his or her home country working on a specific topic. Modern means of communication are presently enabling scientists from the South to enter into dialogue with their peers all over the world.

(ii) Research competition and commercialisation

Many different types of advisory organisations, ranging from public policy bodies to private consultancy companies are taking over one of traditional roles of universities: 'formulation of ideas and concepts'. Universities are finding it difficult to compete with these new knowledge providers. Universities can not rely anymore on their traditional modalities for simply building new scientific arguments by gathering sufficient academic allies to oppose established scientific statements. They have to systematically build networks with peers, in- and outside academic circuits, to compete successfully on the market for research.

When coming into contact with their western peers, scholars from the South soon discover that global competition is also affecting their position as knowledge builders of the country. Increasingly, foreign and domestic consultancy companies are reaping the profits of the expanding knowledge market in developing countries. Although the technical competence of universities in the South may be up for competition and collaboration with these forces of the free market, the financial and managerial capacities of universities in the South often seem to be lacking.

(iii) Changing knowledge demands

Although accessibility of knowledge has increased drastically, demands for expertise knowledge is becoming more complex and diverse. The consumer market for knowledge has widened considerable as a consequence of increased political and socio-economic uncertainty. Because of rapidly changing demands, the very idea of certainty in relation to knowledge is under attack (Welch, 1998). External advice for decision-making is increasingly sought for, ranging from local market analysis to long term scenarios for future development. Therefore, in order to find solutions it is not so much a question of how to develop expertise, but more to identify specific demands of local target groups.

Because of the above three trends, research at universities diversified from a focus on gathering raw data and assembling new ideas to a focus on amalgamating existing knowledge elements. Of course fundamental research is still the core part on which universities build their reputation. However, for academics from universities in developing countries it is extremely difficult to initiate fundamental research and access advanced technologies (e.g. electronics, genetic engineering, polymers and resins) and to put them to use. For this category of knowledge, researchers increasingly have to combine sets of technologies to accomplish achievements in their field of expertise. In addition, it is becoming more difficult for developing countries to obtain advanced technologies by direct ways of technology transfer (e.g. purchase, exchange programmes) because of the high initial investment requirements.

Improved communications facilities for accessing information may not help as industrialised countries are diligently trying to protect their findings by pushing for more stringent patent laws. Actors involved in generating new concepts of knowledge are seeking to protect their ideas and to maximise profit in either academic or financial terms. For the latter purpose, researchers are increasingly opting for patents. The champions of patent protection indicate that patents help to induce a dynamic of technological differentiation (Joly et. al., 1996). Often it is overlooked that most companies could only establish themselves by imitating or building on other technologies to allow further innovations to take place (Hobbelink, 1991). This is further confirmed by other studies indicating that there is no such thing as technical self-sufficiency of research institutions for developing advanced technologies into marketable products (such as monoclonal antibodies - see Mackenzie et al., 1988). In fact renowned research institutes could only develop such technology by building on existing knowledge resources.

There is an additional problem for academics of developing countries in focusing on the more advanced technologies. In most non-industrialised countries there is a lack of confidence concerning domestic technological capabilities. Foreign capital goods are often superior in performance and durability feeding the incorrect presumption that domestic human and non-human resources are not sufficiently equipped to solve local problems. This attitude results almost automatically in an over-reliance on importing the entire set of required technologies, rather than developing proprietary technologies based on the blending of local capacities with generic foreign technologies (Yin, 1992 and United Nations, 1998). For development assistance programmes aiming at capacity building of universities in executing research, the challenge is to keep supporting the formulation of new elements of knowledge, taking into account the above trends.

3. Market orientation of universities in Vietnam, Kenya and Burkina Faso

Introduction: Universities in developing countries have to execute their two main functions, education and research, in an environment that presents them with particular challenges. The economic crisis of many developing countries leads to reduced public support, whereas the demands for higher education and expertise knowledge are increasing. This section examines to what extent two universities in developing countries (Can Tho University in Vietnam, and Moi University in Kenya,) have been able to adapt to local market demands. The comparison is based on experiences of executing the MHO programme at both universities. The MHO programme or 'Joint Financing Programme for Cooperation in Higher Education' was established in 1993 by the Dutch Ministry of Foreign Affairs with the aim of better equipping selected universities in developing countries to carry out their tasks. Objectives of the programme are related to institution building of the recipient university as a whole and secondly to remedy quantitative and qualitative human resource deficiencies at the national level (Nuffic, 1998). In total twelve universities in developing countries are currently participating in the MHO programme. Each recipient university implements about ten projects.

The reason for choosing the two concerned universities is the difference in local market opportunities and the varying degree of autonomy of the concerned institutions. Can Tho University in Vietnam finds itself in a fast changing market environment with many opportunities, and locally almost no competition from other Vietnamese institutions for higher education. Market opportunities for Moi University in Kenya as dictated by limited national economic growth are somewhat less and the institute has little possibilities of competition with the four other public universities. It nevertheless has been able to offer education and research that is unique in the Kenyan context.

The MHO-programme at Moi University, Eldoret, Kenya.:
Context
Moi University is one of the universities participating in the MHO-programme. It is one of the five public universities in Kenya, a Sub-Saharan African country that is undergoing a severe economic crisis. After a relatively prosperous period of growth of the Kenyan economy during the 1970's, the 1980's were characterised by declining exports. The public sector continued to expand, and Kenya's economy became more and more dependent on donor funding. Between 1984 and 1990 foreign aid increased from 7.2 per cent to 13.7 per cent of the gross domestic product (GDP). The economy more or less collapsed when in November 1991 the donors declared that no more funding would be forthcoming, unless major changes were undertaken in the political as well as the economic spheres. The donor community was in particular concerned because of accounts of widespread corruption and human rights violation. Kenya has undergone major economic reforms over the last few years, including price deregulation, removal of exchange controls and privatisation of public services. External debt is estimated at about 80% of GDP, the interests and repayments of which absorb around a quarter of export income. The fiscal deficit of the government and the inflation rate have dropped, but economic growth is clearly not large enough to alleviate the poverty of the largest part of the population. Life expectancy at birth is currently estimated at 56 years. The GDP per capita is around US$300.

Higher education

In Kenya, the structure of the old British education system (7-4-2-3), in which a lot of importance was attached to the O- and A-level exams, has been in place until 1986, when an 8-4-4 structure was introduced (K'Olewe, 1997). Not only the number of years spent at each of the levels of education changed. The reform also intended a major shift in the philosophy of education. Education was to move from a more general approach to a practically and production-oriented curriculum. The new system turned out to cause a heavy burden for the government. The costs for new physical facilities, equipment, teaching methods and curricula at all levels were enormous. The 1986 reform did not include a change of the external examination system, which has a strong effect on the curriculum. The existing examination system contributes to repetition of grades, high dropout rates and a tendency to teach content-matter driven, and merely as a preparation for the exams. There is only little attention for skills such as problem solving, creativity and independent thinking. The fact that there is growing unemployment among school leavers in Kenya acts as a deterrent to parents sending their children to school, particular when they are supposed to co-finance that education. School leaver unemployment also creates great pressure on the Government of Kenya to expand higher education.

Kenya devoted the early years of independence to a rapid expansion of higher education facilities in order to the train enough qualified personnel to man its economic and administrative institutions. Although the results have been impressive in scale, it has to be noted that higher education was expanded but not adapted to the needs of the post-colonial economy. The result was an overproduction of graduates in relation to the available jobs in the formal sector of the economy. At the beginning of the 1980s it turned out that an increasing number of young Kenyans went abroad to study due to the inadequate number of places in the existing university. It was estimated that about 10,000 students were enrolled at universities outside Kenya, which was almost equal to the number of students enrolled at the University of Nairobi, then the only public university in Kenya. To curtail this exodus and to stop the brain drain it involved, other universities were established. Nowadays there are five public universities in Kenya.

Admission to one of Kenya's five public universities is administrated by the 'Joint Admissions Board' by which prospective students are selected and are assigned to one of the universities. The results for 'Kenyan Certificate of Secondary Education' are main instrument for selection. The competition for admittance is severe, as the total of secondary school leavers dramatically outnumbers the intake of the public universities. The expansion of the public higher education system has resulted in a number of problems. While the government of Kenya had been relatively successful in providing physical facilities to the expanded institutes, the growth in the number of staff lagged behind the student increase. Governmental measures to improve the staffing situation have only been partially successful. The Government of Kenya recently has started a process of rationalising the budget devoted to higher education. Over the last few years, government funds for public universities were further reduced, as the Government of Kenya shifted resources towards basic education and secondary education.

Moi University

Moi University is located in and around the town of Eldoret, in Western Kenya, nearly 300 kilometres from Nairobi. Its history, mission and strategy reveal that it has been conceptualised as a development university. In January 1981, a Presidential Working Party was set up by President Daniel arap Moi to prepare detailed plans and recommendations on how the decision to establish a second public university could be implemented. The working party reported that it had found support in the country for the establishment of a university that would be technologically oriented and would focus on problems of rural development in its training and research programmes. It is against this background that Moi University was set up by an Act of Parliament on the 8 June 1984. The establishment of Moi University as a 'development university' should be seen in the light of a shift away from the academic and general orientation of Nairobi University, towards a more applied, practical and technological higher education. To achieve its technologically oriented mission, Moi University proposed predominantly technology/science-based degree programmes. The degree programmes have a strong practical component in the curricula, characterised by on-campus workshop training, attachments in the industries and fieldwork. Moi University is primarily a teaching institute as the preparation of professionals for Kenyan society is one of the main elements of its mission.

In June 1994 the first Indicative Plan for MHO support to Moi University was approved. Subsequently, projects have been set up in various areas, ranging from tourism to civil engineering. In total 8 Dutch institutes of higher education currently cooperate with Moi University. Considerable progress is being achieved in the implementation of the current project package. Infrastructure investments have resulted in the construction and installation of various laboratories and the setting up of computer facilities. Curricula are being renewed. A start has been made with staff development, at various levels (Ph.D.-studies, Master programmes, diploma training, exposure programmes, etc.). The MHO programme at Moi University is focused on strengthening capacities in both education and research. The emphasis is on knowledge transfer and ensuring access to up-to-date scientific information. In addition, the central administrative services are supported. One project is focused on the introduction of new teaching methodologies and the creation of a powerful learning environment. This project, 'Community-Oriented Health', aims at improving the medical curriculum, in the broad sense, by introducing problem-based learning and having students do practicals in rural communities.

The contribution of the MHO programme to the development of human resources for Kenyan society is negatively influenced by the Government policy of cost-sharing, which has serious effects on the access of students (in particular at graduate level) and, consequently, to the quantity of university graduates. A number of changes has been initiated during the execution of the MHO programme. There is an increasing focus on linking education to the needs of the labour market and a willingness to critically review subject matter in the curricula. Research still plays a modest role at Moi University, but various MHO-supported faculties are starting to conduct applied research for various clients, e.g. in environment and engineering.

It has to be noted that the sustainability of the MHO interventions at Moi University is uncertain. Important impediments are the recruitment and retention of staff and limited financial means for recurrent costs. Public higher education in Kenya is in a state of financial crisis. Salaries for university teachers are low. The location of Moi University, in a fairly remote part of Western Kenya, makes it difficult to recruit and/or retain staff. For much (potential) staff it is more interesting to find employment in Nairobi, where prospects for making extra income are better. Another aspect of improving staff recruitment and retention is the importance of creating an interesting working environment, in terms of research facilities and research programmes. In this sense, the MHO projects are directly contributing to improving the working environment for university teachers and researchers.

It is clear that Moi University is providing essential services to Kenya. These are the generation and application of relevant knowledge, the training of professionals for many sectors in society, and the provision of extension and consultancy services to various organisations at national and regional level. It has to be underlined here that it is doing this in a difficult setting. Moi University is functioning in a context that is characterised by political turmoil, ethnic conflict, and economic crisis. As a public university in Kenya, it is woven into a complex web of political and ethnic affiliations. In addition, it has little autonomy to decide about its own direction, as it is subject to central regulations and student influx that is determined by another body. The economic crisis that Kenya is undergoing has dramatic effects on the university.

Recruitment and retention of skilled and motivated staff are a constant difficulty. Financial means for recurrent costs are scarce. One of the university's core tasks, ensuring a high quality for educating young people, may soon be threatened because of increasing financial difficulties of prospective students.

The MHO-programme at Can Tho University, Vietnam:
Context
Over the last decade Can Tho University in Vietnam, located in the Mekong Delta in southern Vietnam, experienced important changes of its external environment. It is important to describe the recent economic and political developments affecting Can Tho University to understand the contribution of the MHO programme to the development of the university.

In 1986, after years of economic depression, Vietnam opened its doors to the world resulting in major economic growth, with annual GDP growth reaching 9.5% in 1995. Despite the present financial crisis in Asia, the Government of Vietnam is continuing its efforts to secure economic growth, aiming to double its per capita GDP to US$400 in the year 2000. Policies are primarily aimed at modernising the banking system and establishing an appropriate legal and regulatory framework. With major support from foreign donors Vietnam is venturing to increase the transport system, telecommunications network and power supply. Such developments are not taking place everywhere at the same pace. Southern Vietnam is remote from the capital Hanoi, the central powerhouse of Vietnam. In southern Vietnam, financial support from central government is considerably less. No less than five years ago, the Mekong Delta was among the poorest regions of Vietnam. At the same time however, government control on centrally formulated policies is less stringent in the south. Once government cautiously allowed private shops to reopen their doors after 1986, the south was first to jump to the opportunity. At present the southern provinces have the highest GDP rates per capita, partly due to the vast production of rice in the Mekong Delta.

Although still being one of the poorest countries in Asia (income per capita of US$ 250 in 1996), Vietnam compares favourably with other countries in the Southeast Asian region with regard to a number of human development indicators. This is especially true with regard to education indicators. The adult literacy rated 88 percent in 1994, which is the third highest in Asia, after the Democratic Republic of Korea and the Philippines.

Higher education
Higher education in Vietnam has a long tradition dating back to the Quoc Tu Giam, the first royal university, which was founded in the year 1070. Until recently the higher education system in Vietnam was organised according to the Soviet model whereby teaching methodologies are largely information based, with a focus on training specialists receiving automatic employment upon graduation. In addition the Soviet model advocated a strong division between institutes focusing on research and on education, resulting in over one hundred mono-disciplinary institutions of higher education. In January 1993, Vietnam undertook the most comprehensive review of education and training since 1945. Prime elements of the new policies affecting higher education were to create a smaller number of larger institutions to allow for economies of scale. To allow students to more easily go from one institution to another and switch between programmes, training programmes were changed to a system with a first cycle providing elementary sciences and a second cycle for specialisation. Furthermore universities obtained more autonomy in developing curricula and organising entrance and final examinations. At present the main challenges ahead for tertiary education in Vietnam are (World Bank, 1996 and Leibbrandt et al.,1998):
a. to allow universities more autonomy for staff development, for establishing international linkages and donor support, and for developing competitive curricula geared towards rapidly changing demands of society;
b. to strike a good balance between public and private financing, reflecting that education is partly a private good, but also a social commodity benefiting all of society. A balanced system is to be sought between one extreme that relies too heavily on households and an opposite extreme that relies too heavily on government;
c. to enhance cooperation between research institutions and universities.

Can Tho University
Can Tho University was established in 1966 and is the only university in the Mekong Delta. From its inception onwards, Can Tho University has been one of the few larger comprehensive universities, offering a broad range of degrees. The university has benefited from recent policies and is viewed by the Vietnamese government as an example of a multi-disciplinary university.

For Can Tho University, the start of the MHO programme in 1993 coincided with the decision of the Ministry of Education to restructure higher education in Vietnam (Sloper, 1995). Nine MHO projects, ranging from institutional development to medicine started in 1995, just as the restructuring of higher education came into full effect. The projects were prioritised by Can Tho University in accordance with perceived needs. It is foremost the leadership of Can Tho University who recognised the importance of having a range of projects for institute-wide capacity building (De Hoop, 1998).

With hindsight it can be concluded that the MHO programme supported the university in two ways. Foremost the MHO programme served as a catalyst of change to reformulate priorities and implement new policies. Without the programme, the university would probably have chosen the same direction, but at a much slower rate. Secondly the support of the MHO programme enabled the university to adjust its training and research to rapid macro-economic developments, such as privatisation of large state-owned farms, large investments to upgrade the infrastructure, and restructuring of the banking system.

An important change coinciding with the implementation of the MHO programme is that responsibilities for management have been decentralised at all levels of the university. For instance deans of colleges are responsible for co-ordination curriculum development, instead of the rectorate. Lecturers are directly responsible for revising lecture notes. Because Can Tho University opted for having MHO projects to benefit all schools and colleges, Can Tho University could actively execute this process of decentralisation throughout the university. In its turn this has led to changing attitude and behaviour of both staff and students towards a more proactive stance. Next to decentralising responsibilities, managerial capacities of individual staff were upgraded, primarily through an MHO project on institutional development. According to the former rector of Can Tho University this has ensured a reservoir of potential managers who can further develop schools and colleges, and in due time, can take charge of managing the university. Although no strategic plan is ready as yet, the MHO programme has enabled Can Tho University to act strategically according to a clear vision of the rectorate. Having more than one project gave Can Tho University the opportunity to make balanced choices. It is primarily thanks to the rectorate that such choices were made systematically and diplomatically, aiming to ensure financial and academic synergy between the various schools and colleges. Financial allocations to different schools and colleges were spread evenly, taking into account contributions by other donors. Foremost the less developed schools and colleges were included in the MHO programme to allow synergy at the institutional level. Other schools and colleges were chosen in view of the need for higher educated personnel in Vietnam and the Mekong Delta.

Although support was prioritised in varying degrees, all colleges and schools benefit from the MHO programme, thus allowing financial synergy in further developing Can Tho University.

Through the MHO programme Can Tho University also took initiative in raising the level of academic synergy between colleges/schools. This is especially important as the university is the only higher education institution in the Mekong Delta and thus includes all disciplines. Enhanced academic synergy can be observed at three levels. Firstly, Can Tho University focuses on enhancing teaching methodologies and curricula up to Bachelor's level at all colleges and schools. Students are encouraged to take a more a pro-active stance in learning instead of simply consuming knowledge. Libraries are modernised and guidelines adjusted throughout the university to facilitate access for students. Secondly, Can Tho University emphasises a multi-disciplinary research approach, thus working towards a problem-solving paradigm instead of a purely theoretical approach. Thirdly, Can Tho University has expanded its academic collaborations at the national, regional (e.g. Thailand and Laos) and international level. Through the MHO programme, the university could systematically widen and deepen its relations with Dutch universities and benefit from academic international networks of new counterparts.

Can Tho University is well aware that funding by external international donors is temporary. The university systematically encourages schools and colleges to pursue income-generating activities on the local market. Almost every college sells products or provides services to companies, public institutions or consumers. Guidelines are in place in that taxes are paid for revenues. Involved staff receives supplementary payments for their efforts and other costs, like hiring extra labour are subsequently paid from revenues.

Concerning Vietnamese policies on higher education, the government may allow for more mechanisms for competition between institutes for higher education, as demonstrated by the start of a World Bank programme. This programme for promoting strategic planning by universities. worth US$ 80 million will have several levels of tendering by national universities.

Also at provincial level Can Tho University is facing more competition. Until recent teacher training colleges were, for most part, reliant on Can Tho university if they wanted to issue degrees at bachelor level. Over the last years some teacher training colleges have started cooperation with Ho Chi Minh City University, or are applying for governmental approval so that they can issue degrees at bachelor's level themselves. At the same time most Vietnamese institutes for higher education receive less financial support per student from the Vietnamese government. Therefore Vietnamese universities will have to find alternative financial sources and to scourge the market, both locally as well as internationally.

For now Can Tho University has been successful in accessing international markets as over 70 percent of its budget is from sources other than the Government. However when such support ceases Can Tho University may find itself in serious difficulties in case no alternative money sources have been found.

4. The impact of market demand: what capacities to build?

Introduction:
The above two case descriptions illustrate that the same capacity building programme, with the same organisational set-up, instruments and similar Dutch partners, is differently implemented and has different effects. This section is comparing the experiences of Moi University and Can Tho University. It attempts to draw a number of conclusions regarding the need to focus on market opportunities and threats.

In comparative education, case study methodology is rarely used (Renkema, 1998). In this paper, a comparison is made between two case descriptions, which are contrasted by first establishing the differences and the similarities (Bereday, 1964) and then arriving at conclusions and 'lessons to be learned', which have the status of working hypotheses. It should therefore be regarded as an exploratory case study.

Can one make a comparison between universities located in countries as diverse as Kenya and Vietnam? The two universities seem to be too distinct to enable the drawing of conclusions on the basis of a comparative analysis. The socio-economic, political and cultural circumstances are quite different. The same can be said of both systems of higher education. Moi University, is one out of five public universities in Kenya, and has only restricted institutional autonomy. Can Tho University is only one of many institutes for higher education in Vietnam, and is more able to set its own priorities.

Despite these differences, there is also a strong resemblance between Moi University in Kenya and Can Tho University in Vietnam. The following similarities can be observed:
a. both countries have experienced substantial reforms of government policies in education;
b. both institutes are relatively young public universities of similar size;
c. both universities are located far away from the capital of the country;
d. both universities strive to be problem-solving and practically oriented in their approach;
e. both universities have experienced a huge expansion over the last decade.

Case comparison:
During the last decade both universities have undergone a dramatic change from a rather small university with provincial status, to a large university with over 10,000 students in the case of Can Tho University. The ambitions of both universities have grown likewise. Both want to further expand, access state-of-the-art technology and become centres of excellence in research. Both universities realise that in order to achieve this they will have to step down from their academic ivory towers and actively search for market opportunities, both nationally as well as internationally. Apart from this increased market awareness, both universities differ in the way they could enter this market.

At Can Tho University the external conditions favour more market opportunities.

A growing economy has resulted in many households capable of paying student fees. Strongly growing young industries look for technical support at the university campus. However, also internal factors are important. The policy at Can Tho University of centralising coordination, while at the same time decentralising decision making and responsibility has balanced the need of the individual academic, and the role of the university developing and disseminating knowledge elements. In the case of Can Tho University, the MHO programme played a supportive role in providing an instrument for capacity building. At present Can Tho University is in the process of systematically improving staff capacities to analyse and distil market opportunities, and negotiate and formulate cooperation agreements. The MHO programme is providing the tools for realising these improvements.

The external environment of Moi University may not be favourable for attempts to strengthen institutional capacities. The university is functioning in a context that is characterised by political turmoil, ethnic conflict, and economic crisis. In particular the economic crisis of Kenya is having dramatic effects. Despite these constraints, the university remains successful in carrying out teaching and research. However, mainly because of the unfavourable external circumstances the impact of the MHO programme in capacity building is currently relatively limited (Renkema et al., 1998). It is obvious that external developments influencing Can Tho University have been more favourable than at Moi University. Foremost this is to be attributed to changing policies in Vietnam, resulting in considerable economic growth. Secondly Can Tho University benefited greatly from a fortunate timing of the MHO programme of which the start coincided with a change of policies of the Ministry of Education and Training in 1993.

However despite the large difference in external developments, it could be argued that Moi University could have tried to balance its disadvantageous position, by actively seeking to improve its internal functioning. This is not the case. For Moi University, the lack of external market opportunities has made it difficult to actively and systematically motivate staff to look for that same market.

Prospects for capacity building:
When looking at the experiences with institutional strengthening of Moi University and Can Tho University, what emerges as 'lessons to be learned'? Three issues seem important: the intertwined relationship between the university and its external environment, the crucial role of university administration, and the need to reflect our concept and practice of capacity building.

It is obvious that the external environment is of major importance to the development of universities in developing countries. It is clear that the higher education sector is deeply affected by in particular the country's economic performance. Whereas structural adjustment programmes are calling for cutting cost and increasing efficiency, there is popular pressure to increase access to higher education. It has been stated that economic strength is a condition for successful implementation of education sector programs and projects (DAE, 1994). However, while acknowledging the relative autonomy of the education system, it would be too deterministic to see the educational development as completely dependent upon economic growth. The external environment consists of more than just economic inputs. It may be helpful to see a capacity building programmes, such as the MHO, also as a factor in the environment of the university. A capacity building programme should not only take into account the effects of changes in the environment, but should itself be understood as an influential component of that environment, able to reinforce or counterbalance external developments. The experience of Can Tho University suggest that indeed the MHO programme was instrumental for the university to adapt to a changing context. An extensive programme, such as MHO, has the potential to assist a university to be better equipped for improving the quality of staff performance in dealing with market opportunities.

Whether that potential in fact materialises, and 'institution building' is actually taking place, for a large part depends on the receiving university. A university linkage programme may offer considerable scope for the institutional development of the Southern partner, but not all universities will profit from such a programme in the same way nor will the results be the same. Such programmes can only facilitate universities inasmuch that strategic choices for types of collaboration have to be made by the institute itself. The actual success of the programme depends to a large extent on the management and organisation of the institution. More than with many other types of organisation, the prime resource of universities is its human resources. Also, more than with other organisations, staff of universities have a desire to decide on the subject matter for research and teaching and to have control over their personal career. The concerted support of one university in the South, such as provided through the MHO programme, creates a spectrum of choices for the management. Depending on the qualities of the managers, at various organisational levels, and the freedom of the university to decide on its own course, such programmes can contribute to capacity building in varying degrees.

A specific point of focus of capacity building programmes should therefore be university administration, in its widest sense. 'University administration' has both an internal and an external meaning. The internal meaning refers to the organisation and internal functioning of a university, e.g. its academic structure and the way material and human resources are organised. The external sense of administration is 'that of service to society by building a culture, the professions, the university extension services, and the relations linking the university to the international and national scene' (Cabal, 1993). It is first of all this second sense of administration that is often lacking in capacity building programmes. 'Service to society' implies that universities in developing countries systematically have to reflect upon external demands. What knowledge is needed by whom? What kind of graduates do employers need? How will students create knowledge, which is relevant to them? What knowledge can we create for the private sector? The 'missing link' in most of the universities in the South is the link between the university and the society and in particular 'academia and ordinary people' (Brock-Utne, 1996). Can Tho University has surely taken the first strides in the right direction but it is to be seen whether they can maintain this course when Vietnam is facing more economic hardship, like Kenya. The aim of institution building programmes therefore should be to build capacities to organise its education and research in such a way that it can consistently service the market needs of society. In other words, university administration should take into account changes in the external context of the university, adjust policies and create conditions for staff to seek out market opportunities.

The prevailing concept and practice of capacity building in higher education is focused on knowledge transfer and delivering up-to-date information through direct curriculum transfer (in the narrow sense) and staff training in the North. When looking at the trends described in section 1, when understanding the impact of the environment and when realising the major role of university administration, it may be necessary to move beyond current notions of capacity building.

To optimise contributions of cooperation programmes, such as the MHO programme, more attention should be given to attune areas of cooperation to deficiencies of the university, often rooted in its external market environment. Moreover, capacity building should focus on improving university administration, thus ensuring a better link of the university to the wider society. All emphasis should be on making universities 'more user friendly, user-responsive and user-participatory' (Girdwood, 1993).

References

Barr, R.B. and Tagg, J., (1995) *From teaching to learning: a new paradigm for undergraduate education.* In: Change, November/December 1995.

Bereday, G.Z.F., (1964) *Comparative method in education.* Holt, Rinhart and Winston, New York, Cf.: Bereday's third step of comparative analysis (juxtaposition).

Box, L., (1991). *Mapping on a Human Scale: Local Knowledge and Institutional Ignorance in Development Research.,* ITC Journal 1991-4, pp. 276-280.

Brock-Utne, B., (1996). *Globalisation of Learning- the role of Universities in the South: with a special look at Sub-Saharan Africa.,* International Journal of Educational Development, Vol 16(4), pp. 335-346.

Cabal, A.B., (1993). *The University as an Institution Today: topics for reflection.,* IDC, Ottawa/UNESCO, Paris. (p. 103).

DAE, (1994). *Issues in the Implementation of Education sector programmes and projects in Sub-Saharan Africa.,* DAE, Paris, France.

De Hoop, M.B., (1998). *Report of a Nuffic Mission to Can Tho University & The International Training Institute for Materials Science.,*Vietnam, 11-25 January 1998, Department for Human Resource and Institutional Development, Nuffic.

Gibbons M., (1998). *Higher Education Relevance in the 21st Century.,* DRAFT - Association of Commonwealth Universities.

Girdwood, A., (1993). *Capacity-Building and Higher Education in Africa: a comment on the capacity building rationale and aid to higher education in Sub-Saharan Africa.,* Compare Vol 23(2), pp. 149-158.

Heyneman S.P., (1998). *The Transition from Party/State to Open Democracy: The Role of Education.*, International Journal of Educational Development, Elsevier Sciences, pp. 21-40.

Hobbelink, H., (1991). *Biotechnology and the Future of World Agriculture.*, Zed Books Ltd., London and New Jersey, p.104.

IIEP, (1995). *Education aid policies and practices.* Report of the November 1994 Meeting of the International Working Group on Education (IWGE)., UNESCO/International Institute for Educational Planning, Paris.

Joly, P.B. and de Looze, M.A., (1996). *An Analysis of Innovation Strategies and Industrial Differentiation through Patent Applications: The Case of Plant Biotechnology.*, Research Policy 25, North Holland, Elsevier Science, pp. 1027-1046.

K'Olewe, O., (1997). *Education Reform as Public Policy in Kenya: the case of the 8-4-4 school system.*, Journal of Practice in Education, Vol 3(1), pp. 5-11.

Latour, B., (1987). Science in Action: *How to follow Scientists and Engineers through Society.*, Milton Keynes, Open University, UK.

Leibbrandt, G., Le Thac Can, Tran Thi Dan, Ursula Nguyen, and Patmo S., (1998). *Review of the Vietnam-Holland Inter-University Cooperation 1975-1997.*, Ministry of Foreign Affairs, The Hague.

MacKenzie, M., Cambrioso, A. and Keating, P., (1988). *The Commercial Application of a Scientific Discovery: The Case of the Hybridoma Technique.*, Research Policy 17, North Holland, Elsevier Science, pp. 155-170.

Moore, M., Stewart, S. and Hudock, A., (1995). *Institution Building as a Development Assistance Method.*, SIDA Evaluation Report 1995/I, Stockholm.

Nuffic, (1998). J*oint Financing Programme for Cooperation in Higher Education: Description of the Programme and its Procedures.*, The Hague, The Netherlands.

Rodrigues Dias, M.A., Director of the Divison of Higher education, UNESCO.

Renkema, W.J.T., (1998). *Knowledge of the traveller: case study research and the problem of generalisability.* Tertium Comparationis, Journal für Internationale Bildungsforschung.

Renkema, W.J.T. and Legerstee A., (1998). *Report of a Nuffic Mission to Kenya.*, Department for Human Resource and Institutional Development, Nuffic.

Sloper, D. and Le Thac Can, (1995). *Higher Education in Vietnam: Change and Response.*, St. Martin's Press, New York, p.11.

Tung, K.C. and Renkema, W.J.T., (1997). *Embedding Capacity building in Institutional Change,* Newsletter of the Association for the Development of Education in Africa, Vol. 6(2).

United Nations, (1997). *Biotechnology in the ESCWA Member Countries: Sectoral Issues and Policies.*, Economic and Social Commission for Western Asia., E/ESCWA/TECH/1997/1, Amman.

Welch, A., (1998). *The End of Certainty? The Academic Profession and the Challenge of Change.*, Comparative Education Review Vol. 42, No. 1, pp. 1-14.

Yin, J.Z., (1992). *Technological Capabilities as Determinants of the Success of Technology Transfer Projects.*, Technological Forecasting and Social Change 42, pp. 17-29.

World Bank, (1994). *Higher education: the lessons of experience.*, World Bank/IBRD, Washington, D.C.

World Bank, (1996). *Vietnam: Education Financing Sector Study.*, Human Resources Operations Division, Country Department 1, East Asia and Pacific Region.

World Bank, (1997). *Revitalizing Universities in Africa: Strategy and Guidelines.*, Washington D.C., USA

Part 3

Civil Society

10

The Current State of the French Education System: A Contrast Balance Sheet

Claude Thélot

1. Introduction

In this chapter I would like to separate out the most significant facts for reflection and, indirectly, for the policy to be pursued in our education systems as the 20th century draws to a close. The major advances during recent years in the information and evaluation system of the French education system allow us, in fact, to describe and analyse its functioning, its resources, its successes and its failures (including in comparison with other developed countries).

It is natural to begin by examining the students and the system: they are, or are supposed to be, central to the system; it was, or is supposed to have been, made for them. This raises the first - descriptive - question: how does the school function, what services does it offer, how has it evolved over the past few decades, etc.? This description must also deal with the cost of education, even if this issue is less visible and sensitive in our country than the issues of students, structures and programmes. After description comes evaluation: what are the results of the school, its successes and its failures? This will necessitate a short detour via its objectives: one does not, in fact, evaluate without having first defined (at least to some extent) the yardstick to be used for evaluation. Both description and evaluation alike will be focused on primary and secondary education, leaving higher education aside, with the exception of admission into higher education since this involves the *lycée*[a][1].

2. Mass School

The most spectacular, immediately visible aspect of the changes in recent years is entry into a mass school:

- children start school well before the age of six since, nowadays, all children

---
[a] State secondary school for ages 15-18

aged three and half of those aged two by the autumn return to school are at a nursery school; the development of younger classes has been spectacular and it is peculiar to France (only Belgium can compare with France on this point), even though this extremely early start - from the age of two - has marked time for the past fifteen years, as if French society hesitated to go further or, better still, judged the situation satisfactory; it is true that while early school attendance is *on average* beneficial in later years, it is not necessarily true for *all* children; we often hear warnings against children starting school too systematically early;

- the primary school has been a mass school for a long time; what is new is that the distance is now covered much more rapidly than before since repeated years have decreased: approximately 40% of 11-year-olds were still attending primary school twenty years ago, in other words they had repeated at least one year; today, this figure is down by half;

- the *collège*[b] is now for everybody: not only do all pupils attend, which dates from the late 1960s but, above all, the course is now genuinely covered by an entire generation, although even 8 to 10 years ago, 25- 30% of pupils entering at age 11 did not stay on until age 15; they would leave school at age 13, which was a major factor for social inequality in the school, since these pupils often came from working-class backgrounds. The gradual elimination (between 1988 and 1992) of the age 14 cut-off point has been a major element in recent years; now, for most of a generation, the first critical point of reference is the end of the *troisième* (first year at a *collège*) (regardless of the type of *troisième*: general, technological, integration);

- the *lycée* is now the mass *lycée*, attended by the majority of young people, in fact by slightly more than two-thirds: 68%. This is a change which dates back some ten years, from the period 1985-1987, and one which has been very rapid since in 1980, for example, only one-third of a generation were admitted to a lycée; besides, it is the rate of this change that worries many adults who have lost their bearings or, worse still, are unaware of what is going on. Analysts too are often slow off the mark, considering the *lycée* on the basis of research carried out ten or fifteen years ago, without seeing or assimilating the changes. The word *lycée* in the singular in fact covers several types of reality: it consists of three separate routes (which is peculiar to France; other countries have only two): the general route (with its literary, scientific and economic and social streams), the technological route (with its industrial technology, tertiary technology, laboratory science and technology, medico-social science and technology and hotel technology streams) and, finally, the vocational route, with some forty or so industrial or tertiary specialities. *Lycée* pupils follow one of these three routes in two different types of establishment: on the one hand, the general or technological route in the general or technological *lycée* (including, in particular, the former classical and modern *lycées*) and, on the other hand, the vocational route in the vocational *lycées* (which are the transformed successors to the former technical schools); a type of *lycée* known as '*polyvalent*' offers all three routes;

- finally, French higher education has likewise become mass higher education,

---

[b] State secondary school for ages 11-15

through diversification: slightly more than half a generation now enter higher education and this may take place somewhere other than at a university (university students in the strict sense, that is to say, not counting those at a technical university institute (IUT), remain in the majority, but increasingly less so, and now represent less than two-thirds (62%) of the total number of students). The various streams of higher education are either selective - IUT (technical university institutes), the *grandes écoles*[c] offering literature, science or business studies, with or without preparatory classes, higher vocational diploma (BTS) classes in *lycées*, etc. - or open, chiefly universities, at least as far as the first few years are concerned (except for medicine, a more or less selective stream with a one-year time difference). This very clear division, mainly peculiar to France, coupled with the fact that the *baccalauréat*[d] is a national examination providing the right to enter into higher education, explains the forms and problems surrounding *entry* into higher education in our country.

This major shift towards a Mass School may be summarised by the length of probable school attendance for a young child starting school: he or she will now stay in the school system for an average of 19 years, in other words, having started school at, say, 3 years of age, he or she will leave at the age of 22. Fifteen years ago, this probable length was less than 17 years; this considerable and sudden protraction of more than two years at school goes some way towards explaining the extension of youth and the very late, indeed excessively late age upon completion of education (22 years is an average age) and the discrepancy in age (for instance, students are adults and therefore citizens and *lycée* pupils at the same time: 43% of *lycée* pupils have reached the age of majority, 56% at a vocational *lycée* and 38% at a general or technological *lycée*, despite the drop in repeated years throughout the school career, which alone transformed *lycées*). It was during the latter half of the 1980s that the movement gathered momentum, in particular in *collèges* and *lycées*, followed, naturally enough, by higher education and, while this met a demand for education (from families, businesses, etc.), it is also, however, the result of the policy pursued since then, that is, it responded first and foremost to a supply of education.

3. Article 3 of the 1989 Vocational Guidance Act

We should mention here the three points central to this policy: the announcement, in 1985, by J.-P. Chevènement, of the need substantially to increase access to the *baccalauréat*, up to 80% for a given age group; the simultaneous creation, again by J.-P. Chevènement, of the vocational *baccalauréat*, intended to extend and to round off vocational studies and, in so doing, to diversify access to the *baccalauréat*; finally, the preparation and passing, in 1989, when L. Jospin was Minister of Education, of the Vocational Guidance Act, Article 3 of which states: 'The Nation sets itself the objective, over the next ten years, of guiding all those in a given age group at least to the level of the

---

[c] Competitive-entrance establishments of higher education

[d] School-leaving certificate taken at a *lycée*

vocational training certificate (CAP) or technical school certificate (BEP) and 80% to *baccalauréat* level'.

Often quoted incompletely, recalling only the '80%', by way of a symbol to be either praised or disparaged, this Article in fact draws together the priorities and, since it contains certain clear, quantified, dated objectives ('over the next ten years' from then, i.e. the objectives were meant to be reached by 1999 at the latest), it might now be interesting to concentrate our discussion and evaluation on this Article. It was inspired chiefly by the fact, which was evident during the mid-80s, that French workers were on average inadequately qualified, particularly compared to those of our main competitors. This teaches us that the relationships between education supply and demand are dialectic: supply, which will shape the broad movement of 'massivisation', has been constructed from a demand, the demand from employers (including public employers) uneasy about the weakness inherent in a certain lack of qualifications among workers. The simplest way to raise the level of qualification of the workforce, beyond the development of in-house training (not very 'credible' in our country), would be to replace retiring workers with young people entering the world of employment who are more qualified and better trained than they are. Hence the ambition stated in 1985 and later confirmed by its inclusion in Article 3 of the law of 1989. In fact, the past ten years have seen us make up most of the ground we lost compared to several developed countries as regards the qualifications of the workers.

The prime objective of this Article, if we choose to take it literally, is beyond our reach because 100% success or, if you prefer, aiming for 'zero-defects' is a slogan or an ideal. It is not an accessible objective in the education system, since it means that *all* the children within one generation will be guided at least to the level of the CAP or BEP or to *seconde*[e] in a *lycée*, which is after all fairly high (without wanting to lower that level substantially, which would be a different policy). Bearing this comment in mind, the objective has in fact virtually been achieved: 91% of a generation now attain at least this level (as against, for example, 67% in 1980 and below 80% when the law was passed) and this proportion, which is without doubt a maximum, will probably remain stable over the next ten years. In terms of numbers of pupils, about 60,000 now leave school without reaching this level, compared to 75,000 in 1989 (and 210,000, or one quarter of a generation, twenty years ago, which illustrates the great progress made by schools). Here too, there is no real likelihood of this number actually decreasing over the next decade, which raises the problem both for schools and society of these young people experiencing major academic and therefore economic and social difficulties in the future.

Since we are thinking in terms of the law, the concept that springs most readily to mind is that of the *education* of young persons, not of their *qualifications*. We know that the two concepts do not coincide: we may have followed an entire stream, for example the two post-*collège* years leading to the CAP, without being awarded the final corresponding certificate (this is possible via the school route, that is to say, in a vocational *lycée* or more often via apprenticeships). Nor should we forget that, in these cases, a certain amount of

---

[e] 15-16 year olds

training has been given to the young person, training that will be useful to him in his professional life, even if it has not been officially recognised by the final qualification. We can therefore refer, in such cases, to young people who are 'trained' without being 'qualified'. The confusion between the two concepts, training and qualification, is often great, reflecting the importance our country assigns to paper qualifications. This confusion bedevils the assimilation of non-qualified persons into professional life, even if they have received a certain level of training. These non-qualified people outnumber the 60,000 'untrained' people, amounting to approximately 90,000, which is less than half the figure for 1980 (200,000).

The second objective of Article 3 of the Act merits a more detailed discussion. We shall begin with an established fact: today, as stated earlier, 68% of a generation now *reach baccalauréat* level (63% within the national educational establishments, 7% outside, especially in agricultural education and apprenticeships), compared with 55% ten years ago and 34% in 1980. We are talking here about *access to the level of the baccalauréat* rather than the proportion of a generation *passing* the *baccalauréat*. Once again, two different concepts are involved, between which opinion does not always draw sufficient distinction. The law accepts reaching the level of the *baccalauréat*, that is, as a general rule, reaching the *terminale*[f] class (general, technical or vocational). Now, a final-year pupil may fail the *baccalauréat*: again, we see the distinction made earlier between level of training and qualification. Bearing in mind repeated years (even years taken three times in certain private education structures), approximately nine out of ten final-year pupils will pass the *baccalauréat*. This means that the proportion of 68% reaching *baccalauréat level* corresponds to a proportion of 61% of students having *passed the baccalauréat* among today's young adult population. The spectacular increase in those reaching and passing the *baccalauréat* may largely be ascribed to a diversification of *baccalauréats*, enabled and encouraged by the creation of and surge in the vocational *baccalauréat*. The general route would thus seem to have lost ground to the other two; this is no cause for regret, since this relative decline is the very expression of this desirable diversification (which was in fact hoped for). The reverse, the retention of the relative importance of the general route, which would imply that access to the *baccalauréat* would have increased without change, in a homothetic manner, would have been serious and would, moreover, have represented a failure of efforts to increase the qualification level of the labour force. Today, to be quite clear, 50% of young people reaching *baccalauréat* level follow the general route (compared to 60% in 1990 and 65% in 1980); 30% via the technical route (compared to 31% and 35% respectively); finally, 20% arrive via the vocational route (compared to 9% and 0% respectively, the '*bac pro*' or vocational *baccalauréat* having been created in 1985): diversification has been very broad and very fast.

Progress in access to the *baccalauréat* has thus been vast, greater than any progress in the general increase in education detailed in the first part of Article 3 of the Act, but the objective this time - 80% of a generation - has not been achieved and it most likely will not be, even pushing back the horizon: in fact, in

---

[f] Final year at a lycée

the next ten years, the long-term forecasts that have been made regularly for some years now show that this proportion will remain stable: for example, according to the last forecast financial year (drawn up in Autumn 1998), it should stabilise at around 67% in 2007[2].

4. The cost of the school

At the same time as the mass school was developing, the resources which the country placed at its disposal increased greatly, as called for by the school. The political priority given to education for at least ten years, which rather surprised other countries, was more than empty words. It also allowed France to catch up other developed countries somewhat. In 1997, France earmarked 619 thousand million francs for education, both initial and continuing, or a good 7.3% of the wealth that it had produced that year, placing France among the front-runners - behind the countries of Northern Europe, but ahead of Germany, Japan, the Netherlands, etc.[3] It is also twenty years since society decided, de facto, in favour of education. The resources for education, that is to say, its cost, have increased more than the national wealth: they have almost doubled since 1974 (they have multiplied by 1.9), whereas the wealth produced annually by the French economy has multiplied by only 1.6. This very substantial increase is not due to an increase in the numbers of pupils: the average pupil costs much more today than twenty years ago: FF 35,700, compared to FF 21,400 in 1975 (in today's francs, of course), in other words, 1.7 times more or 2.4% more on average per annum. This increase in cost is essentially due to two factors: the reduction in the number of pupils per class and the increase in teachers' salaries; it will have to be brought into line with progress in the performances of the education system.

A few additional remarks will shed some light on these very global orders of magnitude.

Firstly, by order of education. In all countries throughout the world, a pupil costs more the further advanced he is in his career path; this is related particularly to the higher qualifications and salaries of staff between primary and higher levels and France is no exception to the rule. But what characterises our country is the shallowness of this progression: a student costs, on average, between 2 and 2.3 times more than a primary school pupil: the gap is slight, among the slightest in the developed world[4]. This is explained as follows: a French schoolchild costs FF 23,900 per year, or roughly what he would cost anywhere else; but, whereas a secondary school pupil costs us a good deal more than elsewhere (FF 45,500 per year), a student, especially a university student, will cost less than in other developed countries. An average student, taking all streams of higher education together, costs FF 48,800 (or, if we take account of the fiscal advantages and the allocation of low-cost accommodation, FF 55,800) per year, a university student in the strict sense, that is, not counting those in the UTIs, costs FF 37,300. France has made an immense effort in recent years on behalf of its higher education, but this drive has, in the main, been directed towards entry into mass higher education, in other words, the growth in resources has followed growth in the numbers of students without exceeding it by much. We are taking a risk as regards the resources we are allocating to our higher education: they are broadly inadequate and they are very (no doubt excessively) unevenly distributed, with a student at a *grande école*, in a preparatory class, IUT or BTS class being very expensive, a university student - particularly during the first years - not very expensive and teaching staff during the first years, whether they have studied for two years (DEUG) or three (*licence*), being too few in number.

Who pays the school? When we say that, in 1997, a pupil cost on average FF 35,700 per annum, this is not what his family paid (or he himself, if he is a student). We arrive at this estimate by adding all the financing together. The main contribution comes from the State: it pays two-thirds of the cost (65%, to be exact). This because, in France, teachers are State civil servants and the bulk of the expenditure on education is accounted for by staff costs, whether they are teaching or non-teaching staff. Education is, in fact, a labour activity (an 'activity', rather than a labour 'enterprise') in both senses of the term: the expensive thing about education is first of all the staff, but what determines its quality is also primarily the staff, mainly the teachers. The State's share in the financing of education has diminished over the past twenty years while, by contrast, in the wake of the laws regarding decentralisation which placed the *départements* in charge of the construction, maintenance and equipment of *collèges* and the regions in charge of *lycées*, the contribution from the local authorities has greatly increased: today, the local authorities (including the *communes*, which have always been responsible for primary schools) contribute 20% of the overall cost of education.

The most significant feature concerns the direct contribution of households: it is small, 7% of the overall cost, and it has fallen over the past twenty years (it amounted to 10% in 1975). In other words, education is an activity financed in a highly collectivised manner - and increasingly so. It is natural that education, an investment which is both individual for those who take part in it and collective for the economy in which they will work and the society in which they will live, should be financed in a combination of ways, both collectively (in particular via taxes) and individually (for instance, through registration fees). The economists have shown for some time that mixed financing would at best ensure the optimum, even if they cannot really say what the exact division should be between the two sources of finance. It is also normal for the collective share of the financing to decrease the further we advance in the hierarchy of the system: 'free' primary education, that is, in reality, financed exclusively collectively ('teaching is free, secular and compulsory'), then secondary education, where the 'consumer', that is, the school student or his or her parents pay proportionately more and the 'taxpayer' relatively less and, finally, higher education, where the student's own share of the financing has to be the highest. This is indeed what we find in France and in all other countries. But the scale of this increase in the individual share of the financing of studies is highly variable and, in our country, it is restrained, probably excessively so. The local authority's share of the financing is falling slightly, for example, between 93% for nursery schools to

80% at university or 90% in a preparatory class for a *grande école*. In substantially increasing student grants and introducing more loans on more favourable terms to avoid accentuating inequalities in higher education, it will no doubt be necessary to increase the contribution made by students or their families to their studies. The establishments, particularly the universities, will then be able to offer improved-quality education, for example, better stocked libraries with longer, more suitable opening hours, which the students will incidentally be justified in demanding because they will have contributed more to them. Unfortunately, minds are not yet prepared for such change. The local authorities might also agree to contribute more to the financing of higher education in our country, which is what the regions have already done in the 'Université 2000' plan, which they financed at the same level as the State but, to carry on down this road, it will no doubt be necessary to define the exact conditions and methods by which they could be effectively associated with the drawing up of university policies (and not exclusively their financing, as currently proposed in the new plan, christened 'U3M').

So much for the operation and resources of the school. We now move on to evaluation, with the emphasis on its results, its successes, its failures, always in a spirit of objectivity.

5. School results

No-one evaluates without objectives. Hence the definition, or timely reminder, of the objectives of the French education system. Again, the recent major legislative texts are of use in this context, for instance, the 1989 Vocational Guidance Act, as amended by the five-yearly 1993 Employment Act, because they have shaped, codified and, on this particular occasion, stipulated and broadened the tasks of the school. Article 1 of the 1989 Act sets four prime targets for the French education system which I will use to evaluate it now:

- imparting knowledge and culture;
- preparing for professional life;
- shaping the citizen of tomorrow and, over and above this, the future adult in a democratic society;
- finally, being fair in achieving the above goals, reducing inequalities in the school (and thereby helping to reduce inequalities in French society).

6. Imparting knowledge

Evaluating what children know at the various stages of their school career has made quantum leaps in recent years, especially as regards primary and secondary levels; we now seem to have a more accurate idea of what pupils know and do not know. Summarising these evaluations suggests more than one conclusion.

First of all, the general level of knowledge acquired by young people has risen. It might be overstating the case to claim automatically that the school achieved this increase (certainly not true in certain cases!) and thus to draw the conclusion that the transfer of knowledge by the school is overall better than it used to be. However, the average level among young people today is higher than that of their predecessors. Witness, first of all, the marked decrease in non-qualified school-leavers mentioned earlier: 210,000 young people left school without attaining the CAP or the BEP in 1973, or one quarter of that generation; today's figure is 60,000 or approximately 8%. Witness also the tests conducted by the Ministry of Defence on young men during their 'three days'; these intelligence and behavioural tests, which have not changed since the early 1970's, reveal that the average level reached by these young men has risen by one quarter in twenty-five years. Witness, finally, the bulk of the evaluations conducted by the Ministry of Education over the past 10-15 years in primary schools, when pupils enter the *sixième*[g] and when they leave a *collège*. In all, if we take the average of the rates of evolution of knowledge as measured by the Ministry of Defence tests and the evaluations conducted by the Ministry of Education, the decline in non-qualified school-leavers and access to the *baccalauréat*, the conclusion would seem to be that our young people's knowledge has progressed by 0.6% per annum on average over the past two decades. This positive overall outcome calls for certain nuances and comments[5].

In the first place, these genuine advances nevertheless fall short of the growing needs of the French economy and the growing expectations placed upon the school, by parents in particular. The result is that these advances are sometimes denied or underestimated but, above all, that they are in reality insufficient. Young people leaving school without training illustrate dramatically the degree to which the needs of the French economy have increased: whereas, 25 years ago, the 210,000 young people who left school each year without training experienced no great difficulty in finding work, today's 60,000 do not find employment. Jobs are much more demanding in terms of training than they were twenty years ago and will remain so. Equally - another example of the gap between progress and needs - pupils now have a better command of English than before (this was evident from many evaluations of *collège*-leavers, for example, but could also be said of young people in higher education, especially in the *grandes écoles*). However, such advances continue to fall short of needs in a world that has become internationalised and, in any case, the command of this language (or its offshoot, that is, the English spoken in international exchanges, 'Esperenglish' if you will) by young French people still lags behind that of young people in numerous other countries. English is, moreover, a good example of yet another point of view: if mastery of this language has increased, it is certainly thanks to the school, but it certainly also the result of other factors.

Secondly, the progress of pupils compared to their elders is not homogeneous: there are areas or disciplines where progress is substantial, others where it is weak or absent and yet others where the pupils have fallen behind. The average, then, while increasing, covers highly disparate situations, which in part reflect the priorities which the school in fact sets itself (from its programmes, from its

---

[f] 11-12 year olds

timetables, its classroom practices) and it is for this reason that a balance sheet of what pupils know is vital for political deliberation. Two examples will illustrate this diversity.

Firstly, by discipline: students leaving a *collège* have a rather better grasp than before of mathematics and history/geography and are rather less competent in French. Even where they have made progress, the level, compared with other countries, may be very mediocre and even unsatisfactory: one case in point is biology which, together with physics and chemistry, is less well mastered in France than in many developed countries, which today represents a handicap. By contrast, the poor performance in French does not alter the fact that reading skills are better by the end of the *troisième* than in other countries.

The second example, which straddles the literary disciplines and the human sciences, can be found in the following outline, which appears very general: today's young people master a certain number of mechanisms less well than some decades ago, but they have more fluency, spontaneity and originality in their expression, both written and oral. This is clear in modern languages, where they speak more spontaneously, but with more mistakes. This can also be seen in French, where spelling and the mechanics of the language are, at around 12 to 14 years of age, less well mastered than during the 1920s, especially among boys, but where essays (those required for the primary school-leaving certificate and again at ages 12 and 13) are better today than before. The decline in the command of mechanisms is also reflected in arithmetic: while addition and subtraction are as good as they used to be, this is less true of multiplication; the contrast is complete with today's improved command of questions of geometry, which corresponds to a marked emphasis in curricula since mid-1985. This general outline - a weaker grasp of the mechanics/more fluent, more original expression, is perhaps not new, since traces of it can be found in certain complaints expressed with regard to the proficiency of pupils in Latin during the 19th century! Be that as it may, this leads us to urgent discussions in the matter of policy: the main challenge of the education system today is to put the emphasis back on the command of a certain number of mechanisms, those considered fundamental, thanks to effective teaching practices (not only methods) today, without losing the progress in terms of originality and fluency of expression that has been made in recent decades.

Finally, the third aspect affording a panoramic view of the evolution in pupils' knowledge involves dwelling upon the disparities: temporal disparities and disparities between pupils.

The temporal disparities first. The developments may be different and even contrasting between the medium and long term and the short term. For example, reading levels by the end of primary school are not very different from what they were ten years ago: stability in the medium term. It is without doubt better than three or four decades ago: improvement in the long term. However, and this is essential for policy, an apparent decline is evident in the very short term: for two or three years in fact, the average skills of pupils entering the *sixième* have been declining. More precisely, the proportion of pupils not mastering basic reading skills when they enter a *collège* has been increasing since 1996, even if it is difficult to make exact comparisons. This figure reached 21% at the start of the 1998-99 academic year (the recent drop is also significant in mathematics: in September 1998, 38% of the pupils entering the *sixième* did not have basic arithmetic skills). These apparently diverse developments can be reconciled as follows: reading skills appear to have increased until the mid-1990s and to have slipped into reverse since. It is certain that such a diagnosis is serious and calls for purposeful action at primary school level: in fact, we should endeavour to avoid this decline through preventive action rather than to make up for it at the *collège*. Generally, these disturbing short-term observations should lead to an education policy that will improve compulsory education as a matter of priority (primary school and *collège*).

Now to the disparities between pupils. The rising levels are not identical for all types of pupils. There is a certain narrowing of disparities in knowledge among all the young people in one generation, since the 'best' pupils have progressed little over the past 25 years (but their level has not dropped, nor has that of pupils passing the *baccalauréat:* a doubling of access to the *baccalauréat* has not been paid for by a fall in levels), while the 'worst cases' have progressed more, becoming less poor. The tests by the Ministry of Defence show, for example, that not only are there now fewer illiterates among young men than before, but that these illiterates are not as illiterate as they used to be. By contrast, and this is serious, it is among young men of CAP or BEP level, or those leaving a *lycée* during the school year that the level of proficiency has decreased. Interpreting this trend is a delicate matter: it is perhaps because the 'best' at this level now carry on as far as the *baccalauréat* (technological or vocational) and pass it that those who do not reach that level or do not hold the *baccalauréat* and who therefore remain at CAP or BEP level, compare unfavourably with those who were previously at this level; this group, which was then terminal, included all young people of this level, the good and the not so good. Whatever the case, this unfavourable development should make us focus in more closely on these young people who only just achieve the minimum level provided for in Article 3 of the Vocational Guidance Act, without exceeding it.

7. Preparing for professional life

As this is a matter of assessing whether school prepares young people for their future professional lives, it is, by definition, a difficult thing to do, particularly in these times of uncertainty. Who can say what their professional lives are going to be and, consequently, how we should train them? However, even if we are very broadly unaware of the jobs which will be held, we can still say without fear of correction that it will be necessary to provide proof of certain knowledge and skills and, most probably, certain professional behaviour, in particular a certain creativity and a certain capacity for adaptation. Evaluating this knowledge takes us back to the previous section. Evaluating types of behaviour and the contribution of the school as regards their prevalence is very difficult, but will be illustrated below when discussing the future citizen. We are left with the evaluation of the acquisition and mastery of skills, intellectual working methods in particular, a subject on which we could say a few words, although these are very new and uncharted waters, making absolute conclusions impossible. Let us consider the case of the working methods of *collège* pupils in the *sixième* and *troisième*[h]. They seem to be good, including in the eyes of the teachers, for a majority of pupils, but seem poor for a large minority (and the pupils least well equipped in this respect tend to deceive themselves, not considering their working methods as mediocre as their teachers do). They change between the beginning and the end of the *collège*, becoming more elaborate and less automatic (there is even 'a certain decline in basic practices and reflexes as well as in the mastery of time management', which is rather disconcerting). Finally, as expected, there is a close correlation between the level of pupils and the 'quality' of their working methods - close, but not absolute[6].

To go beyond these few elements on skills, to evaluate whether the school prepares pupils for professional life should be carried out indirectly, starting with an examination of the links in our economy between education and employment, salary or growth. It is the preferred field of educational economists, who thus conduct an 'external' evaluation of the education system. Four aspects can be emphasised, in an attempt to summarise their contributions.

Firstly, the professional integration of young people in French society is poor and the handicap compared to adults in this respect, measured on the basis of the proportion of people in employment, has worsened. Contrary to the claims of those minds who seek to argue without restraint, schools are not entirely to blame, but they are partially responsible, which therefore represents a minus point in the overall assessment. This should prompt the schools into better coordination with employers (including public employers) for the transition, the 'decompression chamber', between school and adult life. The right to vocational training must be inextricably linked to the development of block-release training. Both the education system and employers must or should be prepared to commit themselves to this with greater determination than at present.

Secondly, the exposure of young people to unemployment is primarily because young people are ill-trained and increasingly so, thus demonstrating the increased importance of a minimum level of education. In this sense, qualifications have not been devalued but rather, revalued, because it provides relatively more protection from unemployment than twenty years ago. This is a plus point in the assessment, since the lack of education is a growing handicap.

Thirdly, turning this time to employment and salaries rather than unemployment, education is less 'profitable' in France than it was 15-20 years ago (the opposite of the United States). That education should be a stronger defence against unemployment and should therefore be revalued from this initial point of view is

---

[h]   14-15 year-olds

'paid for' by a certain 'deskilling' upon recruitment and therefore a certain devaluation from this second point of view. This deskilling is not entirely offset by subsequent promotions and reinstatements. Thus, the same education or the same qualifications do of course, always lead, on average, to an increase in salary with respect to not having these qualifications, but this increase is lower than it was one or two decades ago. Even if the explanations for the reduced profitability of education are many and varied, perhaps this is an indirect indication of a certain weakening in the adaptation of initial education to economic demand.

However, in the macro-economic perspective, rather than individual, the role of education in our economic growth has increased in the past twenty years. As any employer knows, having a trained, qualified labour force is now decisive in order to develop and perform well in national and international economic competition. The qualification of employees has become one of the more important factors (second to the volume of capital) in explaining the rhythm of French growth[7]. This is a positive indication as regards the overall efficiency of our education system in the economic sphere. On the whole, these various indirect indications more or less counterbalance each other and lead us to conclude that the education system is currently achieving the objective of 'preparing for professional life' in a similar way - only slightly better (if we genuinely quantify it, 0.2% a year on average) - than it did in the past. Progress has therefore been too modest to allow us to lose interest in this aspect of the education question and, more particularly, the need to improve greatly the transition of young people from school to professional life. This supposes, among other things, the development and improvement of anything with a bearing on vocational guidance, both in *collèges* and *lycées*, and encouraging block-release training in all its forms.

8. Training the citizens of tomorrow

Training the citizens of tomorrow has, since the French Revolution, been a prime objective of schools. It is more topical today than ever and it may well have to be expanded somewhat: not only training the citizen, but 'socialising the future adult who has to live in a democratic society', in so far as the traditional authorities which, in addition to schools, socialise the young - families, companies, neighbours, churches, as well as the army, political parties, trade unions – have become weakened. Schools do not have to fulfil this role on their own, but they should take this weakening into account, that is to say, they should expand their traditional role.

Two main dimensions should be considered when attempting to evaluate the degree to which schools have attained this goal. Firstly, that of civic skills, then that of behaviour, not only professional this time, but also 'democratic' or 'citizen-like', if we might use such terms. We have only very patchy elements of evaluation for both dimensions and we cannot pretend to draw up a full balance sheet. However, these elements are not uninteresting and they give food for thought.

The civic skills of pupils increase from the *sixième* to the *troisième* and on to the *terminale*[i]: Progress is marked and if the schools are partially responsible, which is probable, it is a sign that the *collèges* and *lycées* are effective to a certain extent. Various surveys give grounds for thinking that young people have fewer civic skills than adults aged thirty to forty, as if these were also acquired after school, as we grow older, in the actual practice of citizenship. Interpretation is therefore, as always with this type of observation, ambiguous: is it an effect of a generation, with young people having less in the way of civic skills than their elders, or is it simply because the young people have not yet reached thirty or forty, in which case it is a simple effect of life cycle? We cannot decide between these two interpretations with a one-off evaluation but, in the case under review, the second interpretation surely carries some weight. That said, we cannot rule out evidence of a certain decline in civic skills among the younger generations compared to their predecessors, which would seem to run parallel with a certain alienation and lack of interest in politics. Consequently, we should not feel too satisfied when we consider the civic skills of *lycée* pupils. However, it is still reassuring that these skills increase between *sixième* and *terminale*.

Judgement of 'citizen-like' behaviour is more delicate, more differentiated and carries higher stakes. Indeed, unlike knowledge, where it is easy to outline a preference (it is preferable to have knowledge than not to have it), the field of behaviour cannot be structured into any obvious or consensual hierarchy (which behaviour should the school be encouraging?) and does not readily lend itself to evaluation (how can the effective behaviour of pupils be assessed?). The measuring method itself raises another question: whereas civic skills are evaluated conventionally, on the basis of several questions of fact, behaviour cannot be as easily grasped. In fact, we collect stated types of behaviour, but this is done on the basis of the simulated situations in which the pupil is placed, by asking him to tell us how he would react. These simulations are numerous and varied enough to eliminate, as far as is possible, the arbitrary nature of the choice of this or that situation and the effects of answers intended to please. The outcome is that we can reasonably believe we are obtaining a fair approximation of various kinds of 'real' behaviour. Once these questions of measurement are settled, two areas may be mentioned where it is possible to rank the answers sufficiently, so as to draw meaningful conclusions.

Firstly, tolerance, a positive value on which there is reasonable, if not unanimous agreement. Tolerance increases throughout the school career, with *terminale* pupils claiming to be more tolerant than those in the *sixième*. Again, if we attribute a certain amount of responsibility to schools in this welcome development, this can be written up to its credit. Secondly, respect for rules and the law, by which we mean respect in both senses of the word – legitimacy which is both recognised and observed. Both the school world and the social world have rules and laws which, when recognised as legitimate and respected, as in the case of tolerance, produce a more desirable situation than the converse and one we must make every effort to achieve. Now, the legitimacy and observance of rules decreases throughout the school career, particularly when it comes to the rules of

---

[i] Final year at a *lycée*, pupils aged 17-18

the school world of school; cheating and 'incivilities' increase from primary school through to *collège* and *lycée*. This decline between *sixième* and *terminale* is especially true of boys and, even allowing for puberty and adolescence, which encourage them to be competitive or rebellious, this has to be written up to the debit of the *collège* or *lycée*[8].

This finding is serious; it forces us, if we take the mission of the school seriously, to make some adjustments. In any case, the school would see it as an honour to achieve this in an information society which regularly distils the dishonesties perpetrated by certain members of the social, economic and political elite. Not setting bad examples is an essential condition, even if it is not enough, from the moment we want to instil in young people respect not only of rights, but also of obligations and rules. The adults in educational establishments, starting with the teachers, must not set bad examples either in their personal conduct (punctuality, professional conscience, etc.) or in their relationships with pupils. Without necessarily assigning it a general value, the fact that many *collège* and *lycée* pupils complain of the 'contempt' in which some teachers hold them is the polar opposite of what is desirable; it is more than unjust, it is also ineffective if we intend to train them to become future citizens. Beyond the conduct of the teaching staff, we must undoubtedly also develop the possibility for pupils to fulfil roles, to carry out functions. A. de Peretti was right to insist at length upon this way of bringing out the everyday conduct of the citizen in *collèges* and *lycées*; recently, a certain number of requests from the *lycée* pupils themselves appeared to point in the same direction[9].

If we now leave the field of development in behaviour throughout the school career, from entry into the *collège* to leaving the *lycée*, in order to try and appreciate the developments which have taken place over time, we can start with the regular surveys conducted by opinion pollsters on behalf of the newspapers in order to see whether young people of today have attitudes which are more or less public-spirited than those of yesteryear. Thus, by way of example, young people aged 18 to 25 vote less than they did twenty years ago, but this is even more true of older citizens, so that, on this point, the 'relative lack of citizenship' among young people is reduced. Or what about the moral condemnation of reprehensible acts (stealing from a department store, the tax office, public transport) which has increased in our society in recent years, but even more so for young people than for others, so that their 'deficit' is once again reduced?[10] The practice of cheating is more widespread among the young than among their elders but, here again, it is difficult to know whether this is a generational effect or an effect of life cycle. Even if it is in part a generational effect, certain very precise forms of cheating are nonetheless very much bound up with life cycle: for example, we cheat more at examinations when we are pupils or students, we cheat the tax office more when we are adults. Falling back on police crime statistics helps us to dovetail these two interpretations, even if this cannot be as convincing as we might wish, given that police statistics are marked by the priorities of maintaining order and by errors in recording. Whether we confine our enquiry to cases of theft, whether we also include more serious crimes or, again, base ourselves on the whole gamut of offences recorded by the police service, the result, qualitatively, is the same: the increase in these offences over the past fifteen years measured against the number of persons is considerable among minors (aged 13 to 18), more so than among adults. For example, the number of cases of theft by minors rose by 18% during the period 1982 to 1997, or an average of 1.1% per annum. This fits in, moreover, with the increase in school violence, more recent but visible, which makes the very conditions of education in certain establishments very difficult without specific, coordinated action between the law courts, the police and the education system[11].

Overall, if we risk synthesising the few indications we have for the acquisition of knowledge and preparation for professional life, we may conclude a slight downturn in the average civic behaviour of young people (to quote an order of magnitude, maybe approximately -0.2% per annum during recent years and decades). The school is not, of course, solely or even chiefly responsible for this trend; but this trend is sufficiently worrying to grant top priority to the emergence, among pupils, of 'citizen-like' behaviour, which is evidently not learnt in the classroom.

9. Reducing inequalities in the school

Reducing inequalities in the school is the fourth objective of the French education system. It is not self-evident; it is not affirmed in all countries with equal vigour and it is only quite recent here in France, dating back no further than the Second World War and chiefly to the early 1960s, that is, the heyday of social change in French society in the 20th century.

Have the inequalities in our education system been reduced? The term 'inequality' is best taken in its widest sense: inequalities between children belonging to the same generation, between boys and girls, between geographical areas, between social groups, etc., and the conclusions are not necessarily the same according to the angle chosen. If we simply remember that knowledge is less unevenly distributed among young people than it was some decades ago (as mentioned earlier with reference to the Ministry of Defence tests) and that the inequalities separating boys and girls have been so far reduced as to be reversed (girls in all developed countries do better than boys at school, which is a 180° reversal of the secular trend and one which, in our country, also dates back to the 1960s), we may now concentrate on social inequalities and, to a lesser degree, geographical inequalities.

The very fact of entry into mass school represents an element of the reduction in inequalities: by definition, many children from the middle or underprivileged social strata, or from regions where pupils left school early, now attain higher academic levels thanks to the 'massivisation' of the school and they are the first in their family to reach this situation. It is because this lengthening of their education took place without any lowering of the overall academic level (even if this judgement does require diversification) that we can talk of progress.

Therefore, far from being a simple translation without importance, with the *baccalauréat* having somehow become the primary school certificate of yesteryear and the inequalities having simply shifted position, as some maintain, this access by middle and working-class strata, the young people from certain regions (for example, the North of the country) to qualifications, to the CAP-BEP, to the *baccalauréat* and to higher education, takes on a capital importance for these young people, for our economy and for our society. Since knowledge in itself is liberating (for instance, should we cite the case of young girls from the Maghreb?), 'massivisation', as long as it is not paid for by a lowering of levels, is a powerful factor for democratisation and development.

But we must go further still and ask the following question: through such 'massivisation', have the chances of access to long-term education for children who had only limited access not only increased (which is the definition of 'massivisation') but actually increased *more* than those of other children, thereby 'really' reducing inequalities, social or geographical? The answer to this question is yes, really: with the 'massivisation' of schooling, inequalities have generally been reduced in varying proportions, sometimes appreciably, sometimes a little. The careers of *collège* pupils today are therefore much less inegalitarian than during the 1980s: without counting the attenuating effect on inequalities of the removal of the cut-off point at the end of the *cinquième*, mentioned earlier, the fewer repeated years are less socially discriminatory or lead to fewer discrepancies between French and foreign pupils; again, entry into the general and technical *seconde* is now less different from one social group to another, etc.[12] Likewise, access to the *baccalauréat* is less socially unequal than twenty years ago, including the general *baccalauréat*. The reduction of geographical inequalities is also considerable: while the rate of access to *baccalauréat* level (regardless of type) has doubled, the disparities between *académies*[j] have been greatly reduced, from 16 points in 1975 (Amiens: 23% of a generation reached this level, Île-de-France: 39%) to 9 points in 1997 (Strasbourg: 55%, Île-de-France again, 64%). Finally, access to higher education is also much less inegalitarian than it was before 'massivisation'. Here again, an illustration will convey the scale of the reduction: today, the child of a blue-collar worker has 7 times less chance of being at university than the child of a top executive, a teacher or a researcher, which is a major inequality. During the 1960s, however, about thirty years ago, he was not just 7 times less likely to be at university, but 28 times less likely[13].

To sum up, the reduction of inequalities at school over these past twenty years has been considerable. Of the four objectives of the school, this is where progress has been the most striking. If, as with the other three, we make efforts to quantify the scale of this evolution, we may conclude that inequalities have been reduced by an average of 2.9% per annum.

This overall conclusion requires two additional remarks. Firstly, some precise and specific analyses to show that the reduction in inequalities has not taken place on the same scale everywhere. Then, an appraisal of the scale of current inequalities, in a society where salary and social inequalities have started to increase again over the past dozen or so years.

---

[j] A regional education authority in France

The development, over the past forty years, in the social intake of four of our most important *grandes écoles* (the *école polytechnique* (engineering), the *école normale* (humanities), *the école nationale d'administration* (civil service college) and, finally, *hautes études commerciales* (business administration)) makes very interesting reading as an illustration of this first point: this intake has only slightly democratised over the whole period, in no way comparable to what we have noted for universities[14]. Around 1950, children from the middle and upper social classes had about 24 times more chance than children from working-class backgrounds (farm labourers, manual workers, non-manual workers, craftsmen or tradesmen) of admission into one of these four *écoles*; in 1990, they had 23 times more chance. The intake of these four *grandes écoles* (which says nothing about that of the others) has thus neither closed, despite what is often said, nor particularly opened. The contrast with the university is stark: it reveals that the democratisation of education has not been homogeneous in all sectors of our education system.

This brings us to our second point: although they have diminished - sometimes greatly, sometimes a little - the inequalities in our education system are still notable. To give a meaningful idea of the situation, we could rightly compare the intake to the various sectors of higher education. 52% of students in preparatory classes for the *grandes écoles* (CPGE) are the children of executives, teachers and researchers, 36% of university students and 14% of BTS students, while approximately 16% of all young people aged 20 to 25 come from these backgrounds. By contrast, manual workers' children represent 7% of CPGE students, 12% of university students and 25% of BTS students, while representing approximately 37% of young people aged 20 to 25. So the discrepancies are considerable. Equally, and despite the reduction in inequalities between *académies* or *départements*, the intake and functioning of *collèges* and *lycées* are very different. Thus, by way of indirect illustration, from one *lycée* to another, the rate of *baccalauréat* success may vary quite considerably and about one-third of that difference can be attributed to the profile of the *lycée* pupils – whether they are more or less socially disadvantaged or older, depending on the *lycée* – and can therefore be explained by the differences in *lycée* intake[15].

Given this situation, and although they function in different ways, our school establishments have not followed the increasing polarisation in this field. Quite the contrary, *collèges* appear to be behaving in a more homogeneous, more uniform manner than before, especially as regards vocational guidance[16]. In addition, while the social environment may be more varied than before between one *collège* and another, this may perhaps be ascribed to a certain flexibility in the academic map, but it is no doubt due more to the polarisation of the national territory (it would, incidentally, be interesting to separate these two effects). Similarly, *collèges* in ZEPs (areas for special educational assistance) have not seen their functioning and results moving away from those of the others in the same way that their environment, which has declined largely due to the pressure of unemployment, has separated itself from that of the others[17]. Looking at these few elements, we are left with the impression that the education system - far from adding to the social and geographical inequality which has grown again over the past twelve years - has mitigated it and, in part, compensated for it.

This impression leads us directly to a major political question which may best be expressed in the following terms. Does success in the Mass School, the *collège* for all, the *lycée* for two-thirds of a generation, necessitate a further differentiation of the system? Quantitatively first of all, by differentiating resources - and this is a policy of positive discrimination that would have to be pursued and enlarged upon (the ZEP policy is one illustration). Qualitatively too, by varying the procedures of education (options, timetables, aids, certain parts of curricula, etc.) and, perhaps, to some extent, the objectives themselves, by 'declension' of the national objectives, as stated in the 1989 Vocational Guidance Act, in other words adaptation to the environment, to the pupils, to the 'education demand' they are expressing.

10. Conclusion: progress in resources and results of the school over the past twenty years.

In conclusion, a comparison can be made between the increase in the resources of the school (or its cost) over the past two decades and the development in its results. We are familiar with the two opposing arguments on this question. To some, having increased the resources of the education system, for example, with the 'revaluations' of careers and salaries in 1988-90, when L. Jospin was Minister of Education, served no purpose: the money was 'lost in the sand', failing to bear fruit in any the sense of any real progress in our education system. To others, on the other hand, the increase in resources is very productive, enabling class sizes to be reduced, for instance, and, in an extreme version expressed by the trade union organisations, it is even a precondition, a sine qua non if the system is to progress.

The two trends below must therefore be compared and contrasted:
* over the past twenty years, the average cost of a pupil, excluding the rise in prices, has increased by 2.4% per annum (that is to say, it has multiplied by 1.7);
* over roughly the same period, the pupils' knowledge has undoubtedly increased by approximately 0.6% per annum, the effectiveness of preparation for professional life having increased by 0.2% per annum, training of future citizens declining by 0.2% per year and, finally, overall inequalities (a combination of social and geographical inequalities) falling by 2.9% per annum.

It is, therefore, not true that the increase in the resources allocated to the school - which expressed the education policy preference of the whole of French society and not only of the State – has not been translated into progress: we must at the very least recognise a certain co-existence between the two increases: resources and results. Yet the genuine increase in results is not commensurate with resources. Weighting the four objectives of the education system differently, we achieve rates of school progress which are certainly different, but are always well below 1% a year (between 0.2% and 0.8% in fact), a much slower tempo therefore than the increase in the average cost of a pupil. Thus, the advances made by the school, which are real but which already fell short of the expectations made of them because of the hopes and needs of the French economy and society, also lag behind the advances made in its resources. In reality, progress no doubt depends on resources, but increasingly less so with the coming of the Mass School: the question of the school has now become principally a question of quality.

Notes

1 Most of the data presented in this text comes from the Ministry of Education, Research and Technology publication, *L'état de l'Ecole* (The State of the School) No. 8, October 1999.
2 See the article by C. Ravel-Szlamovicz in No. 54 of the review *Education et formations* published by the Ministry of Education, Research and Technology, June 1999.
3 One of the three Ministry of Education, Research and Technology Department of Programming and Development publications below may be consulted for all questions on the cost of education: *L'état de l'Ecole*, 1998; or O. Mesnard, C. Ragoucy, C. Berreur: 'Le coût de l'éducation en 1997' (The cost of education in 1997), Note d'Information 9832, October 1998; or *Le compte de l'éducation et de l'éducation supérieure. Années 1994 à 1997*,(The bill for education and higher education. 1994-1997), *Les dossiers d'Education et formations*, No. 105, December 1998.
4 By way of illustration, the figure is 2.8 in Germany and in the United States, 2.5 in the United Kingdom and in Sweden, etc.. See, on these different points, the annual publication of the OECD, based on the work and estimates of the countries themselves, *Regards sur l'éducation* (Education at aGlance)
5 Regarding the level of pupils, see C. Baudelot and R. Establet, *Le niveau monte* (The level is rising), Seuil, Collection L'épreuve des faits, 1989.
6 Reference may be made to the recent Ministry of Education, Research and Technology publications on these various points. See, for example, *Notes d'information* 9624, 9635 and 9733, or A. Stefanou; *Les méthodes de travail des collégiens. Résultats, fiabilité, robustesse* (The working methods of collège pupils. Results, reliability, soundness), *Les Dossiers d'Education et de formation*, No. 96, December 1977.
7 See, on these various points, the work by O. Marchand and C. Thélot, *Le travail en France (1800-2000)* (Work in France 1800-2000), Nathan 1997.
8 All these evaluation elements come from recent work conducted within the Ministry of Education, Research and Technology. Past publications may be consulted (e.g., *L'état de l'Ecole*, No. 9, October 1998, or the studies by A.

Stefanou and D. Fabre-Cornali, e.g., *Notes d'information* 9632, 9634 and 9906, or *Connaissances civiques et attitudes à l'égard de la vie en société en collège* (Civic knowledge and attitudes to life in society and at collège), *Les dossiers d'Education et formations*, No. 77, December 1996), or being published (*L'état de l'Ecole*, due to appear in Autumn 1999).

9 To explore this question in more detail and gain an idea of the variety of roles likely to be held by pupils which A. de Peretti proposes introducing in school establishments, reference may be made to his work, *Controverses en éducation* (Controversies in education), Hachette 1993.

10 These dimensions come from a special analysis of surveys by SOFRES for Le Nouvel Observateur in 1987 and 1994. On this subject, reference may usefully be made to C. Nadaud's article in the work *L'état de l'opinion* (The condition of opinion), Seuil, 1995.

11 On the description and analysis of school violence, reference may usefully be made to one of the following publications: (supervised by) B. Charlot and J.-C. Emin, *Violence à l'école: état des savoirs* (Violence at school: the state of knowledge), A. Colin, 1997; *Les violences scolaires, ni fatalité, ni impuissance* (School violence, neither destiny nor powerlessness), Report by J.-L. Lorain, Senator of Haut-Rhin, April 1998; 'La violence à l'école' (Violence at school), special edition of *Cahiers de la Sécurité intérieure*, No. 15, 1st quarter, 1994, Institut des hautes études de la sécurité intérieure (IHESI).

12 See N. Coëffic: 'Parcours scolaires au collège et au lycée' (School career at *collège* and *lycée*), Note d'information, No. 9801, Ministry of Education, Research and Technology, Programming and Development Department, January 1998.

13 See M. Euriat and C. Thélot: 'Le recrutement social de l'élite scolaire en France. Evolutions des inégalités de 1950 à 1990' (Social intake to the academic elite in France. Developments in inequality from 1950 to 1990), *Revue française de sociologie*, XXXVI, 1995.

14 To study this question in detail, reference may be made to the article mentioned in the previous note. It is true that, today, fewer children from working class backgrounds are found among pupils in these four *écoles*, but it is wrong to draw the conclusion that their intake is closed: this fall is simply the result of and runs parallel to the fall among the working classes (mainly farm labourers and manual workers) in our society.

15 See *L'état de l'Ecole*, op. cit.

16 See D. Trancart: 'L'évolution des disparités entre collèges publics' (The development of discrepancies between state *collèges*), *Revue françaises de pédagogie*, No. 124, INRP, July-August-September, 1998.

17 A very precise and constructive balance sheet is to be found in the recent report by the Inspection générale (school inspectors): C. Moison and J. Simon, *Les déterminants de la réussite scolaire dans les zones d'éducation* (The deciding factors of academic success in education priority zones)

11

University Training for Adults in the Light of the Interaction Between University and Civil Society

Jean-Luc Guyot

1. Introduction

The ageing of the population in our industrialised countries, the adjustments required by the speed of technological progress and the consequences of the current economic upheavals probably lie behind the increasing interest in university education among adults. In addition, 'lifelong learning' is often considered a valuable tool to establish a new form of citizenship and an important instrument in the fight against the mechanisms of social exclusion.

Universities are therefore increasingly being called upon to meet the demands of lifelong learning expressed by various segments of society. They have to cope with the need for vocational retraining linked to the increased mobility within the labour market, the need for refresher courses and courses designed to update skills linked to the constantly increasingly complexity of professions, or the need for personal and social development independent of professional activities. This trend is reflected by an increase, in both relative and absolute terms, in the size of the mature student population in universities. Hence, for example, Graph 1 shows, for French-speaking Belgium, the development of this population in the long term (Bourgeois et al, 1999: 73).

Some major achievements have already been made over the past few decades, but the issue of adult education remains a subject of controversy, particularly as regards the access of mature students to university education. As Bourgeois notes (1990), the position held by those who defend this access is far from univocal. Some people refer to the social mission of universities and the fight against unequal opportunities, stressing the need for universities to reach a public, which has traditionally been excluded from such education. Other people are aware of the 'need for universities to take up the challenge of recent technological, economic, social and cultural changes which, in one way or another, have

Graph 1   *Trend in numbers at French-speaking universities in Belgium in indexed form*

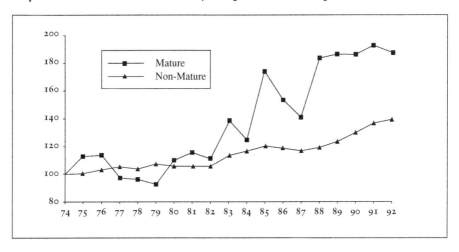

increased the demand for lifelong learning, particularly in the professional sectors where added qualifications have become absolutely essential' (Bourgeois, 1990: 1). Others again adopt a more pragmatic point of view and are concerned above all with the economic and financial viability of universities. On the one hand, opening up universities to mature students would make it possible to offset the financial 'deficit' and the loss of revenue caused by the demographic trend and the decline in the number of traditional university recruitment areas, and adult education would therefore be seen as a beneficial new market. On the other hand, the requirements of the education market are considered such as to make it essential for no university to neglect any segment of this market, and universities therefore have to invest, inter alia, in the range of courses available for adults so as not to develop an inferior position compared with their direct competitors (the other university institutions) or their indirect competitors (the private sector) which are investing in this area.

Given these diverse positions, it is possible to identify certain attitudes which are considerably more reserved and elements which constitute a favourable context.

On the one hand, the innovations, or even revolutions, which the development of university education courses for adults could imply in terms of practices and conceptions, both pedagogic and institutional, give rise to certain reservations within universities themselves. Hence, as Bourgeois points out, the policies for the development of such courses come up against resistance which is sometimes active, sometimes less so, on the part of those for whom adult education is not compatible with the main aims of the university and the requirements in terms of 'excellence' which these imply.

On the other hand, the scope of activities related to university education for adults is still relatively 'new'. Although teaching practices have undergone a relative degree of expansion, scientific research activities continue to be somewhat infrequent. Consequently, the players working in this field are still seeking an identity and legitimacy within universities.

Finally, given the current situation of shortages and economic crisis, the scarcity of resources available to the decision-making bodies of universities often compels these bodies to make choices on the basis of aims which are considered priority, and this often contributes towards crystallising the opposition and tension found in the field of adult education.

Clearly, then, the development of university courses for adults raises numerous questions and poses a whole host of difficulties. Not least the various aspects of the organisation of studies: what mechanisms are available to facilitate access and success for mature students at university? What are the various practices applied in this area? Other question marks relate to the characteristics of mature students at university, the effectiveness of the mechanisms put in place, the organisational processes that are set in motion when access policies are developed, or are not developed, as the case may be...

Research was conducted by two teams, one at the University of Warwick in Great Britain, and the other at the Catholic University of Louvain in Belgium, between 1992 and 1996, to try to find answers to all these questions. Further to this research, a more ambitious project involving five European universities[1] was launched in 1998 with the support of European funding. This project aims, in particular, to arrive at an understanding of the strategies adopted by universities to deal with non-traditional mature students[2].

The research carried out in Warwick and in Louvain (Bourgeois et. al., 1995; Merrill and Guyot, 1995), highlighted the diversity of the situations and practices in the field of university education for adults in the various disciplines of universities. Hence within one and the same university, the proportion of mature students varies considerably from one faculty to another. As an example, Graph 2 shows the situation at UCL for the 1992-93 academic year (Bourgeois et al., 1995: 16).

The research also shows the diversity of practices in adult education, in particular as regard the types of courses on offer and the mechanisms set up to facilitate access to these courses (admission conditions, course timetables, location of activities, structure of curricula, teaching mechanisms, assessment methods, services provided for students). Moreover, divisions between and sometimes even within faculties were also identified. The disciplines differ in their 'degrees of openness' to adults.

As regards courses leading to diplomas, generally speaking, it would appear that at the UCL, arrangements aimed a facilitating the entry and success of mature students are most developed in the human sciences. Conversely, these arrangements are less widespread in the natural sciences. For example, with regard to the arrangements made in terms of timetables, it may observed that the syllabuses in the extra-faculty entities are those in which special timetabling arrangements are most widespread. This is followed by those in the faculty of psychology and education sciences and those in the faculty of economic, social and political sciences. Some faculties, such as the faculty of philosophy and letters, that of applied sciences, that of sciences and the higher institute of

Graph 2   *Proportion of mature students in the faculties of the UCL (1992-93)*

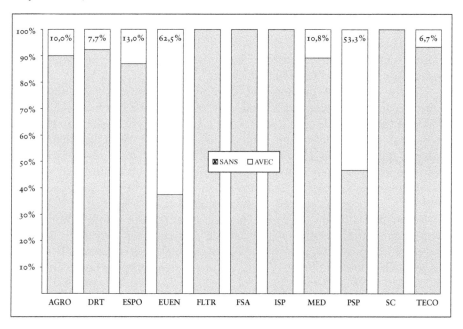

Caption: SC = faculty of sciences; AGRO = faculty of agronomic sciences; FSA = faculty of applied sciences; DRT = faculty of law; FLTR = faculty of letters; MED = faculty of medicine; ESPO = faculty of economic, social and political sciences; PSP = faculty of psychology and education sciences; ISP = higher institute of philosophy; TECO = faculty of theology; EUEN = extra-faculty entities.

philosophy do not have any formal timetabling arrangements. As for admission conditions, arrangements have been made most frequently in the syllabuses of the extra-faculty entities. This is followed by the syllabuses of the faculty of economic, social and political sciences and the faculty of psychology and education sciences. As an example, Graph 3 indicates the proportions of syllabuses at the UCL for which special timetabling arrangements were made in the 1992-93 academic year (Bourgeois et al., 1995: 17).

In addition, the mature students for whom these mechanisms are intended vary from one discipline to another. In the exact sciences, they are mainly adults who have already followed higher education, while initiatives aimed at adults without any previous higher education are more numerous in the human sciences.

As regards courses, which do not lead to a diploma, certain faculties such as that of applied sciences and that of agronomic sciences are more active than they are with regard to courses leading to a diploma. These faculties are developing training courses, which meet certain requirements expressed in industrial and business circles (lifelong learning and specialisations). On the other hand, some faculties, which seem attentive to mature students on courses leading to a diploma, prove less interested in offering courses, which do not lead to a

Graph 3   *Timetabling arrangements in the faculties of the UCL (1992-93)*

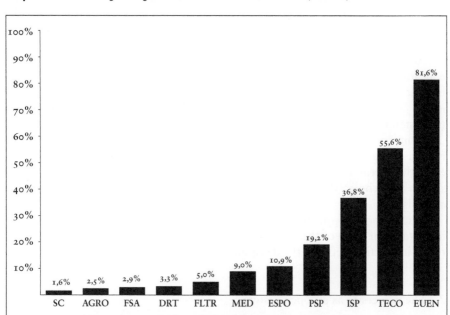

Caption: SC = faculty of sciences; AGRO =faculty of agronomic sciences; FSA = faculty of applied sciences; DRT = faculty of law; FLTR = faculty of letters; MED = faculty of medicine; ESPO = faculty of economic, social and political sciences; PSP = faculty of psychology and education sciences; ISP = higher institute of philosophy; TECO = faculty of theology; EUEN = extra-faculty entities.

diploma. This is the case in the faculty of psychology and education sciences, the extra-faculty entities and the faculty of economic, social and political sciences. The faculties of law and of medicine seem very concerned by lifelong learning for university graduates and are making a special effort for this group. Finally, some faculties, such as the faculty of philosophy and letters and the faculty of sciences, concentrate most of their educational activities, which do not lead to a diploma on lifelong learning for teachers.

Reading these results prompts us to think that there is probably a relationship between the degree of accessibility to a syllabus and the type of mature student following this syllabus on the one hand and the scientific discipline which the syllabus involves on the other. The fact that syllabuses leading to a diploma in sciences such as mathematics, physics, chemistry or biology have virtually no mature students and are devoid of any special arrangements aimed at facilitating access for these students, whereas over half the syllabuses in the faculty of psychology and education sciences include timetabling arrangements and that almost one student in five is an adult is not by chance.

This leads us to wonder about the origins of these differences. The question that arises is not only that of the dynamics of organisational change enabling the development of new policies in adult education at university, but also that of the mechanisms underlying the organisational dynamics themselves. Above and beyond the analysis of the strategic moves of the various players involved in the organisation of a university, there is a need to identify the stakes that cause these players to take action and the referents that structure their action.

We are therefore led to view the measures taken in the field of adult education as being more than purely the result of political will, in a given socio-historical cultural context, within civil society and at the institutional university level. Of course, these elements may not be neglected. They help us to understand the disparities, which may be observed between universities in different countries or between universities in the same country or the same region. Nevertheless, if the aim is to interpret specific features in terms of adult education in each discipline within one and the same university or the university system as a whole[3], the study of other mechanisms needs to be integrated into the analysis.

The purpose of this text is to explore, from a theoretical point of view, the importance of some of these mechanisms and, more specifically, of those relating to the interaction between the disciplines making up universities and civil society.

2. The university as an open system

Before interpreting the range of university courses available to adults in the light of the interaction between universities and civil society, we feel it would be advisable to consider this interaction in greater detail. To do this, we will adopt a point of view similar to that developed in the sociology of organisations by the 'contingency school'. This endeavours to understand how organisations are structured through the influence of contextual variables on the characteristics of these organisations. The term contingency corresponds to the idea that '... environmental constraints render organisational structures contingent, the latter being largely determined by the former '(Amblard H. et al., 1996: 14). For Mintzberg (1982), the organisational structure is loosely linked to its environment and also depends on the aims pursued by the leaders. According to him, the relationship between organisation and environment is adaptive: the organisation adjusts its structures in line with the contextual constraints. This adjustment may give rise to different forms of organisational configuration depending on the dominant type of principle of internal coherence.

Generally speaking, the contingency approach, as this can be applied to universities, proposes to analyse the scientific disciplines and universities from the point of view of interaction with the external environment. In this paper we present the most interesting contributions from various authors, some of whose work is along these lines. We will focus our attention on the organisational and cultural aspects of the disciplines rather than on their epistemological components. We do not intend to develop any socio-epistemological theories here, whose intention is to demonstrate the importance of extra-scientific factors in the definition of scientific content and directions taken by the development of science.

During his work, Becher (1989) focused on the relationships that exist between exist university and society. There are two opposing points of view here. The first presents a socially asexual image of science and university work. Scholars indulge in investigations in their ivory towers and, as scientists, have few relations with the outside world. The other point of view, upheld in particular by Barnett (1988), Rothblatt (1985), Kogan (1987), and Dill & Sporn (1995), sees universities, in our modern context, as being closely linked to civilian society, if only because intellectual activity needs to be supported by an economic surplus. From a material point of view, university research ex nihilo would be impossible. Academic work is dependent on the resources that civil society is able to provide. It is understandable that, in return, universities are expected to produce 'useful' scientific work, in the sense that the investment made in it proves economically profitable. This situation may result in a conflict between this pragmatism expected by society on the one hand and the values and aspirations of the faculty on the other. Hence there is increasing antagonism between the emphasis traditionally placed on the value of the pure sciences in the academic sphere and the importance attached to the applied sciences in economic, social and political spheres4, and in certain situations this antagonism results in the appropriation of applied sectors by non-academic players (partnership between business and university, private research centres, etc.) and the emergence of new rules by which to play the game.

Becher points out that the pressure exerted by society on universities, in particular in terms of 'research and development' sometimes results in the creation of new departments in order to be able to facilitate progress in sectors of investigation which are not perfectly in line with the academic divisions and which, for reasons of size, duration or aim, are not effectively covered by the activities of existing departments. The parallel with certain departments specifically devoted to adult education is inescapable.

The creation of new departments which are more in line with social and economic expectations leads to the emergence of hybrid communities, as is pointed out by Geiger (1985) and Gibbons et al. (1994). These communities bring together scientists from different scientific and non-scientific circles. Consequently, the criteria used to assess the work and the scientific staff tend to alter and become more 'secular'. As Elzinga points out (1987a), we are facing a situation in which two systems co-exist. In the former, traditional system, name awareness feeds on international recognition, expressed primarily by peers. In the second, the source of the awareness is different and lies in recognition of services provided to external, often local, economic or political elites.

The interference of society in universities is not without its consequences for the principles granting it legitimacy as regards the academic decisions and the directions taken. Exogenous criteria such as social relevance, cost, usefulness, etc. will henceforth have to be taken into consideration as well, even for the pure sciences. According to Elzinga (1985), it is therefore increasingly difficult to distinguish between applied sciences and pure sciences. From a traditional system monitored on the basis of reputation and compartmentalised in separate disciplines, we are now moving towards a decompartmentalised system which is subject to regulations that attach increasing importance to non-academic factors, in particular under the pressure exerted by the management requirements expressed by the university institution on the one hand and political requirements expressed by civil society on the other.

According to this author, this shift originates in two phenomena. On the one hand, in a context of increased technocratisation, political and bureaucratic institutions are making increasingly frequent demands of science. On the other hand, market forces are exerting pressure to develop new technologies, which requires substantial basic research work. The first of these phenomena leads to the socialisation, or even the politicisation, of research. The criteria used to justify research can now focus on sectoral problems (health policy, defence, development aid, social problems, etc.) or on social or political movements. The second phenomenon may lead to the commercialisation and privatisation of research.
However, it would be wrong the see the development of the economic and political approach adopted by science as a one-way process. According to Elzinga (1987b), this should rather be seen as a complex interrelationship of the disinstitutionalisation of science on the one hand and the scientification of society on the other.

Moreover, although academics share a series of values, representations, and standards, which are specific to them, they are nevertheless members of civil society as well and as such they have also integrated its culture. The ideals, the philosophical options and the values of members of the discipline[5] are not produced exclusively by this community. Moreover, exogenous cultural or ideological elements can 'interfere' with scientific work, particularly when the disciplines concerned involve human aspects.

The introduction of cultural or ideological elements into research can sometimes be deliberate and the result of a strategic calculation, in particular when the university player has to associate himself with external financial backers or assert his position on institutional or educational markets (Henkel, 1987).

Furthermore, the process of the socialisation of science leads to a restructuring of disciplines. According to Elzinga (1987a), this processes brings about epistemological changes by means of the emergence of new, hybrid scientific communities that are less compartmentalised, listen more to external demands and consequently benefit more often from external resources but are also more likely to be regulated by elements outside scientific and university circles.

The appearance of certain disciplinary fields, their maintenance and/or decline can be analysed in the light of the processes of interaction between university and society, which have just been explained. The creation of new study syllabuses can also be examined from this point of view. Moreover, Becher and Kogan (1980) point this out with regard to vocational training, such as that provided in accountancy or nursing which, according to them, have succeeded in making their mark at university because they are both academically acceptable and fulfil a market demand (and are therefore viable in terms of student numbers).

According to Elzinga (1987a), external change factors concern both the 'technical' sciences and the other sciences. The human sciences, for example, can be used for administrative or ideological purposes. Hence under the pressure exerted by certain social movements, new areas of scientific investigation have emerged, including, in particular, the study of sexual inequalities ('women studies'). According to this author, in such cases the values conveyed by the social movements that instigated the development of the new field of research show through this field, as it is a matter of the scientist agreeing with the ideology of the financial backer. Elzinga sees in the emergence of new disciplines the convergence of different, even contradictory movements and interests. These may be social movements, manoeuvres by academic staff or scientists aimed at safeguarding their own discipline, the professionalisation of certain groups of highly qualified workers or corporatist interests. Moreover, numerous disciplines appeared during the 1970s on the basis of external corporatism or the influence of groups of professionals, or in some cases further to pressure exerted by certain social movements. In all these cases, the innovation came about under the impetus of external rather than internal factors.

For Becher (1989), the various types of science defined on the basis of the hard/soft and pure/applied axes can be analysed in the light of the process of socialisation of the scientific world.

The pure, hard sciences have a great deal of prestige. They are presumed to reveal the general laws that govern the phenomena they study. They are seen as requiring great intellectual effort and therefore have to be entrusted to highly qualified people. Their purity and elitism are, however, offset by the promises of practical applications, which they sometimes offer. These promises help explain the large amounts which society is prepared to invest in them, particularly for the purpose of analysing specific problematic sectors with a view to discovering general causal relations. Funding for this type of science is obtained by particularly effective political and professional lobbying undertaken by highly organised associations of specialists. Even in less costly sectors of research, the art of obtaining funding has to be cultivated. Winning external funds plays a positive role in professional recognition and advancement. The material dependence of these sciences on external resources opens up the path for political and commercial interference and in some situations can lead to work considered socially applicable being favoured to the detriment of areas of investigation directed mainly by epistemological considerations.

The applied hard sciences, where the primary function of research is to develop techniques aimed at production and more specifically products as such, display a different profile. The work involved covers a broad field, rather than focusing on a limited number of specific issues. It is therefore more difficult for one interest group alone to become organised and to put forward unified and coherent projects to financial backers. This difficulty can be offset by the utilitarian criteria referred to above in relation to the pure and hard sciences. More particularly, the views of non-academic, professional practitioners in the sector of application often exerts a degree of influence by bringing new dimensions into the decision-making mechanism of the group of academic peers.

These two types of science require an active commitment from their faculty in the race for funding and imply dependence on the goodwill of the public and private spheres of the economy.

This pressure weighs less heavily in the fields of the pure and soft sciences, which are related to non-applicable and largely a-theoretical knowledge and which focus on the particular rather than on the general and on comprehensive rather than causal research. The way in which the outside world perceives this form of knowledge is ambivalent. On the one hand, teaching in these areas is considered an attribute and a respectable activity. However, knowledge in such fields is shown as esoteric, speculative and largely pointless. That which academics sometimes represent as being the pursuit of knowledge in itself is seen from the outside as being of no great practical interest and therefore attracts hardly any public resources. This type of discipline is considered too specific and particular to benefit from major investment. This attitude is backed up by the opinion that the pure and soft sciences require but few resources. In a context like this, the quest for funds is not an important activity in these sectors, and specialists do not feel obliged to cultivate a very developed network of public relations outside the university. This element, together with the fact that these sciences are characterised by a certain amount of individualism in the work, means that professional organisations, as interest groups and political players on the social scene, are relatively weak.

In comparison with the pure and hard sciences, the pure and soft sciences seem more heterogeneous to the extent that they also include fields that aspire to the nomothetism of the pure and hard sciences or which may have practical repercussions.

The main characteristic of the applied soft sciences, from the point of view of their relationship with society, is the possibility of seeing their research projects guided by non-academic interests. Because by maintaining close links with the academic community, which, moreover, sometimes includes some of their own members, professional associations of practitioners often play a significant role in defining the problems to be investigated and the methods to be adopted. Moreover, thanks to the control they exert over research budgets, local authorities attempt to direct scientific activities into sectors deemed 'useful'. This may also be done by pressure groups.

3. University education for adults and the socialisation of disciplines

The central theme of the contingency approach as we saw it is the analysis of disciplines and universities from the specific point of view of relations and interactions with the external environment. We feel that this approach is particularly fruitful for the analysis of the processes leading to the development of study programmes designed for adults or special arrangements aimed at promoting their presence at university.

A number of monographs, such as that prepared by Bourgeois (1990), point to the importance of the interaction between university and civil society when creating syllabuses for non-traditional mature students. In addition, the theories put forward by some authors, such as Becher, Kogan or Elzinga with regard to the process of 'socialisation' in universities provide an analytical grid that can be applied to the problem of adult education. In fact, it is difficult to ignore the parallelism between the creation of new research departments which are better adapted to the demands of social and economic spheres in the field of research and development and the launch of entities devoted specifically to adult education, such as the FOPES (faculté ouverte de politique économique et sociale – open faculty of economic and social policy) and the FOPA (faculté ouverte pour enseignants, éducateurs et formateurs d'adultes – open faculty for teachers, educationalists and instructors for adults) which, at least when they were created, were independent of the traditional faculties.

The central hypothesis which we will uphold here is that the more 'socialised' a discipline, that is the more open it is to the influence of civil society and the more it interacts with this society, the more likely it is to listen to the calls for adult education or for special arrangements which are expressed in this society. There is therefore considered to be a positive relationship between the degree of socialisation of the discipline and the extent to which arrangements are made and adults are included in this discipline.

Apart from the quantitative aspect, that is the extent of the frequency of the mechanisms and the number of mature students involved, the contingency approach could also be used to take into account the qualitative dimension of the variances observed in terms of the type of mature students following the syllabuses. In fact, it may be asserted that, depending on the type of player in society with whom members of the discipline interact on a preferential basis, the nature of the demands in terms of courses or special arrangements will vary and, consequently, so will the profile of the mature students concerned.

Generally speaking, numerous people, including Kulich (1987) and Duke (1992) have stressed the increasing importance of the demand for lifelong learning coming from various segments of civil society. Sometimes these demands correspond to requirements in the field of vocational retraining, sometimes to requirements in terms of proficiency courses or courses designed to update skills linked to the increasing complexity of professions or to requirements relating to personal and social development independent of the economic sphere. We believe that the legitimacy of this increasing pressure may be found in the economic requirements referred to above as regards scientific research and as identified by Barnett (1988) and Rothblatt (1985).

As we have pointed out, scientific activity at universities can often be guided by requirements in terms of the profitability of the economic investments made. This can create tension between the traditional criteria of academic excellence, enhancing the value of scientific 'purism', and the interest shown by economic, social and political circles in the applied sciences. Given this trend towards the interference of society in the direction taken by scientific production at universities, it may justifiably be assumed that this interference is not confined to the field of the creation of knowledge, but also affects the transfer of knowledge.

Hence if market forces exert certain types of pressure for the development of new technologies, it is difficult to see why such pressure would not also concern learning to use these innovations. Similarly, the increasing technocratisation of economic, social and political management is no doubt leading civil society to increase its demand for advanced education, since this technocratisation means that managers need to update their skills or acquire new, more suitable skills. Is there any need to recall here the examples of university courses in accounting, nursing, management or engineering and the process of the 'professionalisation' of certain professions?

What is more, social movements, which sometimes initiate new centres of research and, according to Henkel (1987), are responsible for the ideologisation of research, mainly in the human sciences, could come to consider university education as a vehicle to be used to increase awareness of their claims or to defend and disseminate their concepts of social reality, which would make them actual or potential applicants for education. This demand would concern the adult public in particular, or certain fringe groups within this public, either because these people are expressly concerned by the claims made and the plans proposed by the social movement calling for education, or because adult education is part of the liberating aims of this movement.

Finally, social-democratic ideology, which seems (seemed) to dominate our industrialised countries, may also lie behind a general movement calling for lifelong learning (within or outside university), corresponding in particular to its aims of fighting against social exclusion, and of socio-economic integration and participation. This ideology, as well as the underlying social movement, is believed to be particularly capable of making its demands heard in university circles, given its privileged position among institutionalised political players, who are the main financial backers of the education system.

In a global context like this, it is understandable that the process of university 'socialisation' affects not only the field of research and that of community services, but also that of teaching and training activities. Moreover, some academics may be particularly sensitive to the socialisation of the definition of the content of university courses because they consider this process to be an opportunity for the emergence of new, highly reputed markets offering an interesting alternative to the conventional academic markets and structured by recognition of the educational services provided and no longer by the system of assessment and reciprocal recognition among peers.

Nevertheless, although there can be no doubt that universities are confronted with this complex process of 'socialisation', it does not seem as if all disciplines are experiencing this process with the same intensity or speed. This disparity may be attributed to various elements, which may lie behind the diversity in situation as regards adult education that may be observed between the disciplines. Some of these elements refer back to the ideas expressed by Becher (1989) with regard to the epistemological components of the disciplines and their classification along the 'pure/applied' and 'hard/soft' axes.

Generally speaking, it is probable that it is the applied disciplines that experience the effects of 'socialisation' most, by the nature of the subject of their work. As regards the definition of educational content, they would therefore be more likely to pay attention to the expectations of civil society. In this respect, the professional associations of practitioners can also play an important role since, given their close relations with the academic community, they provide the relay between the education demands put forward in economic and socio-political spheres and this academic community.

The role played by the professional associations refers us back to another element, which may be seen as related to the varying levels of 'socialisation' of the disciplines in the field of adult education. Apart from the importance of the interaction developed between the discipline and its external environment, it is important to take into account the latter's degree of organisation. This organisation may be the result of action by professional groups which, as we have said, can be the link between the parties involved in the interaction between universities and civil society, but also the result of the action taken by institutional agents, such as local authorities, pressure groups or social movements, which structure the demand for education. The presence of agents capable of undertaking this structuring process and expressing this demand collectively, whether they are professional groups or other types of agent, enables members of the discipline to gain a clearer idea of the precise content of the training requested and therefore to respond to this more easily, or even more effectively. Conversely, in the absence of such structuring of demand, the balance between demand, which will be more dispersed, and any supply will follow market logic.

From an epistemological point of view, the pure and hard sciences have enormous prestige, not only within the academic world, but also outside. They are considered to require a high level of intellectual ability. This elitism, which is said to be shared by universities and their environment, it is not thought to be without its effects on the level of the demand for non-traditional adult education in these disciplines. On the one hand, anxious to preserve this academic prestige, the university teaching staff working in these disciplines could be inclined to reproduce this elitist argument and reserve access to these disciplines for a limited number of students. This idea is confirmed in certain observations made at the university of Warwick (Merrill and Guyot, 1995). On the other hand, this argument can have a significant dissuasive effect among potential mature students wishing to join syllabuses in the 'pure and hard' sciences. This same mechanism could also apply to the 'pure applied' sciences. As regards the qualitative aspect of the courses and mechanisms provided, as well as our hypothesis with regard to the relationship between the type of player in interaction with the members of the discipline, the nature of the demand and the profile of the adult public in question, it is difficult to identify the points of consistency characterising this relationship. However, we can identify a number of different situations.

In the case of courses designed for non-traditional mature students, the players in civil society involved in structuring demand seem to belong to the social or political sphere. At least, this is what is confirmed by the work of Bourgeois (1990) with regard to FOPES. Nevertheless, 'professional' players can also be identified as for the FOPA syllabuses, which are worked out in conjunction with professionals from the educational world, or the school of public health.

Lifelong learning or specialist courses, which are therefore designed primarily for mature students who already hold a university degree, reveal a certain amount of intervention (which should be identified more precisely) by professional groups, particularly if these courses do not lead to a diploma. We are thinking in particular here of certain syllabuses in law, medicine or engineering, as well as numerous courses that do not lead to a diploma.

The other types of situation, chiefly 'reorientation' syllabuses, that is those which offer special arrangements in terms of conditions of admission for adults who already hold diplomas of higher education, and further training courses, do not appear to be characterised by the presence of specific groups in civil society. It could rather be maintained that the development of mechanisms in these syllabuses corresponds to the trend in favour of exploring new, unstructured markets.

4. Conclusions

Our aim was to provide food for thought to understand how the process of socialisation in universities may lie behind the disparities between disciplines which might be observed in terms of the supply of university education for adults. We realise that these are not the only processes at work in the differentiation of the disciplines from the point of view of policies for adult education at university. Hence in our doctoral these (Guyot, 1998), we considered to two other types of factor likely to influence the emergence of such policies and to lead to features specific to different disciplines at this level.

On the one hand, we have looked at the role played by the special sociological characteristics of members of the disciplines, that is the academic sub-cultures that they convey and create. From this point of view, each discipline refers to its own sub-culture which expresses, in dynamic terms, a symbolic complex (production and allocation of meaning) and a normative complex (making a system of values hierarchical and certification of rules of behaviour, attitude, integration and adaptation within the group). These elements are considered to have an impact on the investment made by academics in developing the adult education courses provided.

On the other hand, we have used the analytical grid proposed by Bourdieu (1984) and attempted to establish the relationship between, on the one hand, the importance of adult education in the various disciplines and, on the other, the type of principle of academic legitimisation predominant in these disciplines. In this respect, we have put forward the hypothesis that university teaching staff involved in disciplines where academic authority is based chiefly on scientific criteria will concentrate mainly on the development of their intellectual resources (investment in scientific production and research) to the detriment of other activities (teaching, services to society), which could in particular explain the very low level of interest in adult education.

These various ideas were explored at the empirical level as part of the survey conducted concerning UCL during our doctoral thesis (Guyot, 1998). The results have revealed a certain balance between these interpretative frameworks and the actual situation observed. Nevertheless, these results were probably not all we could have hoped, in particular because they did not enable us to definitively establish the validity of the three approaches adopted (contingency approach, culturalist approach and the approach of Bourdieu), at least as far as our purpose was concerned. However, we may well wonder whether this is feasible at all, given the complexity of the mechanisms in action and the epistemological status of these approaches.

References

Amblard, H., Bernoux P., Herreros G. & Livian Y.F. (1996) *Les nouvelles approches sociologiques des organisations*. Paris: Seuil.

Barnett, R. (1988) Limits to academic freedom. In Tight M. (Ed.) *Academic Freedom and Responsibility*. Milton Keynes: Open University Press.

Becher, T. (1989) *Academic Tribes and Territories*. Buckingham: Society for Research into Higher Education and Open University Press.

Becher, T. & Kogan, M. (1980) *Process and Structure in Higher Education*. London: Heinemann.

Blume, S. (1985) After the darkest hour... integrity and engagement in the development of university research. In Wittrock B., Elzinga A. (Eds) *The University Research system*. Stockholm: Almqvist and Wiksell.

Bourdieu, P. (1984) *Homo Academicus*. Paris: Editions de Minuit.

Bourgeois, E. (1990) *Formation d'adultes et prise de décision à l'Université*. Louvain-la-Neuve: FOPES-UCL.

Bourgeois, E., Duke, C., Guyot, J.L. & Merrill, B. (1999) *The Adult University*, Buckingham: Society for Research into Higher Education & Open University Press.

Bourgeois, E., Duke, C., de Saint Georges, P., Guyot, J.L. & Merrill, B. (1995) *Comparing Access Internationally. Admission, Provision and Adult Participation in Two Universities*, Working Paper 14, june 1995, Continuing Education Research Centre, Department of Continuing Education, University of Warwick.

Dill, D., Sporn B. (Eds) (1995) *Emerging Patterns of Social Demand and University Reform: Through a Glass Darkly*. Oxford: Pergamon Press.

Duke, C. (1992) *The Learning University Towards a New Paradigm?* Buckingham: Society for Research into Higher Education and Open University Press.

Elzinga, A. (1985) Research bureaucracy and the drift of epistemic criteria. In Wittrock, B. & Elzinga A. (Eds) *The University Research System*. Stockholm: Almqvist and Wiksell.

Elzinga, A. (1987a) Internal and external regulatives in research and higher education system. In Premfors, R. (Ed.) *Disciplinary Perspectives on Higher Education and Research*, Report No. 37. Stockholm: University of Stockholm GSHR.

Elzinga, A. (1987b) *Politicization of science and epistemic draft*, Mimeo, Dalarö 1987 International Conference, Swedish National Board of Universities and Colleges, Research on Higher Education Program.

Geiger, R. (1985) The home of scientists: A perspective on university research. In Wittrock, B., & Elzinga, A. (Eds) *The University Research System*, Stockholm: Almqvist and Wiksell.

Gibbons, M., Limoges, C., Nowotny, H., Scwartzman, S., Scott, P. & Trow, M. (1994) *The new Production of knowledge. The dynamics of science and research in contemporary societies.* London: Sage Publications.

Guyot, J.L. (1997) *Accès de adultes à l'université en Communauté Française de Belgique. Etude comparative avec le Royaume-Uni. Etude de cas*, rapport de recherche final, Louvain-la-Neuve: FORG-FOPES, UCL.

Guyot, J.L. (1998) *Particularismes disciplinaires et formation des adultes à l'université. Analyse des facteurs sociologiques des politiques de formation d'adultes à l'université.* Thèse de doctorat en sociologie, Louvain-la-Neuve: UCL, Département des sciences politiques et sociales.

Guyot, J.L. & Merrill, B., (1998) Departmental Cultures and Academic Disciplines: Implications for the Access of Adults in Universities. In Alheit, P. & Kammler, E. (Eds) *Lifelong Learning and its Impact on Social and Regional Development. Collected Papers*, Contributions to the First European Conference on Lifelong Learning, Bremen 3-5 October 1996, Bremen: Donnat.

Henkel, M (1987) *The discipline: Still the dominant force in higher education?*, Mimeo, Dalarö, 1987, International Conference, Swedish National Board of Universities and Colleges, Research on Higher Education Program.

Kogan, M. (1987) *The responsiveness of higher education to external influences*, Mimeo, Dalarö 1987 International Conference, Swedish National Board of Universities and Colleges, Research on Higher Education Program.

Kulich, J. (1987) The university and adult education: The newest role and responsibility of the university. In Leirman, W. & Kulich, J. (Eds) *Adult Education and the challenges of the 1990S*, London / New York / Sydney: Croom Helm.

Kuhn, T. (1962) *The Structure of Scientific Revolutions*, Chicago: Chicago University Press.

Merrill, B. & Guyot, J.L. (1995) Access of Adults to the University: A Comparative UK/Belgian Study, in Hamilton M. & Withnall A. (Eds) *Innovation in Continuing Education Provision, Teaching and Learning*, Papers from the conference held on 27 April 1995 at Lancaster University as part of the UACE/SCUTREA/SRHE Seminar Serie, Lancaster: Lancaster University Department of Continuing Education and Department of Educational Research.

Mintzberg, H. (1982) *Structure et Dynamique des organisations*. Paris: Editions d'Organisation.

Rothblatt, S. (1985) The notion of an open scientific community in scientific perspective. In Gibbons M. & Wittrock B. (Eds) *Science as a Commodity*, Harlow, Lorigman.

Notes

1   The Catholic University of Louvain, the University of Warwick, the University of Bremen, the University of Barcelona and the National University of Ireland.

2 That is, those going into university education for the first time, following an interruption in schooling.

3 Our work concerns the case of U.C.L. only. We are not in a position to express an opinion on the consistency of the disparaites observed between disciplines at other universities. Some work (Guyot et Merrill, 1998) suggests that, as a whole, the situation as regards the disciplines remains relatively stable from one university to another, at least as regards the issue of adult education.

4 It would be interesting to transpose this anatagonism to educational aspects, particularly as regards access for adults and the higher degree of accessibility of courses in the applied disciplines.

5 As Kuhn (1962) stresses, for example, a discipline is not characterised exclusively by a group of peoples sharing the same knowlegde and a field of investigation, but also by the members of the discipline. These members for a community characterised by a number of paradigms, ways of looking at things, ways of thinking, around which a strong consensus has developed them.

12

Pakistani Immigrants: A Challenge to Norwegian Schools and Social Equity

Gunn Marie Hansen

1. The Education of Linguistic, Cultural, and Immigrant Minorities in Europe

The complexities of the education of minorities and immigrants present many problems to the European Community of Nations. Torsten Husen (1992, 1993) explains these complexities in the context of the European nations. This introduction will examine the key factors – curriculum, equity, and educational goals - that might have an influence on the interaction and subsequent education of minority groups, whether the situation of the group is permanent (involuntary minorities) or temporary (immigrant minorities). This is a relevant distinction for understanding the context of educating minority children. Gibson and Ogbu (1991) expand on the contrasting situation of immigrants and involuntary minorities or ethnic minorities. It is especially interesting in the case of Europe where generations of ethnic and immigrant minorities reveal differences in patterns of adaptation to the cultural majority. Husen refers to this concept as Ethnicity, which can be delineated into components - biogenetic, territorial, linguistic, cultural, religious, economic and political. The degree to which each of these aspects are present will determine much of the situation of the immigrant group. Research literature from the USA and Europe, using various terms or definitions of sociological and cultural interpretations of minorities provide similar evidence for the situation of minority groups.

National minorities in Europe are not a new phenomenon. The nation-states have throughout history accommodated within national borders many different minorities and cultures. Their longevity and self-assurance regarding their culture/language within the national majority characterise more permanent minorities. Some historical minorities who have maintained much of their ethnic identity over generations and have participated in the political process of the nation do have educational success and do become productive members of society (Wirt, 1979). These groups achieve parity or equity with the dominant population.

European minority problems (and American) in education are viewed as problems dealing with language or culture. Explicitly the problems are represented through such factors, however; the real complexities of the education of minorities has to deal with political and sociological factors addressing schooling and institutions which empower or disable minority educational achievement. Political and cultural dominance over a minority group is implicitly represented through allocation of resources and policy planning. It is explicitly displayed through issues of linguistics and cultural pluralism in national curriculums and educational goals. At a time when Europe is moving towards a greater unity, minority language and cultural groups cling more fiercely to their identity. The European nations should make policy and curriculum to deal with these new demands and the notion of the integrated European citizen.

Currently, there are three ways in which countries are dealing with the issue of language as and educational goal for immigrants. First, the minority language may be used as the medium of instruction, as is the case in Catalonia, Spain. This can become problematic where minority group members are dispersed across the nation. If concentrated in one area, mother tongue instruction is much more feasible. Second, the minority language may be taught compulsorily as an alternative national language, official national status. This is the case in Belgium, where both Flemish and Walloons have to learn either French or Dutch as the second national language. Third, the minority language may not be taught as part of the national curriculum, but may be an 'optional extra' to the standardised curriculum. This is the case in France and Britain.

Clearly, each immigrant situation should constitute a different type of policy or curriculum based on the nation's educational goals for the immigrant student. However, few governments have looked at the research into minorities when establishing programming and competencies that deal with equity for immigrants. Most decisions are based on governmental policy. Unfortunately, as in the United States, minorities lack political power or community action in order to advance their linguistic needs. Although there may be an ethnically sensitive policy in view of the tensions, few schools have actually been able to enact a language curriculum that can bring success to immigrant minority students due to lack of educational goal setting and the divisive nature of bilingual education and mother tongue teaching.

The overall picture of immigration in Europe today is a movement due to economic hardship rather than political or religious persecution. In Europe the movement has been mainly from developing countries, former colonies, and from the Mediterranean area to the more prosperous North. Restrictive measures by the host countries have begun to deter this movement. Further complications have arisen with the burgeoning democracies of Eastern Europe. Movement has shifted from east to west. Whether permanent or temporary, legal or illegal, the problems of immigrants and minorities pose a great question to the civil society of the nations of Europe. Modern immigration is much more heterogeneous. Denmark, for example, has a work force consisting of only two percent foreigners, but between them they speak over a hundred languages. The diversity of ethnic origins - not only from every quarter of Europe, but also from Asia,

Africa and the Caribbean - further complicates matters, as do the various religious allegiances - Christian, Moslem, Hindu, Buddhist (Council for Cultural Cooperation). In France, Islam has now become the second largest religious grouping after Catholicism.

The EC Directive of 1977 charged member states with the duty of ensuring for migrants adequate and equitable teaching in the official language, and the language and culture of origin in cooperation with the States of origin, and with the training of teachers able to fulfil these tasks. This resulted in consternation, as nations counted the cost of full implementation. Hosts began to offer financial inducements for migrants to return home due to economic problems and host unemployment. Few takers were found. Social conflicts were beginning to turn racist in nature, and concepts of the civil society with common educational goals were and continue to be challenged.

Some initial curriculum policy reactions were assimilationist since nations believed that most immigrants were to reside permanently and become citizens. This alienated many immigrants, and later schools took on multicultural education, requiring all children to learn various cultures. Present policies of integration or interculturalism are developing communication between the various cultural identities. This concept is vague and European countries have adopted their own varieties of interculturalism to small degrees. Negative forces in Switzerland and France claim there is no place for immigrants when unemployment is already high. In these situations it may be difficult to even become a citizen, much less receive equitable treatment. The stance of rejection continues, as EC census of November 1989 demonstrates.

The teaching of language and culture become the educational rhetoric of the majority school system trying to deal with the immigrant minority issue. Some form of language or cultural curriculum is presumed to increase the success of language minority students. . Although nations are confronted with increased racism, many countries are not addressing the realities of these inequities that are linked to socio-economic and political implications. The Dutch, who have long accepted numerous immigrants and who are acclaimed for their linguistic competence, explain the problems of immigrants in regard to language and culture. Acknowledging the over representation of immigrants among low achieving students, Dutch researchers, as Cummins (1989) in Canada, consider the most important element in the successful education of immigrants lay in the mastery of languages as an educational goal. Success depends on the degree of mastery in literacy of the primary language; however, resources are not identified to accomplish this goal. Equity in curriculum planning has not enabled immigrants to often achieve educational goals similar to the mainstream.

In numerous countries pilot educational incentives have been developed, such as Bilingual kindergartens in Belgium, native language schools in The Netherlands, and Finnish schools in Sweden. The magnitude of the problem surrounding the educational goal of language for minorities is controversial both in Europe and the United States. In the investigators' experience where literacy in the native language may not be prioritised as an educational goal due to political resource allocation, simply reinforcing language and empowering the community with genuine acceptance of the immigrant culture is often enough for successful academic achievement. An operational bilingual program is difficult to enact given resources and power relations. It is unlikely that the well-intended rhetoric of the EC Directive is in operation in any country in Europe.

In the teaching of culture there is a similar problem. If the OECD report (1989), *One School, Many Cultures* is reliable, the discussion is primarily academic, and 'for everywhere multicultural education is practically non-existent'. No one can deny the fact that a greater mingling of cultures creates the empathy and understanding necessary for multiculturalism. However, few communities are integrated in Europe. There are mostly pockets of racism, where the nationals wish to separate contact with the minority, especially in education because these schools are not desirable for host students.

The sociological implications of previous power relations between the majority culture and the countries from which the immigrants originate appear to be important in understanding the continued subordination or inequity. The position of religion in the culture is also a very important point in the immigrant's educational experience, which may inhibit success. Gender subordination in the Moslem faith causes problems for these students in achieving success with the curriculum. Communities dealing with these immigrants in order to promote educational access and equality in schooling must more keenly identify many special circumstances of culture.

Immigrants and school performance is an important issue for discussion in determining successful integration in the host country. Successive failure of immigrants in the majority schools often lead to the development of an underclass as is the case with migrant workers in Belgium (Eldering, L and Jo Kloprogge, 1983). This group experiences generational failure that creates a sense of helplessness explained by researchers as a psychological trait ascribable to lack of confidence. The school is said to exercise a therapeutic function. Others such as Ogbu (1991) attribute failure to society and continued reinforcement of the caste system - where immigrant minorities become caste-like after a few generations of failure when they perceive their situation as insurmountable because working in school does not contribute to eventual success in the dominant culture by obtaining desirable jobs. A civil society would not allow a system of castes to develop due to unequal attainments in school and society at large. The curriculum and programming used to assist minority immigrant students becomes critical in educational goal setting.

Another major area of academic rhetoric surrounding immigrants in Europe has been how to teach the children of the minority the skills, knowledge and competencies required to be successful in the majority culture while at the same time preserving their distinct linguistic and cultural identities. It is not clear that this rhetoric is useful to solving the situation of immigrants. Certainly schools must adopt diverse curriculum that is culturally sensitive to the diverse needs of students. However, the real question in schooling minority groups appears to be the policy of the institutions, such as the schools, which establish the rhetoric in relation to the immigrant minority communities themselves. Until researchers and immigrants alike begin to speak the 'same language' in regard to mainstream and minority social policy and educational goals, little will be accomplished. Merely changing curricular guidelines will not deal with the successive failure of minority students across generations. Researchers must begin to look at the existing realities in schools and districts that are required to adopt such policies and curriculum of interculturalism and bilingual education. Such factors as teachers attitudes and institutional failure must also be addressed.

Allocations of resources and resistance to policy and curriculum implementation seem to be the core of the problem. Bilingual programs that are deemed a failure are in actuality not true bilingual programs, because they lack qualified teachers and resources. Programs at the local level are often misinterpreted and substantive change does not occur. Much more research is needed in a comparative setting looking at immigrants internationally and exploring their unique sociological, cultural and historical experience in the context of the dominant majority culture. Experimental programs in Germany and the success of the Dutch policy are good places to begin exploring these dynamics and comparing to the situational variables of other areas. This study will add to that comparative literature by examining the situation in Norway based on the student situational factors and opportunities available for them to gain competencies.

2. Nature of Immigration from Pakistan to Norway

'It is good if I reach the target of my savings, before the children reach their school age, so they could start school in Pakistan and continue there. We are being discriminated in everyday life, in the labour market, and at the workplaces.' (Pakistani immigrant residing is Oslo since 1971) (Chauhdry, p. 90.)

In 1968 many western European countries began to tighten their borders to immigrants from the south. Consequently, immigrants sought out other labour markets, and Norway became a destination of choice. In 1966, it was also suggested by government officials and the Organisation for Economic Co-operation and Development (OECD) that Norway begin to look into a foreign import of labour. The first group of Pakistani immigrants came in the early 1970's from West Germany. In 1970, seven thousand work permits were issued to Pakistanis, and the number increased to ten thousand in 1971 (Kommunaldepartementet, 1990). The workers were easily absorbed in the Oslo job market. At this time Norwegian immigration laws were relaxed.

Prior to this immigration Norway can be characterised as a homogenous culture with very little diversity, except for the Sami population of Northern Norway. The Sami Nation, the ethnic minority people of Scandinavia, number approximately 30,000; however, estimates have gone as high as 50,000 (Koskinen, 1995). The Sami (also know as the Lapps) are an indigenous culture with their own language and customs. They have traditionally engaged in nomadic reindeer herding and other local crafts. Today a great number of the Sami people have assimilated to the mainstream Norwegian lifestyle. However, recent attempts have focused on cultural maintenance through mother tongue teaching and the establishment of unique Sami schools (Aikio, 1991).

The population of Norway is approximately 4.2 million of which 2 million 93 thousand are men and 2 million 140 thousand are women (Statistical Reports of the Nordic Countries, 1991). The land area is 325 thousand square kilometers, and it covers the longest and most dramatic coastline of Europe. Remoteness between city and countryside has always been an issue in the development of education.

Estimates by the OECD report of 1990 indicate that immigrants have not significantly changed the homogeneous picture of Norway. The number of immigrants from the south today reveals a number close to that of the Sami minority group, approximately 1% of the population. These immigrants are concentrated in the capital of Oslo. An additional 2% of the immigrant population come from Western Europe and the United States.

A major reason that the population has not been severely impacted by the rise of immigrants from the south is the freeze on immigration which occurred in 1975, not long after the first groups of men obtained work permits. Initially only Pakistani men came to work in Oslo to save money to return home. Eventually the wives and families followed, as jobs and homes were secured. In 1975, the government curtailed immigration to only those persons reuniting with families, having refugee status, and having specific expertise (especially in the growing North Sea oil industry). In 1976 these laws were even stricter making it very difficult to get a work permit in Norway without special circumstances.

Today, the situation of Pakistani immigrants can be distinguished as uncertain and confused. Initially Pakistani immigrant workers came to Norway with the hope of economic gain and eventual return to their homeland. Most engaged in a form of service work and some even started businesses, such as grocery stores. However, the reality of the numbers indicate that few returned, and most instead petitioned for their families to come to Norway.

Some Pakistani immigrants have sent their children home to go to school to maintain the traditional culture. However, some have now reacted to the difficulty of returning home by enrolling children in Norwegian schools so they may learn about the host society. School authorities have recognised the effects of home language and culture on education. Programs have been devised to deal with these needs in the compulsory grades 1-9 and in adult education classes. Some classes for all Pakistani girls have also been in operation to address unique cultural concerns (Riaz, 1994). Prior to this the Norwegian officials believed the Pakistanis to be 'guest workers', and no supports were available in the schools until mid 1980's because it was believed that most would soon return home.

The process of socialisation through the schools and cultural transformation of the Pakistani immigrant students has been discussed as 'stressful' by those from the culture. The contact of the two cultures has caused difficulties due to differences in equality of sexes, independence of women and girls, and other western norms that have left the students affected by the experience of schools. Norwegian officials are familiar with the minority issue from the situation of the Sami, and have attempted to make educational opportunities available to the Pakistanis to promote academic achievement. Have they significantly contributed to this aim from the Pakistani student perspective and what is the relationship between these opportunities and curriculum programs? This study will determine the effects of these variables.

3. Policy and Curriculum

Eide (1992), Randall (1991), Debeauvais (1992), and Skuttnabb-Kangas (1985) are researchers who actively acknowledge the growth of the immigrant and minority issues in Europe and advocate alternative and cooperative efforts to try and uproot the circumstances of minority citizens' lives. In the situation of Norway, there is not a great deal of evidence that shows the perspectives of the minority / immigrant in the context of experiences with the dominant culture. Given the fairly recent development of this issue, it is not unlikely that works are in progress. However, the researcher only encountered representatives from the Institute for Social Research engaged in the issue. Policy and curriculum formulation should prove to be very interesting given the prior experience with the Sami.

Norwegians should begin to educate themselves about the nature and context of immigration to the country to set goals for the educational system that might promote the equal attainments of these students. Given the current emphasis on Norwegians' attitudes toward the minority, it is evident education regarding 'difference' and 'other' is necessary to eliminate some of the social stigma associated with being an immigrant. Recent archival records from newspapers demonstrate reoccurring negative episodes with new immigrants. However, the *Stavanger Aftenblad* dated January 23, 1996 stated that the Cabinet Ministers' have adopted an action plan to combat racism and fear of foreigners. The party acknowledges that immigrant children are a new underclass and have set out to develop better integration and conditions for young immigrants and asylum seekers. This policy recognition is promising and warrants further attention. In addition to this policy, social scientists and practitioners should begin to merge understandings of Norwegians and a long history of egalitarian policy to encompass the minority as the point of research. It is at this juncture the researcher intended for the investigation of urban schools in Oslo to impact the culture, community, and key policy creators.

4. Subjects of the Study

The general population for the study was derived from the Pakistani immigrant group in Oslo with school-aged children in participating middle schools. A total of one hundred twenty five (125) subjects were formally interviewed for the study. The subjects were directly involved with the two selected schools. These subjects consisted of Pakistani students aged 13 to 16, their families, their teachers and the administrators. Subjects were also interviewed from the Oslo School Authority and the Royal Norwegian Ministry of Church, Education and Research. The sample population of formal interviews does not include the countless informal conversational interviews that took place during the five months of the ethnography. These conversations were of tremendous value. These 'informal spaces' were on the school grounds, as well as in the school community at activity clubs for youth, adult learning centres, immigrant women's networks, the local ethnic restaurants, the train and bus stops, the Children's Clinic, the nursery schools, the parent's homes, the parent's grocery stores, the Pakistani Student Society at the University of Oslo, and numerous social functions with teachers and administrators.

In addition, the investigator visited several key social agencies that impact the lives of Pakistani immigrants. These include the Social and Welfare Office, the Unemployment Office, the Urban Neighbourhood Committees, the Oslo Child Welfare Secretariat, the Directorate of Immigration, and the local Police Departments. The locations provided excellent spaces to evaluate the coordination of services for immigrant families. It also provided opportunities to verify information and informally discuss the context of the data. The data describing the question of educational opportunities are distinguished from the students' interviews from each school by their responses to items that related to curriculum, instruction, options support services, partnerships, and incentives.

The Oslo Suburb School

Twenty-two of the 29 Pakistani students at The Suburb School were interviewed. The demographic make-up of the middle school (grades 7-9; ages 13-16) is diverse, with 40% of the population coming from foreign countries. Two hundred and twenty students are split between eight classes of the 7th, 8th and 9th grade. The school has a separate class for minority-speaking pupils who need intensified language instruction in Norwegian. This 'reception' class in for newly arrived immigrants. There are ten students in this class. Students may also take Norwegian as a second language as opposed to Norwegian I. The two classes have equal status in the curriculum. The national origin of most of the students of foreign background is Pakistani and Vietnamese. There is a total of 22 different languages spoken at the school, including Arabic (Morocco), English (Ireland), Tamil (Sri Lanka), Vietnamese, Spanish (Chile & Peru & Dominion Republic), Turkish, Albanian, Somalian, Hungarian, German (Germany), Polish, Portuguese, Gambian, Setsuana (South Africa), Berber, and Eritrean. Twenty-nine of the eighty-eight minority language pupils are Pakistani. The largest group of foreign students is from Pakistan, 33%.

The school is situated in a suburb of Oslo in the northeastern section of the city, and it was built in 1972. During the fieldwork (April to October 1997) the school celebrated their 25 year anniversary. This city suburb is known for industrial factories and service industry jobs. The housing and apartments are middle to low-income to accommodate the local workers. Some residents commute to the Oslo City centre, twenty minutes by train, to work in service industry jobs.

Table 1 *Interview subjects of the Oslo Suburb school*

Pakistani Students	Pakistani Families	Teachers	Administrators/ Community Leaders
8 girls	16 mothers	8 female	3 female
14 boys	11 fathers	3 male	3 male
22	27	11	6
Total subjects = 66			

A total of sixty-six (66) subjects were interviewed at the Oslo Suburb school, surrounding community centres and the homes of the families.

The Oslo Inner City School

Pakistani students from The Inner City School were randomly selected to be interviewed. The demographic make-up of this middle school (grades 7-9; ages 13-16) is diverse, with 84% of the population coming from foreign countries. Three hundred and fifty-three students are split between the 7th, 8th and 9th grade. A total of 296 students are foreign born. Of these, approximately 60 % are of Pakistani origin.

The Inner City School is located in the inner-eastern section of the Oslo City centre. Unlike The Suburb School, this school has a long reputation as a working class middle school. Before becoming a 'immigrant school' it was characterised as a lower class inner-city school. Quickly, immigrants began to ghettoise themselves in this area due to government subsidies for apartments. Also, there are approximately 19 Mosques in this area of 10 city square blocks. This is the centre of the immigrant experience in Oslo, with many local groceries specialising in various country delicacies. Halal butchers are on every street corner, as is the cuisine of many nations.

Table 2 *Interview subjects of the Oslo inner city school*

Pakistani Students	Pakistani Families	Teachers	Administrators
10 girls	2 mothers	5 female	2 female
10 boys	3 fathers	1 male	2 male
20	5	6	4
Total subjects = 35			

A total of thirty-five (35) subjects were interviewed at the Oslo Inner City School, surrounding community centres and the homes of the families.

5. Educational Opportunities for Pakistani Students

In the introduction several factors were introduced that contribute to the successful schooling experience of immigrant minority pupils. Among these factors were primary language instruction (mother tongue teaching), teacher attitude in building trust, empowering pedagogy and assessment based on student experiences, real-life incentives for social promotion in and out of school, parent and community partnerships, and collaboratives that provide enhanced instruction and support. The analyses of the student perspectives of these factors are illustrated by their responses to several of the items in the interviews.

The following summaries describe the male and female student responses to questions dealing with educational opportunities in the Suburb School and Inner City School. These items specifically dealt with assistance and support at school, special programs, mother tongue instruction, parental involvement, after school and weekend activities, and concepts of social assistance and public services. The responses have been grouped into a narrative for each sub-topic of the research questions.

Male Responses to Educational Opportunities at the Suburb School

Assistance in School: All fourteen boys at the suburb school stated that they receive the help they need in school from their teachers, and ask for the help in subjects that they have difficulty. One student stated that he did not require help, so he did not need to ask the teachers for additional assistance. Another boy said that he had often gone to the Social Teacher (school counsellor and resource specialist) for problems he had with disciplinary actions. This student had been involved with the police because of graffiti painted on the school campus. He felt the Social Teacher helped him with the problem. All other boys acknowledged additional assistance to be sufficient from the teachers. Cross case analyses with teacher comments on similar questions reveal that some of these students do need a great deal of additional assistance. Some Pakistani boys deny that they have academic deficiencies, rather accepting their low performance because they enjoy other aspects of school.

Special Programs: The two boys who had lived in Norway for only two years both attend the reception language group. This group received the core curriculum - math, language, science, and social studies - with the support of the mother tongue teacher in Urdu. They also received intensive Norwegian instruction. These two students were mainstreamed for art, physical education, and home economics. Two other students were in special education classes because of an identified learning handicap. These two students received instruction in Norwegian, math, and English in a special reduced class-size support group with a special education teacher. Their other classes were mainstreamed with an elective class that the special education teacher instructed science and social studies. All these students were also enrolled in Norwegian as a Second Language. Four additional students were in this class instead of mainstream Norwegian. Six of the students were in the mainstream Norwegian class and did not attend any of the special programs at the school. The other eight attended the Norwegian as a Second Language class. Several stated they elected to do this because 'New Norwegian', a requirement in the curriculum of that course, was too difficult. They felt being in the Norwegian as a Second Language course would be easier for them. One of the students had a special behavioural modification program developed by the school social teacher. He was beginning to show improvement and would no longer require this supervision.

Mother Tongue Teaching: In general, the students stated they had from two to four years of Urdu instruction in the grades one to four. All students stated they could speak Urdu, but would have difficulty if asked to write the language. Table 3 displays the self-professed language abilities, years in Norway and the number of years in mother tongue instruction for the males at the Suburb School.

Table 3   *Years of mother tongue instruction in Urdu and student self-professed language ability relative to years in Norway for males at suburb school*

Subject number	Years in Urdu instruction	Language most proficient	Years living in Norway
54	5 yrs. in Pakistan; 2 yrs. Urdu support instruction - Norway	Urdu and Punjabi	2 years
24	7 yrs. in Pakistan; 2 yrs. Urdu support instruction - Norway	Urdu and Punjabi; 'Confident in Norwegian now'	2 years
18	2 yrs. Mother Tongue - 1st/2nd grades in Norway	Norwegian; 'Urdu is confusing, I mix it with my Norwegian'	13 years
6	2 yrs. Mother Tongue - 1st/2nd grades in Norway	Norwegian; '1st/2nd grade Urdu helped me to remember my language'	15.5 years
8	2 yrs. Mother Tongue - 1st/2nd grades in Norway; Father instructed Koran 4 yrs.	Urdu; 'I always speak Urdu, but Norwegian is also easy'	Born
11	4 yrs. Mother Tongue - 1st/4th grades in Norway	Norwegian; 'I have forgotten how to write, but I speak Punjabi with my friends'	13 years

Table 3

Subject number	Years in Urdu instruction	Language most proficient	Years living in Norway
17	2 yrs. Mother Tongue -1st/2nd grades in Norway; Mother instructed language	Same in Urdu & Norwegian; 'I didn't learn much in those 2 years but mother helped me keep it up'	Born
16	3 yrs. Mother Tongue 3rd-5th grades in Norway.	Norwegian and Punjabi; 'I can read and write in Norwegian but I speak Punjabi with family'	9 years
31	6 yrs. Mother Tongue -1st - 6th grade in Norway	Norwegian/Urdu 'I can write Urdu, and my mother helps me'	Born
33	None; just read the Koran with Father	Punjabi/Urdu; 'I cannot read Urdu, but like to speak Punjabi'	Born
34	2 yrs. Mother Tongue in Norway; started Koran, but quit	Norwegian/English; 'I did not learn the Urdu language. My parents had separated'	Born
55	2 yrs. Mother Tongue -1st/2nd grades in Norway	Norwegian/Urdu; 'I liked the Urdu teacher, but my Norwegian is best now'	13 yrs. 7 mths.
56	3 yrs. Mother Tongue -2rd-4th grades in Norway.	Urdu/Norwegian; 'I speak Punjabi with my family, and use Norwegian at school - both are easy for me'	11 years
59	3 yrs. Mother Tongue -2rd-4th grades in Norway; and Koran teaching at Mosquechool.	Urdu/Norwegian; 'I speak Urdu with family and use Norwegian and I feel I need more instruction in Urdu'	8 years

Ten of the fourteen boys either claimed they were most proficient in Norwegian or that both Norwegian and Urdu were equally as easy for them. Follow-up with parents and teachers did indicate that very few could read or write Urdu. Only in rare instances when the father or mother instructed at home could they become fully literate in Urdu. Most students spoke Punjabi, the local dialect of their region in Pakistan, on the schoolyard with friends. Parents used the local dialect of Punjabi in their communities. The more educated the family, the more frequent signs of Urdu instruction in the home. Most families did not speak the official language of Urdu, although the schools refer to Punjabi and Urdu as one in the same.

The boys took great pride in socialising in the language of Punjabi with their friends. In free periods, most male students were speaking their language. Only four of the boys held consistent with speaking Norwegian, and this became a characteristic of those attempting to assimilate to Norwegian life. These boys made clear distinctions between the language of school and language of the home. They emphasised the need to practice Norwegian to gain better vocabulary usage and proficiency.

All the boys seemed to value the mother tongue instruction in the elementary school years, but admitted that it did little to increase their literacy in Urdu. The language which they proclaim proficiency is Punjabi and this is an oral proficiency. The two boys who had only been in Norway for two years were making good progress in Norwegian. The oldest boy was able to express himself almost more fluently than those who had been in Norway since birth. The issues of language as a cultural element of being Pakistani will be discussed further in the family case studies. It is important to note that most of the students were in Norwegian as a Second Language Instruction even though most had been in Norway since birth or early childhood. The lack of adequate proficiency in Norwegian is a concern of many teachers. Students claim that they are fluent in Norwegian, but there are definite language deficits.

Support and Recognition in School: Twelve of the fourteen boys felt that they received the support and recognition they needed from the teachers in the school. Only two boys distinguished their status in the school as different from the mainstream Norwegians. As immigrants, they felt that the teachers treated them differently. One of the boys was in special education and felt his foreign status may have put him in this special class. He also had a long history of behaviour problems at the school. The other student took a more positive outlook stating, 'As a foreigner, I get special classes to help me do better with the Norwegian language'.

Parental Involvement: Seven of the fourteen boys stated that their parents never came to the school unless there was a problem. These students stated that neither parent spoke sufficient Norwegian to engage in dialogue at the school. The Urdu teacher would call the home and provide information when necessary. The students who parents were involved in the school attended the two parent conferences during the year. In all cases, the father attended these meetings because the mother could not speak Norwegian. There is sever lack of parental involvement at the school, and the students are aware that the problem is culturally and language determined.

Weekends and After School Activities: All of the boys engage in after school activities that involve family and friends. Four of the boys have weekend jobs delivering papers and advertisements in the neighbourhood to help support the family. Only three of the boys said that they do homework after school. The rest of the boys had other activities that involved - TV, helping in the home, soccer, parties, youth centre activities, computer games, and basketball. Only one student mentioned the Mosque as a weekend or after school activity. Some students take the train to the Oslo City centre on the weekends. Two students mentioned that they partied and had started drinking and going out with girls on the weekends. There are no additional structured activities for the students after school and on weekends, except for the sports clubs, which few are involved.

Concept of Norwegian Government and Social Policy: Four of the male students stated that they were unimpressed with the Norwegian Government. They said that there were many racist politicians who passed laws making life difficult for immigrants and foreigners. Four other boys had no comment on the status of Norway's policies and regulations regarding immigrants. Six of the boys felt that Norway had done a lot to help the status of immigrants and foreigners. Seven of the boys had a mother or father collecting a form of public assistance, either welfare of disability insurance.

Female Responses to Educational Opportunities at the Suburb School

Assistance in School: All the girls stated that they asked their teachers for assistance in school. Some girls always asked the teacher who is instructing the class because they felt comfortable asking for help. One girl asked her favourite teacher in the support class. Another girl asked the lead teacher for her grade level. Three girls specifically stated that they like their teachers. Another girl said she asked for help especially in Math because that subject was more difficult. Girls are more comfortable asking for help in school and take subject matter more seriously.

Special Programs: Seven of the eight girls were enrolled in Norwegian as a Second Language. One girl received special education support instruction in Norwegian lessons. Another girl received some help in Math by the support of Urdu primary language instruction. Most girls did not attend any special programs, but opted to take Norwegian as a Second Language as opposed to Norwegian I.

Mother Tongue Teaching: Most of the students stated they enjoyed speaking Urdu or Punjabi with their parents and friends. Some of the students go to special school after school to learn Urdu. One student stated she would like to read Urdu. Many students acknowledged that they could not read Urdu even though they received Koran teaching in Arabic since very young. Their fathers wanted this and had helped them to learn; however, one student stated that she was not really interested in this. Another girl liked to speak Norwegian most; but speaking Punjabi was easiest. This student also acknowledged that her written Norwegian was superior to Punjabi and Urdu. Half of the girls stated that they used to go to Koran school to learn to read and write Urdu. However, this did not occur any more. However, the girls did state they also learn Punjabi when they go home to speak Punjabi with Mom and Dad. Communicating in Punjabi was classified as fun. Most girls did state that Norwegian was also easy. One of the girls liked to learn Urdu in the Mosque but stated it is difficult. She said one of the mothers also works with us in small groups to test us in the language. In general, the girls believed that both Norwegian and Urdu are good to speak; however, it is complex to write Urdu. One student mentioned that Social Studies is difficult in Norwegian because her vocabulary was not so advanced in Norwegian as in Punjabi. Most of the girls qualified language into what that they liked to speak – Punjabi, what they could read easiest – Norwegian, and what their parents stressed as important – Urdu.

Support and Recognition in School: Six of the girls confirmed that they received the same support and recognition in school as their Norwegian peers. Two of the girls felt they somewhat received the same recognition and support as other students. These two girls had indecision in their eyes and felt in a way they may be treated different from the rest of the Norwegians. These were the same two girls who stated a political opinion on the Norwegian government and social system.

Parental Involvement: In all cases the fathers came to meetings at the school. The fathers came to the school for meetings and parties when they were pre-arranged and officially invited. All girls made it clear that the fathers came when called into a meeting or conference only for the purpose of discussing school progress. Three of the girls stated that parents do not come to school, but the father made special arrangements to come in to school to discuss the academic progress. Girls made no mention of the mothers having any contact with the school. This is a critical factor in the schooling of the Pakistani students.

Weekends and After School Activities: One girl said that they spend time with their Norwegian and Pakistani friends after school. Another girl visits Pakistani in the neighbourhood during the week, but does not go out on weekends. She said it is wrong to drink and party at discos like the Norwegian youth are doing. Many of the girls mentioned sewing workshops and homework as after school activities. Some of the girls go to the local activity centre to socialise with other youth. Other girls practice Urdu at home and stay with their mother. Many of the girls mentioned helping their mother in the home and preferring to stay at home. One girl liked to talk on the phone and visited friends together until 10pm only during the week. On Saturday she stayed home with mother to help in the home. She also went to youth clubs to dance and play billiards. Only a few of the girls watched TV, saying instead that they sit and talk with family and play with Pakistani friends after school. On weekends one of the girls visited the city centre. Most preferred to stay home. If they went any place on the weekend, it was with their mother to the sewing den or with girls in the neighbourhood. One girl played soccer only with girls after school. In general girls liked staying at home doing homework or helping mother in the home. During the summer the girls could go out; however, not during the winter when it is too dark. Girls had very few activities.

Concept of Norwegian Government and Social Policy: Two of the eight girls had not really thought about Norwegian government or politics. These two girls and another girl did mention the child subsidy that their family received each month to take care of expenses. This they liked. Another girl stated, 'There is discrimination towards the Pakistani. I feel like the Norwegians and want to be accepted like them'. Only one student did not receive help from the government. Most of the girls stated they did not really understand politics and had not much thought about this. Two girls said they were not interested, but their father gives

Table 4   *Years of mother tongue instruction in Urdu and student self-professed language ability relative to years in Norway for females at suburb school*

Subject number	Years in Urdu instruction	Language most proficient	Years living in Norway
29	2.5 yrs. in Pakistan; 2 yrs. Urdu support instruction - Norway	Urdu Norwegian/English are mixed.	13 years
30	3yrs. Urdu Mother Tongue -2nd-4th grade in Norway	Punjabi and Urdu, 'Norwegian is getting better'	12 years
23	2 yrs. Mother Tongue -1st/2nd' grades in Norway. Koran Urdu teaching.	Norwegian 'I speak Punjabi with my Parents'	Born
26	3 yrs. Mother Tongue 1st-3rd grades in Norway	Norwegian; 'Urdu teaching helped me to remember my language'	Born
35	3 yrs. Mother Tongue 1st-3rd grades in Norway; In Mosque instructed Koran.	Urdu & Punjabi, 'I am not able to read it very well'	Born
50	3 yrs. Mother Tongue -1st-3rd grades in Norway. Koran School Instruction	Urdu/Norwegian; 'I speak Punjabi with my friends, but not write'	Born
25	2 yrs. Mother Tongue -1st/2nd grades in Norway; Read Urdu at home with family	Norwegian/Urdu 'I speak both well, but cannot write Urdu. Punjabi is popular to speak as well.'	Born
14	3 yrs. Mother Tongue 1st-3rd grades in Norway. Read Koran with family.	Norwegian and Punjabi; 'Both languages are equally easy'	8 years

much advice. These two girls had opinions based on what parents talk about. These girls said there maybe discrimination, and they did not like politics in Norway. One of these girls stated, 'Karl I. Hagen (Conservative Party Leader) should not be that way. He is against immigrants, and he should not think that. He can move if he wants to. We are Norwegian too.'

Male Responses to Educational Opportunities at the Inner City School
Assistance in School: One student stated that sometimes help was available from the teachers. Another student indicated that he rarely received some help from the teachers. He has a friend who is smart in Math and assisted with the assignments. Five of the boys indicated that they ask the teachers for help and that they get the assistance they need. One student stated he did not go to the 'homework help class' after school like other students who need help. Another boy confirmed that the teacher helps him, but that it was not that much help. One boy said that most of the assistance with schoolwork came from home. Finally, one boy stated that he did not do the work in school because he did not understand and did not like to study.

Special Programs: One student participated in the alternative school workshop that focused on learning a trade. Five students were part of this program that met on Wednesdays and Thursdays to learn the trade of auto and bike mechanics. Other days these students attended the regular instruction in the classes at school. This particular student requested the alternative school. He was not sure why his grades were poor in the other classes, but he wanted to be in the alternative school. Five of the students were in Norwegian as a Second Language. One of these students stated he might later do the Norwegian I class. Another of these students received resource assistance in English and Norwegian as a Second Language. A student mentioned the special sculpture elective as a special program. One of these boys took Norwegian as a Second Language in a special reception class to learn more vocabulary. Three other boys were in the Norwegian I class, which is not a special program. However, one of these boys did get extra resource assistance in the Norwegian I class. Another student mentioned he got special assistance in math support class with three other boys,

Mother Tongue Teaching: One student said he was not so good in Urdu but claimed this was his best language. Often there appears to be a conflict with what the boys speak, either Punjabi or Urdu, and their written language, Norwegian. One of the boys said his mother taught him Urdu, but he was most comfortable speaking in Norwegian and Punjabi. He also preferred to write in Norwegian. Another student spoke both Norwegian and Urdu with short responses. He was clearly uncomfortable with the questions being asked of him. Another student did not like Urdu primary language instruction. However, another stated he liked to learn Urdu and this was the easiest language to speak. It is likely he was referring to Punjabi that was easier to speak. Few students speak Urdu. One of the boys said he learned to write a little Urdu, but was more comfortable in writing Norwegian. A student said that he spoke Urdu and English, two official languages of Pakistan, with his parents, and Punjabi to his friends. He also practised Norwegian at home with his parents. Still another student valued learning Urdu, but acknowledged that he needed help to write the language. Only one boy said Urdu is the easiest to speak but used Norwegian at home to practice. Most of the Inner City School boys classified Urdu as very difficult to learn and Punjabi easy to speak. Most had Urdu teaching and cannot write a word of the language. Most boys had forgot all that they learned in Urdu, and prefer to speak Punjabi.

Support and Recognition in School: Four of the boys said they did obtain the same support and recognition in school as other students. One boy said that he received more support from the good teachers. Another stated that some of the teachers to support and recognise them. Two boys stated that there was some racism and that support was not the same. These two students felt that some Norwegians were racist. Another student stated that teachers 'did not have much respect for us'. He said, 'Teachers always blame me for doing something wrong.' A final student did also agree that they were not treated the same as other students.

Parental Involvement: One boy said, 'My mother comes to school with my brother who is twenty-four years old. His job is to translate for her because she does not know how to speak Norwegian.' Another student's father checks on his son at school often. He is worried something might happen to him at school, and he is very strict. The rest of the fathers only came for the parent meetings that are scheduled twice a year for parents to discuss with teachers the student progress. The majority of boys stated that their father only came for the parent meeting when formally invited. The father visited the school and the doctor's or other official offices because the mothers do not speak Norwegian well. The emphasis of parent involvement was seen as the formal invitation to conferences at the school. Because fathers speak Norwegian, mothers were rarely seen on campus. Parents seldom came to the school to visit or participate in their child's learning outside of the formal parent teacher conference.

Weekends and After School Activities: The boys mentioned a variety of weekend and after school activities. Three of them participated in training for a local basketball team. Another two boys did participate in other sports such as swimming and soccer. Only two of the boys mentioned studying or doing homework as an after school or weekend activity. Three boys went to youth clubs on the weekends near their home. Two of the boys mentioned visiting other Pakistani families in their free time. Two of the boys revealed taking care of the family and staying home on weekends. Three boys mentioned going to the movies with family or friends. Two boys went shopping on the town with friends. One of them said that he could do whatever he wanted as long as he told his parents where he was going. Four of the boys went to nightclubs in town and sometimes to parties on the weekends. One of these boys went to the club because his older brother knew the doorman to get in free. Two of the boys had a paper route job after school to earn extra money. The one boy delivered advertisements to earn money for himself. Most boys enjoyed being friends and getting together with siblings.

Concept of Norwegian Government and Social Policy: The Inner City School boys had varied responses to concepts of Norwegian government and social policy. One of the students believed the Norwegian system was good because his mother received a disability pension. Another student liked the labour party and youth party movement because he could follow what was going on in politics. He also appreciated the pension that his family received. Yet another boy only knew of the labour party and had little comment. Four other boys stated that they liked

Table 5 *Years of mother tongue instruction in Urdu and student self-professed language ability relative to years in Norway for males at inner city school*

Subject number	Years in Urdu instruction	Language most proficient	Years living in Norway
2	3 yrs. Mother Tongue- 1st-3rd grades in Norway.'	Urdu and Punjabi 'I am good speaking Urdu, but not so good writing Norwegian'	Born
3	4 yrs. Mother Tongue 1st-4th grade in- Norway; Mother taught me Urdu.	Urdu & Norwegian; 'I speak Urdu well, but I write best in Norwegian.'	9 years
12	4 yrs. Mother Tongue -1st-4th grades in Norway	Norwegian and Urdu Student had difficulty articulating.	Born
13	2 yrs. Mother Tongue -4th/5th grades in Norway	Norwegian/English & Urdu; 'Urdu instruction was not useful'	Born
14	2 yrs. Mother Tongue -1st/2nd t grades in Norway.	Urdu; 'It was good to get Urdu instruction; I can now read the Koran along'.	Born
15	2 yrs. Mother Tongue -5th/6th grades in Norway	Norwegian; 'I learned to read and write a little Urdu'	Born
16	3 yrs. Mother Tongue -1st-3rd grades in Norway	English/Norwegian & Urdu; 'Father helped me learn English; don't know Urdu too well'	Born
17	1/2 yrs. Mother Tongue -4th grade in Norway; Koran' reading for 8 years with father.	Urdu & Norwegian; 'Would like to know how to write Urdu better'	Born
18	2 yrs. Mother Tongue instruction, 3rd/4th grades-too difficult.	Punjabi & Norwegian 'Urdu is too difficult'	Born
19	2 yrs. Mother Tongue -1st/2nd grades in Norway.'	Punjabi & Norwegian 'I cannot write a word of Urdu, too difficult'	8 years

the Labour Party in Norway. One boy in particular gave a very smart analysis of the new coalition government of centre parties having difficulty coming to consensus. He would rather see a labour party in power. Another boy who mentioned he liked the government also discussed his dislike of Karl I. Hagen, a conservative politician. He said that this politician was the one against criminals and immigrants. 'He wants to stop the foreigners from coming to this country' said the boy. Another student also said the Conservative Party is racist and that the public often throws tomatoes at Karl I. Hagen when he speaks. This student' parent also goes to unemployment courses for learning new skills and receives a stipend. Another boy said that he liked the labour party because they did not distinguish between a 'dark or blond issue: to them we are all Norwegians.' His sister is also on disability since she lost her fingers in a meatpacking factory. A final boy did not really think about politics, however; he acknowledged that his mother goes to Norwegian classes and his father gets a pension since he is retired. In general the Oslo Inner City School boys had much more interest and had developed opinions about politics than the Oslo Suburb School students.

Female Responses to Educational Opportunities at Inner City School
Assistance in School: Five of the girls stated they received the help they need from teachers who were willing to answer questions. Some of the girls stated that they did not need the 'Homework Help Course' after school and others said that they received assistance, but it was not always necessary. One girl stated that the teachers ask if they need help and that would make it easier to get assistance in school. Four of the girls were more negative about the support they received in school. One girl stated she did not get much help, but that the women teachers did often ask if they needed more time on lessons. Another girl said that students are constantly talking back to teachers in class and this prevents the teacher from helping others. A girl also said that they (the girls) need an *all-girls* school because they would have more freedom to be involved in school and get help. She also said that the teachers do not always have time to answer questions. Another girl said that students have much more respect at schools in Pakistan. This same girl said that she has no problem asking for help, and that one of her girl friends assisted her. However, like another student she felt she needed to do most of the work herself.

Special Programs: Four girls took Norwegian as a Second Language. Three girls attended Norwegian I course. One girl had no answer. Two girls attended the language reception class because they had no school prior to coming to Norway. Three of the girls were part of a special program to make food in the canteen for students during and after school

Mother Tongue Teaching: One student spoke more in Urdu and Punjabi than Norwegian. In 4th grade this girl went to the language 'reception class' because she had just moved from Pakistan. Another students' mom and dad helped with Urdu instruction in school, and this girl claimed to be comfortable in both Norwegian and Urdu. One student claimed to be fluent in Norwegian because she could write and speak the language. Similarly, another girl had just learned a few words in Urdu, but stated that she was equally good in Norwegian and

Urdu. This is unlikely, but due to the strong cultural identity linked to language students are quick to claim this. One student asserted that she read Urdu, and could write Norwegian, although Urdu was claimed to be equally easy overall. Another girl claimed that speaking good Norwegian was important for equality and to become rich. She said Urdu was difficult and the Koran too strict. Another girl said Urdu was too hard, and she was most at ease in Norwegian. This was true for most of the girls who did not learn much Urdu and found it too complex and strict. One girl summed up the experience well, 'Father shows us how to read but it is too difficult. I can do both languages equally well, but I speak Urdu to my parents and other adults.'

Support and Recognition in School: Five girls said they get the same support in school as other girls. Two of the girls were not sure of the recognition question. Four other girls said that they did not get the same recognition in school from their teachers. One girl made reference to her father not speaking to her brothers who did not complete the high school. She spoke of some racism because Pakistanis are singled out for trouble.

Parental Involvement: Two girls said, 'My father is the only one to come for the school meetings.' One more girl said her father comes for parent night and that is not often. Three other girls said parents come only to the meetings at school. Another student said that her parents were not involved, and the teachers only send letters home for being bad not good. Two girls said that their parents did not come to school, only for parent meetings. A final girl said that her dad came for meetings, but 'I am not a problem so he does not come so often.'

Weekends and after school Activities: Girls did not participate in many activities. Most of the girls stated that they help their mother. One girl helped in the local grocery we own. She also liked to watch TV, make food, do homework, and play with her friend from Sir Lanka. One girl did go to the Mosque five times a week to read the Koran, otherwise she had to stay home with her parents most of the time. Some girls visited Pakistani families in the neighbourhood. Many mentioned doing homework, going to the library and taking care of smaller siblings. In general, the girls were not allowed to go out and had to stay close to home with their mother. Some girls did go to music concerts, but were not allowed to go into the Oslo Parks. Girls were not allowed to go to town with friends, especially at night when the bars are open. One girl claimed that, 'we are not to have fun, and have to stay at home with mom to help. Sometimes I can go to a new film, Another girl stated that she could do nothing with Norwegians except in Gjovik, a rural town. I did have Norwegian friends and so did my parents. We did things together.

Concept of Norwegian Government and Social Policy: Three girls believed that the government did a good job. Two of these parents received a pension from the government. The other girl who supported the social policies said that her parents did not need help from the government, but knew that it was there if they did need anything. Five other girls did not think about the concepts of social policy and government assistance. Another girl said that the government makes promises that are not followed. One of the girls discussed her father's political views. He voted the conservative right wing party, but she did not know too

Table 6   *Years of mother tongue instruction in Urdu and student self-professed language ability relative to years in Norway for females at inner city school*

Subject number	Years in Urdu instruction	Language most proficient	Years living in Norway
1	3 yrs. in Pakistan; 1 yr. Urdu support instruction Norway	Urdu and Punjabi; Norwegian last.	5 years
4	7 yrs. in Pakistan; 2 yrs. Urdu support instruction - Norway	Urdu and Punjabi; 'Confident in Norwegian now'	Born
5	2 yrs. Mother Tongue -1st/2nd grades in Norway	Norwegian; 'Urdu is confusing. I mix it with my Norwegian'	13 years
6	2 yrs. Mother Tongue -1st/2nd grades in Norway	Norwegian; '1st/2nd grade Urdu helped me to remember my language'	15.5 years
7	2 yrs. Mother Tongue - 1st/2nd grades in Norway; Father instructed Koran 4 yrs.	Urdu; 'I always speak Urdu, but Norwegian is also easy'	Born
8	4 yrs. Mother Tongue -1st-4th write, grades in Norway	Norwegian; 'I have forgotten how to but I speak Punjabi with my friends'	13 years
9	2 yrs. Mother Tongue -1st/2nd grades in Norway; Mother instructed language	Same in Urdu & Norwegian; 'I didn't learn much in those 2 years but mother helped me keep it up'	Born
11	3 yrs. Mother Tongue -3rd-5th grades in Norway.'	Norwegian and Punjabi; 'I can read and write in Norwegian, but I speak Punjabi with family'	9 years
10	3 yrs. Mother Tongue -2nd to 4th grade in Norway	Norwegian & Urdu; 'I did not understand much in Urdu. Just some words'	10 years born in Germany
20	3 yrs. Mother Tongue -2nd to 4th grade in Norway.	Norwegian & Urdu; 'Don't know Urdu so well. My father helps me to read it'	

much about it. She said that he attends employment training and believes these programs to be good.

5. General Student Perceptions

A total of 42 students were interviewed at both schools. Students were asked questions regarding their schooling experience in Norway and subsequent socialisation and satisfaction with school. Current findings suggest satisfaction by students with their experience in Norway. Those that reported they enjoyed school and felt that they benefited from the experience also revealed the lowest grades. This was the tendency for most of the boys. The boys did not study as many hours as the girls did. The girls studied more and were serious about school.

The student responses were broken delineated by gender and type of school. Most of the girls in the Suburb School felt that they did receive recognition and support from their teachers. They did not have to go to special programs and were comfortable asking for assistance in school. The boys at the suburb school did not ask for assistance, but required more help in school. The boys were in special programs for identified learning handicaps and behavioural problems. Most of the boys at the Inner City School asked for assistance and were confident in the support they received in school. The boys did attend special alternative programs to learn a trade. All students stated they preferred learning Norwegian as a second language as opposed to Norwegian I. This was considered more difficult. The girls in the Inner City School had much confidence in asking for assistance, although they would prefer to have all-girls programs where they would be able to ask for more help and receive individualised attention

All girls and boys indicated that their friends were of many cultures. When asked about Norwegian friends, they indicated these were the Norwegians in their class. However, in free time after school they did not interact with Norwegians. Some of the boys who were involved in soccer or other sports did engage in activity with Norwegians after school. However, the majority of the students and their families stayed isolated within the sub-culture of the immigrants in the local community. When asked about after school activities, all boys were lacking in mentioning homework. Girls frequently mentioned homework as an after school and weekend activity. Most girls had to stay home and be close to their mother. Girls from the Inner City School mentioned that if they had all-girls activities they would be able to be more active. Boys had an abundance of activities with their Pakistani male friends. Girls remain more isolated.

Students referred to Urdu as the language they speak most frequently with parents as a sign of respect; Punjabi on the schoolyard with their friends and Norwegian was the language that they could read and write. Only five students claimed to read and write Urdu. Parents teach their children in the Mosque, and several of the students had been recent immigrants and had attended over 6 years of school in Pakistan. In general, students in the Inner City school had a better identify related to their language than the Suburb students.

Parental involvement was lacking at both schools. Parents visited the schools when formally invited or if problems occurred in the classroom. Mothers rarely attended meetings at the school because of the language barrier. Fathers and older siblings visited the schools for conferences on student progress.

Students viewed policy and curriculum determined by the government to be generally good. Inner City students had a stronger sense of politics and their place as immigrants did in the Norwegian society. Students had views of what the government could do for them and what politicians might be helpful to their cause. Suburb students did not have clear understandings of social and curricular impacts on their education. These students tended to view their experiences as mainstream more Norwegian.

6. Conclusion and Implications for Education

Specifically, the Pakistani student evidence described a lack of integration of students to the mainstream population. It will be necessary for Norwegian educational policy makers to maintain caution when discussing aspects of schooling which address integration. What is apparent from this research is the conflict between the family's emphasis on enculturation (learning the first culture, Pakistani values) and the Norwegian educational goals of assimilation or integration. Responses to questions regarding levels of acculturation (learning the second culture, Norwegian customs) indicate that Pakistani students are experiencing conflict in reconciling the differences between parent expectations and schooling. Second generation Pakistani-Norwegian students are struggling with social identity in school and the one which they must maintain in the home and their extended community. Adapting their behaviours to the local Norwegian lifestyle for purposes of schooling appears to have made assimilation fragmented. They have not totally integrated because the family preservation is extremely relevant.

Students do not take the mainstream courses, opting for Norwegian as a Second Language. Boys attend alternative programs, and girls feel that to be successful they need to attend all-girls schools. Concepts of opportunity and equity become challenged when differences are apparent in the schooling experience of the Pakistani students. Language instruction has left most students in the Suburb School, both girls and boys, with a loss of identify. Urdu has become irrelevant as a language of communication. However, with Inner City students it is still used as a sign of respect to parents and older Pakistani community members. Identity and fluency in the native language would most likely provide competency for all students in the mainstream knowledge of becoming Norwegian. Most students appear to lack this connection, and find the language to be separate and unique identity to their own culture. Language policy has not significantly increased opportunities for success for students. Schooling has also isolated the family from the socialisation process and not enabled the students and their parents to become competent citizens.

The students often relate their success in school to the local Norwegian standards, where as the family members maintain levels of accomplishment based on standards in Pakistan. There are subtle differences, and in both there is a sense of failure for students due to an inability to accomplish either. While the family has high standards for education for their children, it is only within the context of traditional Pakistani roles for men and women. As Norwegian policy makers negotiate multicultural education and concepts of integration, it would be wise to keep in mind the power of families in determining the path of second generation immigrants. The parents of Pakistani-Norwegian students lack formal experiences with education and the information to empower their children within the mainstream system. Necessary accommodations should be made to build on the strengths of the families to familiarise them with the schools to better prepare the students for success.

References

Aikio, M., (1991). The Sami language: Pressure of change and reification. *Journal of Multilingual and Multicultural Development*. 12 (1&2), 93-103.

Cummins, J., (1986). Empowering Minority Students: A Framework for Intervention. *Harvard Educational Review,* 56 (1).

Cummins, J., (1989). *Empowering minority students.* Sacramento: Xalifornia Association for Bilingual Education.

Debeauvais, M., (1992). Outcasts of the year 2000: A challenge to education in Europe. *Comparative Education*. 28 (1), 61-69.

Eide, K., (1992). The future of European education as seen from the north. *Comparative Education*, 28 (1), 9-17.

Eide, K., (1983). A researcher's assessment of the autonomy problem. In *The education of minority groups: An enquiry into the problems and practices of fifteen countries*. Organisation for Economic Co-operation and Development, England, Gower Pub. Co. Ltd.

Eldering, L. and Kloprogge, Jo, (1989). *Different Cultures Same School - Ethnic Minority Children in Europe*. Swets North America Inc., Berwyn, PA.

Fetterman, D.M., (1984). *Ethnography in educational evaluation*. Beverly Hills, Sage Publications.

Gibson, M.A. & Ogbu, J.U. (Eds.), (1991). *Minority Status and Schooling: A Comparative Study of Immigrant and Involuntary Minorities*. New York & London, Garland Publishing, Inc.

Husen, T., (1993). Schooling in modern Europe - Exploring major issues and their ramifications. *International Review of Education*. 39(6): 499-509.

Husen, T.,A.Tuijnman, & Halls, W.D. (Eds.), (1992). Schooling in modern *European society A report of the Academia Europaea*. Oxford, Pergamon Press.

Husen, T. & Opper, S., (1993). *Multicultural and Multilingual Education in Immigrant Countries*. Wenner-Gren Centre International Symposium, Stockholm, 1982, Pergamon Press, Oxford.

Kommunaldepartementet, (1990). *Norsk innvandringspolitikk og EFs indre marked.* (Norwegian immigrant policy and the European Union's internal market) Oslo, Otto Falch A/S.

Koskinen, A., (1995). Language policy towards ethnic minorities in northern Norway and on the Atlantic coast of Nicaragua. *International Journal of Educational Development.* 15 (3), 221-230.

Lather, P., (1986). Research as praxis. *Harvard Educational Review.* 56(3), 257-277.

Lauglo, J., (1995). Populism and education in Norway. *Comparative Education Review.* 39 (3), 255-279.

Nordisk Statistical Secretariat, (1991). *Educational Indicators in the Nordic Countries: Describing educational status and student flows.* Copenhagen, 56, Statistical Reports of the Nordic Countries.

OECD, (1990 & 1978). *Reviews of National Policies for Education: Norway.* Paris, OECD Publications.

Randall, S., (1991). Europe's Thirteenth State: 1992 and Europe's Minority Communities, *Adults Learning.* 2 (8), 222-224.

Riaz, N., (1994). *A comparative study of Pakistani high school girls' education in Oslo.* Unpublished doctoral dissertation. Educational Research Institute, University of Oslo, Oslo, Norway.

Skutnabb-Kangas, T., (1981). Guest worker or immigrant - Different ways of reproducing an underclass. *Journal of Multilingual and MulticulturalDevelopment.* 2 (2), 89-115.

Skutnabb-Kangas, T., (1985). Who wants to change what and why - Conflicting paradigms in minority education research. In Skutnabb-Kangas, T. & Phillipson, R (Eds.) *Educational Strategies in Multilingual Contexts.*

Tjeldvoll, A., (1995, March). *Quality of Equality? Scandinavian Education Towards Year 2000.* Paper presented at the annual meeting of the Comparative and International Education Society, Boston, MA.

Wirt, Frederick, (1979). The Stranger within my gate: Ethnic minorities and School Policy in Europe, *Comparative Education Review.* 23:17-40.

Yin, R.K., (1994). *Case study research: Design and methods.* Thousand Oaks, CA, Sage Publications.

Acknowledgements

This research was sponsored by the generous support of a Norwegian-Marshall Fund Award from the Norge-Amerika Forening (Norwegian-American Association).

13

University Selectivity and Employment: A Comparison Between British and French Graduates

Jake Murdoch, Jean-Jacques Paul & Julien Zanzala

1. Introduction

Research into graduate employment has become more and more frequent over the last twenty years. In France, many studies have been carried out either on a local basis by universities, or on a national one by 'l'Observatoire des Entrées dans la Vie Active', which belongs to the Cereq. In the United Kingdom for the last fifteen years all universities have carried out their own surveys on the employment of their graduates in the framework of a national survey centralised, first by the 'University Statistical Record' and then by the 'Higher Education Statistics Agency'.

Often results into graduate employment focus on differences between subject areas or levels of study but do not take into account the differences that exist inside a given subject area or level of study. These studies ignore the fact that there can be a variation in graduate employment linked to individual characteristics (gender, social background), as well as ones linked to different higher education institutions. Indeed, a part of the differences in employment prospects could be explained by the differences in quality of the courses taught and the curriculum given at the different institutions. This matter is important from an 'equity' point of view.

The idea of differences in quality is reinforced by the occasional publication of so-called 'University league tables' in the United Kingdom as well as in France. The aim of the article is thus to analyse to what extent we can estimate the impact of an 'institutional ' effect on graduate employment in two countries that have different forms of higher education organisation, i.e. the United Kingdom and France.

First we shall discuss quickly the theoretical framework of such a question and present the studies already carried out on this theme. Then we shall reiterate the different types of entry into higher education in the United Kingdom and in France. Finally we shall present the data used, the different variables taken into account and the results of the models. In conclusion we shall compare the models tested in each of the two countries.

2. Studies on the effect of the quality higher education institutions on employment prospects

Theoretical framework

There are differences in the extent at which higher education institutions select students for entry into different courses. These differences in selection can be linked to national rulings (French *universités* are not allowed to select students on entering the first year at an *université*) or to the particular policies of the institutions. This raises the question: To what extent is it better to select students on entering higher education?

If we assume that there is a difference in the academic level of students on entering higher education, we can also assume that certain institutions can attempt to select the best of the students in order to promote more demanding teaching. This in turn would enable the students to reach a high level of the knowledge. The other institutions would take on the other students and would adapt their teaching to the ability of their students, who in this case would reach a lower level of knowledge (only if the financial resources of the latter institutions are the same as those of the former). If there is indeed a matching between the academic level of the students and the teaching demands of the institutions, reputation differences between the different institutions become very noticeable. This system appears to be more efficient due to the fact that if teaching is adapted to the ability of the students, the system produces a lower rate of drop outs than a system where selection takes place more during the course of study than on entry.

However, selecting students on entry has the disadvantage of tying individual prospects strongly with students' grades at the end of secondary school. This system may be more efficient but less equitable, as long as institutions who take on the students with a lower academic level, do not receive more teaching funds.

We can ask ourselves if employers believe the selection processes to be justified. Indeed, to what extent do employer take notice of the self-ranking of the institutions? Do graduates from the most selective institutions have better employment prospects?

The answers to these questions do not however allow us to judge the teaching that takes place. We can argue that the students' good academic level on entering higher education means that the institutions in question do not have to have a higher level of teaching. Indeed, the students' academic level at the end of secondary school and social background are very often strongly linked. The function of selecting students on entering higher education has thus more a function of social reproduction than of academic one, which has consequences on the equity of the system.

French and British universities differ in their selection methods of students on entry into higher education. French universities can only select their students at the level of the maîtrise or more especially at the level of the DEA/DESS, whereas British universities select their students on entry into higher education. To what extent do these different practices have an effect on the integration in labour market, i.e. to what extent do British and French employers take notice of the differences in the degrees of selection carried out by the universities?

These questions echo the already long-dated discussions by educational economists, which oppose the human capital theory with the filter theory.

If we consider either the human capital or filter theory, we can assume that if there are differences in the quality of educational institutions. These differences could have consequences on the employment prospects of their graduates. Indeed, according to the human capital theory, education increases individual productivity and thus the labour value of a person receiving training. If certain institutions offer better quality teaching (i.e. they have more competent teaching staff, better teaching resources (lower pupil/teacher ratios, better stocked libraries, easily accessible computer hardware and software, etc.), up to date and demanding course material and a good working atmosphere), their graduates will be more productive and receive better wages than the graduates from institutions of a lesser quality, all other things being equal.

For the filter theory frame of reference the education system seeks instead to select individuals according to their intrinsic skills and competences, rather than develop others. In this case, the best quality institutions will be those who attract the individuals whose intrinsic skills are valued most by employers. Up to a certain point, there is no need for there to be any real differences in the quality of the courses taught. There only needs to be a screening or filter mechanism that picks out the right individuals. Entry requirements heavily linked to social background (for example high inscription fees), or heavily linked with skills previously singled out (past grades and institutions attended), can serve as a filter mechanism.

For the human capital theory the difference in the quality of the course taught leads clearly to skill and competence differences, however for the filter theory, it is more of a case of 'wishful thinking': all it takes is for us to believe that an institution is better for it to attract the applicants whose profile fits best the one expected.

The question here is whether in the United Kingdom and in France there are differences in the employment prospects linked to the quality of the higher education institution attended. This question is pertinent in as far as little research has been carried out in the field of economics or sociology (and even less as far as France and the United Kingdom are concerned) and where the entry requirements are different in these two countries.

Studies already carried out in the field

There have been a dozen or so studies on the effect of the quality higher education institutions on graduate employment; a large majority dealing with the United States. There have been various variables indicating institutional quality and also rather contradictory results.

We can single out five groups of variables indicating institutional quality: the budget per student of the institutions; the status of institutions (research oriented institutions vs. teaching institutions in the U.S.A., universities vs. polytechnics in the United Kingdom, Universitäten vs. Fachhochschulen in Germany); entry requirements of institutions; size of institutions; student/teaching staff ratios.

Whereas budget per student has positive and significant impact on graduate wages according to Wachtel (1976), this impact is less important according to Morgan and Duncan (1979), and even insignificant according to James et al. (1989) when individual or course characteristics variables are taken into account as well labour market variables.

As far as the status of institutions is concerned, Solmon and Wachtel (1976) find that graduates from 'research oriented institutions' have higher wages, though according conclusions of James et al. (1989), the effect is insignificant. The latter show also a positive and significant effect on wages of diplomas awarded at private institutions on the east coast of the United States; but this effect is greatly reduced when course characteristics are taken into account.

In the United Kingdom according to Brennan et al. (1996), graduates from universities have on average higher wages to those from polytechnics. Though if social background, degree class and subject area are controlled for, the difference is much less important. In Germany according to the same authors, there is on average a slight positive wage difference for graduates from Universitäten in relationship to those from Fachhochschulen, which becomes even less pronounced when subject area is considered.

Studies taking into account entry requirements show a positive and significant effect of the variable in question on wages (be they the studies by Morgan and Sirageldin (1968), Reed and Miller (1970), Wales (1973), Morgan and Duncan (1979), James et al. (1989) in the United States or Roizen and Jepson (1983) in the United Kingdom). Though this effect is reduced and even disappears according to Reed and Miller (1970) and according to James et al. (1989) when variables linked to individual characteristics of the graduates (grades on entry, social background, subject area) are introduced.

The effect of the size of the institution is slightly significant according to James et al. (1989), however, the effect of student/teaching staff ratio is positive but insignificant.

3. Entry requirements to higher education in France and the United Kingdom

Entry into higher education in France is different to that of the United Kingdom. In France there coexists a selective sector of entry to higher education alongside an open access one. The selective sector of entry to higher education is made up of classes *préparatoires aux écoles d'ingénieurs*, *classes préparatoires aux écoles de commerce* (preparatory schools for science and business schools) and the latter schools themselves. The open access sector accounts for most of the université departments.

In the United Kingdom entry into higher education is selective and is based on A-level exam grades at the end of secondary education. In fact the institutions fix the minimal number of A-level required to enter each of their departments. Thus certain more prestigious universities can be more selective than others (this selectivity maintaining their prestige). Also at a same university the selectivity can vary from one department to another.

In France given that the *universités* cannot legally select their students at the level of first year courses, it is likely that the school grades of the students vary little from one institution to another. Despite open access, in France, into first year courses at *universités*, there is a different picture in the higher levels. Indeed, entry into some *maîtrises* (which corresponds to the fourth year of study at an *université*) can be limited and give rise to selection of the students beforehand. In addition, entry into troisième cycle, i.e. *diplôme d'étude approfondie* (DEA) and *diplôme d'études supérieures spécialisées* (DESS) is systematically selective and based on a dossier and an oral interview.

There is a true national examination system at the end of secondary school in France (the 'baccalauréat') and in the United Kingdom (A-level exam) which gives a standardised measure academic level of the pupils. This is not the case for higher education. We can thus look to identify the quality of the graduates from the higher education institutions by using the quality of the students on entry.

Though the question of the impact of the quality of higher education institutions (linked to the level on entry of the students) on their graduates employment prospects, must be dealt with differently in France and in the United Kingdom. Whereas in France it is better to look at the *maîtrise*, DEA and DESS diplomas, in the United Kingdom the *first degree* (which corresponds to the first three years of higher education) is a good level of reference.

The limit of this methodological constraint, i.e. identifying the quality of the institutions by the quality of the students on entry to course in question, is that it does not of course allow us to take into account the teaching process during this course. If we identify an institutional effect we can not deduce whether it is a real effect due to better skills acquired by the students during their training or if it is a pure effect of reputation linked to initial quality of the accepted students. It is not possible to opt between an approach in terms of human capital or in terms of a filter.

4. The data used

Data

The British data comes from a survey carried out by each university on whereabouts of their graduates six months after the end of their studies. This data is centralised by the Higher Education Statistics Agency (H.E.S.A.). The number of full-time students possessing a *first degree* is 162,635. Nevertheless, the absence of certain information for some departments reduced the initial number of students.

The French data comes from a survey carried out by the Cereq in June-July 1997 on a sample of higher education graduates. This survey gives with precision the whereabouts of graduates on the labour market for each month after they leave the education system. There is nevertheless a limitation in having only part of the total number of 'université' departments, this reduces the possible analyses of the effect of the quality of the institutions on employment prospects.

In the two countries three subject groups were kept for the analysis. In the United Kingdom the sample encompassed finally 25 institutions catering for three

Table 1   *Proportion of graduates for each of the different variables in the British analysis*

	Social Sciences	**Languages**	**Computer Science**
2<Average A-level points<12 (select1)	9.8%	4.3%	22.5%
12<=Average A-level points<20 (select2)	39.0%	19.2%	42.5%
20<=Average A-level points<25 (select3)	36.4%	55.2%	26.2%
25<=Average A-level points (select4)	14.8%	21.3%	8.8%
Proportion of male graduates 49.2%3	0.3%	86.5%	
Age<21 years (Age1)	50.4%	26.4%	34.5%
Age 21-22 years (Age2)	30.6%	46.7%	35.9%
Age 22-23 years (Age3)	8.3%	18.8%	14.9%
Age>=23 years (Age4)	10.7%	8.1%	14.6%
Pass/third class honours (Class4)	3.3%	2.1%	12.3%
Lower second class honours (Class3)	38.3%	33.1%	36.7%
Higher second class honours (Class2)	53.9%	58.1%	38.0%
First class honours (Class1)	4.5%	6.6%	13.0%

subject groups 'Social Sciences', 'Computer Science' and 'Languages', which amount to 5,705 total graduates. In France the subject groups are 'Economics/Management', 'Languages/Humanities' and 'Science'. Given the constraints due to the size of the sample the number of departments encompassed finally three for the maîtrises in 'Languages/Humanities', four for the 'maîtrises' in 'Science', five for the DEA/DESSs in each of the three subject groups and nine for the 'maîtrises' in 'Economics/Management'. In the full survey for the maîtrises, eleven departments were in the sample for 'Economics/Management' and 'Science' and nine for 'languages/Humanities'; for the DEA/DESS, the number of departments is eight, nine and fourteen.

The variables in the analysis
The variables of the British data models
In the United Kingdom selectivity is indicated by the average A-level points score of the students in each of the departments/universities (cf. Table 1). For Computer Science and Social Sciences the mode is in between 12 and 19 points; it is between 20 and 24 for Languages. The control variables are the individual student A-level points scores, gender and age at the moment of the survey. We can note that male students are clearly the majority in computer science whereas female students are more numerous in Languages. The Social sciences graduates are younger (half of them are under 21 at the moment of the survey). The graduates in Languages and to a lesser extent those in Social Sciences have more often upper second class honours, whereas it is an more even spread in Computer Science.

The quality of graduate of employment is indicated by two variables: unemployment and the occupational category. Those who are unemployed are the graduates who put down as their main activity: 'seeking employment'. The occupational category opposes high-grade occupations (administrators, managers, professionals and associate professionals and technicians) to the others.

The variables of the French data models
The idea of selectivity in France has been calculated in relationship to the average age on obtaining the baccalauréat (cf. Table 2). Selective departments are those where the average age of the students on obtaining the *bac* is less than the average age of the students on obtaining the *bac* for the whole subject group. The less selective departments are the other departments.

The quality of the employment is indicated by three variables: being unemployed in March 1997, the occupation in January 1995 (seven months after leaving university) and the occupation in March 1997. We have grouped together the occupations in two sub-categories, *cadres moyens et supérieurs* in one sub-category and clerical (*employés*) and manual (*ouvriers*) in the other. As there is only a wage variable in the French data and not the British data, we decided not to use the French wage variable.

The average age on obtaining the *baccalauréat* corresponds to that of the theoretical age, i.e. 18. Nevertheless, we can note that the average age of students is less for *DEA/DESS* graduates than for *maîtrise* graduates. This is likely to be due to the more systematic selection of students before entry into the troisième *cycle* (post-graduate research degrees). The proportion of graduates from the selective departments is between 60 % and 73 % according to the level of study and subject group. We can remark that given how the selective departments were defined, the proportion of graduates obtaining their *baccalauréat* before they were 18 is higher in the above mentioned departments. Nevertheless, there is not a large difference to the average of the whole subject group. This enables us the see the impact of the higher education institution variable to some extent independently from the academic performances of the graduates themselves.

There is, as in the British sample, a higher proportion of male graduates in the scientific subject groups and a higher proportion of female graduates in the arts

Table 2   *Data from the French graduate sample*

	Economics/ Management		Languages/ Humanities		Science	
	Maî-trise	DEA-DESS	Maî-trise	DEA-DESS	Maî-trise	DEA-DESS
Number of departments	9	5	3	5	4	5
Average age on obtaining the bac for the subject group	18	17.7	18.1	18	18.1	17.9
Number of selective departments	3	3	2	3	2	3
Total number of graduates	359	397	61	105	133	147
Proportion of graduates from selective departments (in %)	66.0	72.7	63.9	65.7	60.1	66.7
Proportion of graduates obtaining their bac at 18 or under (in %)	74.8	81.8	75.6	77.9	68.4	78.5
Proportion of graduates obtaining their bac at 18 or under coming from selective departments (in %)	78.5	83.6	78.8	83.8	70.0	80.1
Proportion of male graduates (in %)	50.4	57.4	38.5	41.7	70.3	79.5
Proportion of graduates with fathers who are cadres	47.0	52.1	34.6	41.7	44.9	38.7
Average age of graduates in (2.8)March 1997 and standard deviation	26.3 (2.0)	28.0 (2.7)	27.9 (2.8)	28.3 (2.8)	27.0 (2.4)	27.3 (1.9)

subject groups: The economics/management subject group in France and social sciences in the United Kingdom have equal proportions of male and female graduates.

We could also remark that the proportion of graduates whose fathers are *cadres* is higher in the *DEA/DESS*s than in the *maîtrises* for Economics/ Management and Languages/Humanities. The average age at the moment of the survey is between 26 and 28 for the *maîtrises* and 27 and 28 for the *DEA/DESS*s. The average ages appear to high given that the average age on obtaining the *baccalauréat* in sample is the same as the theoretical age of 18. This reflects no doubt the low internal efficiency of French 'universités', where repeating a year and changing of course is frequent.

Along with the institutional selectivity variable, three other variables were introduced to reduce the risks of over estimating the weight and significance of the selectivity variable: gender, age in 1997 and social background. The gender variable eliminates the effects on employment, of there being a higher proportion of male or female graduates in certain departments of the same subject group. In addition, the introduction of the social background of graduates is aimed at reducing the institutional effects due to the fact that the selective departments attract students from more well off backgrounds. Finally taking in account of the age of the graduates in 1997 enables us to control for the effect of the selectivity variable of the department linked is linked to the level of the students themselves.

5. The results

The results of the British data

We remind the reader that the British data concerns only *first degree* graduates and their professional whereabouts six months after leaving university. The latter is indicated by the probability of being unemployed (graduates on the labour market only) and the probability of having a high-grade occupation (also graduates on the labour market only).

Two models have been tested for each department and each of the two employment indicators, unemployment and occupational category. The first basic model has only the selectivity variable as explanatory variable. The selectivity variable has the four categories shown earlier (SELECT2 is taken as reference). The second model includes the control variables. Along with the explanatory variables presented earlier (average selectivity of department, gender, age, degree class), we have included the individual A-level points scores of the graduates (ALEVPTS). There are thus twelve models, six basic models and six with the control variables.

The effect of the selectivity appears in nine models out of twelve, both significantly and in accordance to our predictions. Graduates from the most selective departments are less likely to be unemployed (cf. Table 3) and more likely to have a high-grade occupation (cf. Table 4). The three models where the prediction is not corroborated are: the occupational probability model with the control variables in Computer science (the significance of the selectivity disappears when the control variables are included); and both occupational probability models in Languages (the two opposite categories of selectivity, SELECT1 and SELECT4 have both significant coefficients but both are positive) (Cf. Table 4).

The fact that the more selective departments offer better employment prospects does not imply in itself that the training is of a better quality. Indeed, the departments that have a better reputation can at the same time attract the most academically able students and offer them better employment prospects. Thus it is not possible to arbitrate between either a filter function (filter theory) or a function of the increase in productivity (human capital theory).

We will not comment in detail the coefficients of the control variables, however we can underline the interesting results relative to degree class. Indeed, graduates who obtain the highest degree classes for their degree are less unemployed and obtain the most often high-grade jobs. This result seems to indicate that employers take notice of the quality of the training of the individual graduates and as a consequence the selectivity variable could be seen in itself more as an indicator of quality. In conclusion, we could thus arbitrate more in favour of the human capital theory, the institutions where the students were trained being appraised in the light of the quality of the teaching (this quality being the product both of the initial quality of the students and quality of the teaching process).

The results from the French data

As their was a smaller number of graduates we grouped variables more together than in the British sample.

As before, we will start with an extremely basic model that looks at the relationship between employment prospects and the selectivity on entry into departments. The latter being measured in the way we have mentioned above. Then we will add to the model in question the three control variables: gender,

Table 3: *Probability of British graduates being unemployed (6 months after leaving university)*

Model 1	Social Sciences	Languages	Computer Science
Select 1	0.577***	-0.044 n.s.	0.31 n.s.
	0.168	0.294	0.299
Select 3	-0.269**	0.402***	0.192 n.s.
	0.131	0.149	0.285
Select 4	-0.279 n.s.	-0.863***	-1.244*
	0.177	0.203	0.743
Intercept	-1.717***	-1.478***	-2.281***
	0.086	0.294	0.194
Level of significance	0.0001***	0.0001***	0.0803*
Somers' D	0.116	0.146	0.127
Number of individuals	2661	2245	799
Average probability	14.5%	13.5%	9.9%

Model 2	Social Sciences	Languages	Computer Science
Select 1	0.53***	0.062n.s.	0.891**
	0.187	0.312	0.361
Select 3	-0.18n.s.	-0.237n.s.	-0.258n.s.
	0.149	0.183	0.331
Select 4	-0.103n.s.	-0.597**	-2.017**
	0.208	0.26	0.801
Alevpts	-0.001n.s.	-0.009n.s.	-0.065***
	0.012	0.013	0.024
Male	0.36***	0.677***	0.39n.s.
	0.115	0.13	0.421
Age 1	0.232*	0.288*	0.418n.s.
	0.136	0.153	0.319
Age 3	0.497**	0.065n.s.	0.273n.s.
	0.207	0.177	0.383
Age 4	0.521***	0.308n.s.	0.468n.s.
	0.2	0.226	0.378
Class 4	-0.348n.s.	-0.118n.s.	-0.311n.s.
	0.306	0.389	0.368
Class 2	-0.503***	-0.519***	-1.03***
	0.118	0.135	0.297
Class 1	-1.319***	-0.702**	-1.418***
	0.403	0.307	0.507
Intercept	-1.491**	-0.792***	-3.018***
	0.248	0.257	0.489
Level of significance	0.0001***	0.0001***	0.0005***
Somers' D	0.256	295	0.363
Number of individuals	2661	2245	799

*: significant at 10%   **: significant at 5%   ***: significant at 1%
(the standard errors are in italic)

social background and age in 1997 (the first two variables are binary variables and age is a continuous variable).

The first important result to note is that the selectivity variable is rarely significant for the models concerning the *maîtrise* level. The variable in question is in fact only significant in 4 out of 18 models tested (six models by subject area, three basic models and three models with the control variables): two basic models concerning the probability of being a *cadre* for Economics & Management *maîtrise* graduates and two models concerning the probability of Science *maîtrise* graduates being *cadres* thirty months after leaving university. The rare significance of the models illustrates the homogeneity of employment prospects of graduates from different departments, is due to in part to the organisation of French universities, where only part of the *maîtrises* are selective. Hence, the student characteristics and the teaching processes do not vary from one department to another.

Table 4   *Probability of British graduates entering high-grade occupations*
(6 months after leaving university)

Model 1	Social Sciences	Languages	Computer Science
Select 1	-0.305*	0.831***	-0.186n.s.
	0.16	0.256	0.3
Select 3	0.187*	0.458***	0.509n.s.
	0.096	0.126	0.327
Select 4	1.126***	0.971***	1.02*
	0.143	0.149	0.619
Intercept	0.011n.s.	-0.415***	2.039***
	0.067	0.11	0.187
Level of significance	0.0001***	0.0001***	0.0613*
Somers' D	0.151	0.15	0.17
Number of individuals	2248	1903	707
Average probability	52.2%	52.3%	89.9%

Model 2	Social Sciences	Languages	Computer Science
Select 1	-0.201n.s.	0.780***	-0.112n.s.
	177	272	362
Select 3	0.081n.s.	0.331**	0.427n.s.
	112	15	378
Select 4	0.96***	0.773***	0.782n.s.
	166	192	709
Alevpts	0.011n.s.	0.008n.s.	0.019n.s.
	9	1	27
Male	0.37***	0.080n.s.	0.225n.s.
	9	106	352
Age 1	-0.167*	-0.324***	-0.0179n.s.
	101	115	326
Age 3	0.466***	0.050n.s.	0.269n.s.
	179	129	392
Age 4	0.459***	0.129n.s.	0.609n.s.
	171	19	447
Class 4	-0.072n.s.	0.618*	0.194n.s.
	251	343	389
Class 2	0.503***	0.278***	0.614**
	95	106	287
Class 1	1.205***	0.941***	2.629**
	249	215	1028
Intercept	-0.291n.s.	-0.606***	1.331***
	198	213	466
Level of significance	0.0001***	0.0001***	0.0017***
Somers' D	282	215	387
Number of individuals	2248	190	3707
Average probability	55.2%	55.2%	89.9%

The Selectivity is more frequently significant in the models concerning the DESS and DEA graduates: ten times in eighteen models tested.

If we consider the basic model on unemployment, we find that as our hypothesis had predicted, graduates from the more selective departments are less frequently unemployed than the other graduates, no matter the subject area (cf. Table 5). The difference is the greatest in Science departments. Nevertheless, if the effect of selectivity is controlled for by the graduates individual characteristics, the models concerning Economics & Management and Language departments are no longer significant, even though the selectivity variable remains itself significant. The reason for this result can be found in the small number of observations. The model remains significant in Science.

The models concerning the probability of being *cadre* (6 and 30 months after leaving university) are only significant for Economics & Management graduates (cf. Appendix Tables 6 and 7). Graduates from the more selective Economics & Management departments are more often in *cadre* level occupations on leaving university than the other graduates and this advantage remains over the period of the survey.

6. Conclusion

First of all, it can be underlined that the selectivity has the expected impact. The graduates from the more selective departments on the one hand obtain more rapidly a job (their rate of unemployment is lower six months after the graduation in the United Kingdom and thirty months after graduation in France) and on the other hand they find better jobs (the proportion of high grade occupations is higher).

It seems to result that employment prospects vary more according to institutions of study in the United Kingdom than in France. Indeed, in the United Kingdom a departmental effect appears as early as the first degree where as in France we have to wait until the level of the DEA-DESS for a real departmental effect to influence employment prospects. The departmental effect is linked in both countries to the selectivity on entering courses. This selectivity was indicated in the British data by the average A-level points score of students admitted in each department. In the French data, selectivity was indicated by the average age in each department of the graduates when they passed the *Baccalauréat*. It is a pity that the data did not give the *baccalauréat* grades of each graduate, as they would have been a more pertinent indicator as far as the academic level at the end of secondary school is concerned.

If we assume that there is a difference in the academic level of students on entering higher education, we can also assume that certain institutions can attempt to select the best of the students in order to promote more demanding teaching. This in turn would enable the students to reach a high level of knowledge. The other institutions would take on the other students and would adapt their teaching to the ability of their students, who in this case would reach a lower level of knowledge (only if the financial resources of the latter institutions

Table 5   *Probability of French graduates being unemployed*
(30 months after obtaining the diploma)

Model 1	Economics/ Management	Languages/ Humanities	Science
Select	-0.843**	-1.294*	-1.575**
	0.382	0.681	0.682
Intercept	-1.7918***	-1.386 n.s.	-1.504***
	0.288	0.500	0.451
Level of significance	0.0243**	0.0458**	0.0127**
Somers' D	0.19	0.285	0.363
Number of individuals	352	103	124
Average probability	8.80%	9.70%	8.06%

Model 2	Economics/ Management	Languages/ Humanities	Science
Select	-0.770*	-1.340*	-1.953**
	0.397	0.694	0.771
Male	0.427n.s.	0.350n.s.	-1.088n.s.
	0.405	0.754	0.832
Father cadre	-0.458n.s.	0.397	0.418n.s.
	0.696	0.538n.s.	0.741
Age in 1997	-0.046n.s.	-0.045n.s.	-0.045n.s.
	0.076	0.148	0.183
Intercept	-0.578n.s.	-0.419 n.s.	-0.560
	2.096	4.074	5.034
Level of significance	0.1015n.s.	0.3472n.s.	0.0995*
Somers' D	0.292	0.278	0.519
Number of individuals	352	103	124
Average probability	8.80%	9.70%	8.06%

*: significant at 10%   **: significant at 5%   ***: significant at 1%   (standard errors in italic)

are the same as those of the former). If there is indeed a matching between the academic level of the students and the teaching demands of the institutions, reputation differences between the different institutions become very noticeable. This system appears to be more efficient due to the fact that if teaching is adapted to the ability of the students, the system produces a lower rate of drop outs than a system where selection takes place more during the course of study than on entry. Consequently, since the matching device takes place earlier in the academic career in the British universities than in the French ones, a better internal productivity can be expected in the first case. In fact, if we look at data from

'Education at a glance' published by the OECD, it appears that with a lower rate of attendance in higher education than France, the United Kingdom shows a higher rate of graduation. In 1994, 23.6 % of 18 to 21 years olds attended higher education in the United Kingdom compared to 33.2% in France. In the first country, 52.1% of a cohort obtained a first degree, which is the case for 39,1% in France. These rough data indicate that the internal efficiency is higher in the United Kingdom than in France.

The British system may be more efficient however this may be at the price of equity. Since the access to higher education is based on the achievement at the end of the secondary level, those who are not accepted in prestigious universities will not have the opportunity to reveal potential that has not been discovered up to then. Some universities, aware of this phenomenon, try to select students who have not necessarily the minimum entry requirements. This goes to show that efficiency and equity are not necessarily incompatible.

No doubt we would have found different results concerning the effect of institutions on employment prospects in the United Kingdom and in France, if for the latter country we had taken into account the whole of the French higher education system. This is particular the case with Economics & Management on the one hand and Science on the other. This is because the institutional effect would have been clearer if we could have taken into account the *Grandes Ecoles de Commerce* and the *Grandes Ecoles d'Ingénieurs*. Nevertheless, it remains true that the effect in question would still have only appeared after a diploma awarded after five years of successful study, whereas in the United Kingdom the effect appears as early as three years of university study.

In conclusion it is difficult draw a hierarchy between the two systems using our analysis. If we can consider the British system to be more efficient as it enables a earlier distinction of skills between graduates, the French system can be considered more equitable, at least as far as the *université* sector is concerned, as the training on offer is more homogeneous.

References

Alwin D., (1974). College Effects on Educational and Occupational Attainments, *American Sociological Review,* 39

Arrow K., (1973). Higher education as a filter, *Journal of public economics*, 2.

Astin A., (1968). Undergraduate Achievement and Institutional Excellence, *Science,* 161.

Brennan, J., Kogan M., Teichler U., (1996) a. Higher Education and work: A Conceptual Framework, *Higher Education and Work*, Jessica Kingsley.

Brennan J., Lyon S., Schomberg H., Teichler U., (1996) b. Employment and Work of British and German Graduates, *Higher Education and Work,* Jessica Kingsley.

Crawford D., Johnson A., Summers A., (1997). Schools and Labor Market Outcomes, *Economics of Education Review,* Vol.16, N 3.

Griffin L., Alexander K., (1978). Schooling and Socioeconomic Attainment: High school and College Influences, *American Journal of Sociology,* 84.

Harvey L., Moon S., Geall V., Bower R., (1997). *Graduates' Work,* Centre for Research into Quality University of Central England, Birmingham, in *The Guardian higher education,* 11 Febuary 1997

Higher Education Statistics Agency (H.E.S.A.) a, First Destinations Dataset 1994-95.

Higher Education Statistics Agency (H.E.S.A.) b, First Destinations - Summary Statistics 1994-95.

James E., Alsalam N., Conaty J., To D., (1989). College Quality and Future Earnings: Where should you send your children to college? *American Economic Review,* 79.

Morgan J., Duncan G., (1979). College Quality and Earnings, in *Research in Human Capital and Development,* 1 .

Morgan J., Sirageldin I., (1968). A note on the quality dimension in education, *Journal of Political Economy,* 76.

Murdoch J., (1997). *L'effet de la sélectivité relative des départements universitaires britanniques sur la qualité de l'insertion professionnelle des diplômés du supérieur,* Mémoire de Diplôme d'Etudes Approfondies, Irédu, Université de Bourgogne.

Reed R., Miller H., (1970). Some Determinants of the Variation in Earnings for College Men, *Journal of Human Resources,* 2.

Roizen J., Jepson M., (1983). *Expectations of Higher Education: An Employers' Perspective,* Uxbridge, Brunel University.

Solmon L. and Wachtel P., (1975), The Effects on income of type of College Attended, *Sociology of Education,* 48.

Spence M., (1973). Job market signalling, *Quarterly journal of economics,* 3.

The Guardian (1997). New Earnings Survey(1996), The Guardian 26 Mai 1997.

The Guardian Education (1995). Degrees of difference, The Guardian Education 12 September 1995.

The Independent (1997). U.C.A.S. listings, The Independent 18 August 1997.

The Independent (1996). U.C.A.S. guide, The Independent 25 August 1996.

The Times Higher Education Supplement (1996). University league tables 1996, The Times Higher Education Supplement 17 Mai 1996.

The Times Higher Education supplement (1995). Graduates are ill prepared for jobs market, The Times Higher Education Supplement 19 Mai 1995.

The Times Higher Education Supplement (1993). University league tables, The Times Higher Education Supplement 14 Mai 1993.

Turner R., (1960). Sponsored and Contest Mobility and the School System, *American Sociological Review,* 25 October.

Universities and Colleges Admissions Service (U.C.A.S.) a, The *Official U.C.A.S. Guide to University and College Entrance,* Sheed & Ward Ltd, London.

Universities and Colleges Admissions Service (U.C.A.S.) b, Applications to degree courses at each University or College, by subject group, 1995 entry .

Universities and Colleges Admissions Service (U.C.A.S.) c, Applicants accepted to degree courses at each University or College, by subject group, 1995 entry .

Wachtel P., (1976). The Effect on earnings of School and College Investment Expenditures, *Review of Economics and Statistics,* 58.

Wales T., (1973). The Effect of College Quality on Earnings: Results from the N.B.E.R.-Thorndike Data, *Journal of Human Resources,* 8 .

De Weert E., (1996). Responsiveness of Higher Education to Labour Market Demands: Curriculum Change in the Humanities and Social Sciences, *Higher Education and Work,* Jessica Kingsley.

Wise D., (1975). Academic Achievement and Job Performance, *American Economic Review,* 65.

Zanzala J., (1993). Mémoire de D.E.A., *L'effet de la qualité de l'université d'origine sur les salaires des diplômés,* IREDU, Université de Bourgogne.

Appendix

Table 6 *Probability of French graduates having the status of cadre in January 1995 (6 months after obtaining the diploma)*

Model 1	Economics/ Management	Languages/ Humanities	Science
Select	1.709***	0.196n.s.	0.847n.s.
	0.4120	0.644	0.747
Intercept	-1.223***	-0.693n.s.	0.00n.s.
	0.359	0.547	0.632
Level of significance	0.0001***	0.7599n.s.	0.2577n.s.
Somers' D	0.326	0.040	0.165
Number of individuals	149	52	40
Proportion of cadres	50.33%	36.53%	65.00%

Model 2	Economics/ Management	Languages/ Humanities	Science
Select	1.625***	0.568n.s.	0.929n.s.
	0.426	0.714	0.835
Male	0.173n.s.	-1.338*	0.471n.s.
	0.364	0.748	0.850
Father cadre	0.504n.s.	-0.708n.s.	1.348*
	0.373	0.605	0.788
Age in 1997	0.155*	-0.313 **	0.228n.s.
	0.089	0.144	0.194
Intercept	-5.815n.s.	-9.001**	-7.276n.s.
	2.542	4.070	5.540
Level of significance	0.0002***	0.1301n.s.	0.1771n.s.
Somers' D	0.394	0.486	0.506
Number of individuals	148	52	39
Proportion of cadres	50.67%	36.53%	64.10%

Table 7 *Probability of French students having the status of cadre in March 1997 (32 months after obtaining the diploma)*

Model 1	Economics/ Management	Languages/ Humanities	Science
Select	1.767***	0.198n.s.	-0.143n.s.
	0.277	0.496	0.516
Intercept	-0.154***	0.753*	1.504***
	0.210	0.428	0.451
Level of significance	0.0001***	0.6896n.s.	0.7815n.s.
Somers' D	0.375	0.037	0.026
Number of individuals	365	104	131
Proportion of cadres	78.90%	71.15%	80.15%

Model 2	Economics/ Management	Languages/ Humanities	Science
Select	1.563***	0.324n.s.	-0.173n.s.
	0.286	0.515	0.536
Male	0.062n.s.	-0.384n.s.	0.390n.s.
	0.290	0.481	0.508
Father cadre	0.554*	-0.116n.s.	0.689n.s.
	0.286	0.451	0.492
Age in 1997	0.146**	0.117n.s.	-0.009n.s.
	0.063	0.086	0.107
Intercept	4.066**	-2.465n.s.	1.231n.s.
	1.726	2.456	2.966
Level of significance	0.0001***	0.7005n.s.	0.5546n.s.
Somers' D	0.484	0.147	0.223
Number of individuals	363	104	129
Proportion of cadres	79.06%	71.15%	79.84%

About the authors

Robert Cowen is a Reader in Comparative Education in the Academic Group, Culture, Communication and Societies at the London Institute of Education in England. His contemporary interests include comparative education theory work, the evaluation of higher education systems and teacher education.

Anne Bert Dijkstra works at the Department of Sociology of the University of Groningen, the Netherlands. His main interest is public and private schooling and its effects on outcomes of education. The co-author *Jaap Dronkers* is professor in Sociology of Education at the University of Amsterdam, the Netherlands. He is also the conductor of the league tables of Dutch schools, which started in 1997.

Henri Folliet holds an 'agrégation' of philosophy. He has been in charge of administrative responsibilities, first as cultural councellor in Algeria and Austria, later on as 'inspecteur d'Académie' in different French regions and the Ministry of Education. He retired in 1994 and is the secretary of the 'Association Francophone d'Education Comparée'.

Jean-Luc Guyot wrote his dissertation on adult education at the Catholic University of Leuven. Presently he works at the Belgian Ministry of Education (Wallonia) on issues of employment and training.

Gunn Marie Hansen works currently as an educational site administrator for the Montebello Unified School District of Los Angeles County, USA. She completed her dissertation on immigrant-education in Norway at the University of Southern California.

Bram de Hoop is an expert on modes of international technology and knowledge transfer. In this capacity and on behalf of the NUFFIC in The Hague, the Netherlands, he was responsible for the administration of 13 bilateral university cooperation projects in Vietnam en Burkina Faso.

Hans-Georg Kotthoff works at the Department of Education and Pedagogy at the University of Münster, Germany. He conducted a large study on Inspectorates of Education in several European countries.

Jean-Michel Leclercq holds a PhD in sociology. He is a researcher in comparative education, especially interested by educational policies in industralised countries (European Union, Central and Eastern Europe, Japan). He is also a consultant at the directorate of Education of the Council of Europe and chairman of the 'Association Francophone d'Education Comparée'.

Stavros Moutsios did his PhD in Comparative Education at the Institute of Education University of London. He has published in the areas of curriculum theory, international systems of school governance and educational 'marketisation'.

Currently, he works for the Education Office of the Greek Embassy in London, England

Jake Murdoch is a PhD student in educational studies at the Institute of Research in the Economics of Education in Dijon, France. His thesis will be on the comparison across several European countries and Japan, of the effect on graduate wages of the quality and reputation of higher education departments. The co-author *Jean-Jacques Paul* is professor of economics of education at the University of Bourgogne, Dijon. *Julien Zanzala* works and lives in Angola, after finishing his thesis on the effect on graduate wages of the quality of French university departments.

Jules L. Peschar is professor of Sociology of Education at the University of Groningen, the Netherlands. He was chair of national evaluation programmes in education and consultant to the Ministry of Education and OECD. His main interest is in cross-national research and international education indicators, in particular Cross-Curricular Competencies.

Wim Jan T. Renkema holds a Master's Degree in Education. After working for the UNESCO in Paris, where he was engaged in a capacity-building programme of African educational planners and statisticians, he has worked for the Department for Human Resources and Institutional Development of the Nuffic in The Hague, the Netherlands from 1997. His main topics are policy development and meta-evaluation studies

David Reynolds, originally at the University of Cardiff, Wales is professor of Leadership and School Effectiveness at the School of Education, Exeter, England. He has researched and written in the areas of school effectiveness, school improvement and education policy. Together with the co-authors *Bert Creemers*, professor of Education at the University of Groningen, the Netherlands, *Charles Teddlie*, professor at the Louisiana State University and *Sam Stringfield*, professor at the Johns Hopkins University, USA he conducted a large research study on school effectiveness in several Asian countries

Claude Thélot is *Conseiller Maître* at the *Cour des Comptes* (State Audit Office). From 1990 till 1997 he was director of evaluation and economic forecasting at the French Ministry of Education. Thélot lives in Paris, France.

Marieke van der Wal is a PhD Student at the Department of Sociology at the University of Groningen, the Netherlands. Sociology of Education has her general interest. Cross-Curricular Competencies is the subject of her dissertation. Her dissertation will go into a conceptualisation and measurement of Cross-Curricular Competencies and can be expected in autumn 2002.

Hans N. Weiler holds the chair in Comparative Politics at the Europa University Viadrina in Frankfurt a/d Oder, Germany, of which university he is also Rector Magnificus. He also held chairs in Freiburg, Germany and at Stanford University, USA. He has been active in the field of comparative education for many years.

Author Index

Subject Index

Verlag GmbH, Wolfratshausenstraße 21, 80331 München, Germany

T - #0012 - 230425 - C0 - 234/156/13 [15] - CB - 9789026516306 - Gloss Lamination